"*Enhancing Inclusive Instruction* ad
ment in discussions of inclusive practice: student voices. Drawing on quantitative data that reflects student experiences of their learning and individual student voices that bring those patterns of experience alive, the book also offers a range of useful approaches for assessing practices and specific advice for historically marginalized instructors and their allies. In these multiple ways, the book enacts the inclusivity it encourages."

Alison Cook-Sather, *Mary Katharine Woodworth Professor of Education, Bryn Mawr College, USA*

"By how they teach and assess, faculty disable students when they build barriers into their curriculum, either by intent or by design. This book provides valuable inclusive teaching strategies for faculty who actually want students to learn."

Mary Lee Vance, *Axelrod, Grossman and Vance Consulting, USA*

"Student voices matter. Why, then, does much of the equity work not center them? The authors of this innovative book seek to do just that—center student voices to understand how instructors create, or fail to create, inclusive courses. Reflective questions throughout the book, as well the dedicated second part that provides tools and methods to obtain and use feedback, invite readers to carefully consider their own inclusive teaching practices. *Enhancing Inclusive Instruction* is an essential resource for anyone who strives to create courses that are equitable and welcoming for all students."

Stephanie M. Foote, *Gardner Institute, Vice President for Teaching, Learning, and Evidence-Based Practices; and Stony Brook University, Lecturer, USA*

"*Enhancing Inclusive Instruction* provides practical advice about what practices to include and avoid doing in the college classroom. Each piece of advice includes quotes from students. These student voices are so important for understanding the effect instructors can have on their classroom culture."

Michelle Smith, *Senior Associate Dean for Undergraduate Education, College of Arts & Sciences, Ann S. Bowers Professor, Department of Ecology and Evolutionary Biology, Cornell University, USA*

"The authors of *Enhancing Inclusive Instruction* have created a book that serves both as a compendium of the research literature on inclusive teaching and as a resource for instructors to use for their own teaching and course design. The book goes far beyond a set of 'tips' by providing evidence-based suggestions for different contexts, including the support needed from departments and institutions for instructors to accomplish the goals of inclusive teaching."

Gabriela C. Weaver, *Assistant Dean, College of Natural Sciences, Professor of Chemistry, University of Massachusetts, Amherst, USA*

ENHANCING INCLUSIVE INSTRUCTION

Enhancing Inclusive Instruction centers the voices of students of diverse backgrounds to explore how instructors can approach equitable, inclusive teaching.

Grounded in student perspectives, this book is a powerful call to action for instructors to listen to the voices of their learners, take steps to measure the impact of their approaches, and meaningfully reflect on their efforts. The authors provide practical tools that instructors can use to obtain ongoing feedback on their inclusive teaching efforts, and supply guidance on difficult and emerging topics such as how instructors from diverse backgrounds can navigate inclusive teaching in academe, as well as the implications of generative artificial intelligence on equity and inclusion.

Modeling the importance of continuous growth, *Enhancing Inclusive Instruction* provides the knowledge and skills to further any college instructor's inclusive teaching journey.

Tracie Marcella Addy is Associate Dean of Teaching and Learning and Director of the Center for the Integration of Teaching, Learning, and Scholarship at Lafayette College, USA.

Derek Dube is Associate Professor of Biology and Director of the First-Year Seminar program at the University of Saint Joseph (CT), USA.

Khadijah A. Mitchell is Assistant Professor of Cancer Prevention and Control at Fox Chase Cancer Center within the Temple University Health System, USA.

ENHANCING INCLUSIVE INSTRUCTION

Student Perspectives and Practical Approaches for Advancing Equity in Higher Education

Tracie Marcella Addy, Derek Dube and Khadijah A. Mitchell

NEW YORK AND LONDON

First published 2024
by Routledge
605 Third Avenue, New York, NY 10158

and by Routledge
4 Park Square, Milton Park, Abingdon, Oxon OX14 4RN

Routledge is an imprint of the Taylor & Francis Group, an informa business

ISBN: 978-1-642-67569-6 (hbk)
ISBN: 978-1-642-67571-9 (pbk)
ISBN: 978-1-003-44292-9 (ebk)

DOI: 10.4324/9781003442929

Typeset in Galliard
by Taylor & Francis Books

CONTENTS

ILLUSTRATIONS

Figures

Table

FOREWORD

During my time at Lafayette College, I had the privilege of working directly with Dr. Tracie Addy as a part of the Student-Faculty Pedological Partnership Program. Under her leadership in my college's center for teaching and learning, I was trained as a student fellow and collaborated with instructors to provide data and feedback to advance instructors' inclusive teaching practices. This experience ignited my passion for the pedagogy of inclusive teaching and learning. I was honored to collaborate again with Dr. Addy and other student fellows to develop, refine, and publish the Protocol for Advancing Inclusive Teaching Efforts (PAITE). This tool is used to give higher education instructors productive feedback on discernible inclusive teaching practices. My time as a student fellow underscored that the voices of my peers and I were integral to Dr. Addy's scholarship.

Although my college expedition was soon coming to a close, my curiosity and excitement for the dialogue on equitable education had only begun to take root. Dr. Addy soon introduced me to Dr. Khadijah A. Mitchell and Dr. Derek Dube, who were expanding on their initial book *What Inclusive Instructors Do*. Their new work is a captivating extension of their inclusive teaching and learning initiatives. What distinguishes this book is its focus on amplifying learners' voices, and I can attest that the authors have successfully achieved that mission. Through close collaboration with them during the research and analysis process, I witnessed firsthand their unwavering dedication to developing *Enhancing Inclusive Instruction*.

The book explores student voices and experiences with higher education teaching practices. The authors' research and analyses delve into the intricate layers that shape the student's academic experience. Additionally, they provide educators with resources rooted in students' perspectives on inclusive teaching practices. Through interviews and surveys, the authors intentionally prioritized learners' voices, affirming that they are the experts of their experiences—insight that instructors can learn from and engage with as they read. At the heart of equitable teaching lies the relationship between educators and their students. The shared purpose is to foster a communal space where students can engage in the pursuit of knowledge, curiosity, and discovery. To achieve this, instructors must cultivate an environment where students can actively be involved in shaping their learning experiences. *Enhancing Inclusive Instruction* precisely embodies this ethos. By placing the student experience at the center, valuing my contributions to the research process, and allowing a student and recent graduate to pen this foreword, the authors consistently exemplify the principles they advocate for in their book.

So, you may ask why you should read *Enhancing Inclusive Instruction*. The authors unequivocally demonstrate the value of students' voices. As you delve into their analysis, you'll understand why all educators seeking inclusivity should engage with this work and gain insights on assessing and advancing their own teaching practices. Since the conversation around inclusivity is interdisciplinary, I encourage all professionals seeking to foster equity in their communities to engage in dialogue with the authors' work and see how inclusive teaching practices are applicable and imperative in all communities. As a recent graduate and young professional, I've witnessed how inclusive teaching practices transcend the classroom. *Enhancing Inclusive Instruction* holds the key to reshaping the traditional professor–student dynamic, highlighting the shared goal of learning from one another. We are all lifelong learners—together let's make the journey more inclusive along the way.

—Monica Rizk, Class of 2022

As a brown international student navigating the vast academic landscape in the United States, I have often found myself belonging to the minority in my classes. Therefore, my experience in the classroom was often shaped by the subtleties of inclusive teaching. The environment in which I learned, and the way in which material was presented, directly impacted my level of comfort, engagement, and thus performance in the class. This personal connection to inclusivity led me to a transformative experience during my sophomore and junior years when I joined the Inclusive Instructors Academy at my college's center for teaching and learning as a student fellow.

In this role, I was partnered with faculty from across different departments as I observed their classes and worked together with them to explore methods to refine and bolster an atmosphere of equity and inclusion in their classroom. This endeavor was not just an academic exercise, but a practical journey, rooted in real experiences and genuine feedback.

For example, one anecdote shared by a fellow student resonates deeply: During a class observation, a student partner noticed that a professor frequently checked in with the more vocal students during group sessions, unintentionally overlooking the quieter ones. This observation, once shared, allowed the instructor to adapt, ensuring a more even distribution of attention in subsequent sessions. Such firsthand accounts, embedded throughout our partnership, reinforced the very essence of our mission—continuous growth through collaboration.

From realizing how small practices like using a student's name can bolster confidence to witnessing shifts in pedagogical strategies, this experience was insightful for me. Similarly, many of my, as well as my fellow students', faculty partners lauded the tools and frameworks introduced by the Inclusive Instructors Academy, finding them invaluable for making actionable adjustments to their inclusive teaching methodologies. Most importantly, underneath all these tools was the foundational value of using student perspectives as a lens to revisit teaching practices. I saw this in everything from the guidelines I used during observations, which recorded not just the actions of the teacher but also the reactions of the students, to the very function of a student fellow, who serves as a learner's lens to teaching.

Many of our faculty partners remarked on the benefits of a student fellow who could offer them a way to better understand how their students experience their class and teaching methods. For them, this unique lens provided insights that might have otherwise remained obscured. This book, therefore, represents more than just a collection of teaching pedagogies. It is unique in its efforts to do so through highlighting the voices of students in understanding effective pedagogy, because truly inclusive classes require collaboration and a two-way stream of learning where the ideas of both students and teachers are heard and influence each other.

—Tanushree Sow Mondal, Class of 2024

PREFACE

Enhancing Inclusive Instruction centers the voices of students on what makes equitable, welcoming learning environments. Part One shares the themes that emerged from a national students' perspectives study and findings at the levels of course design, classroom climate, and the daily teaching approaches of inclusive instructors. Part Two focuses on getting started with reflection on practice, observation of inclusive teaching, and measuring outcomes of such efforts. Part Three explores critical issues in higher education such as advice for instructors from groups historically excluded, and the departmental and institutional support needed to build more inclusive teaching environments, as well as the potential and challenges of generative artificial intelligence in building more inclusive courses. This book gives tools for instructors to empower themselves to be more inclusive in their courses.

With the ongoing threats against equity work in higher education, inclusive instruction is as important as it ever has been to educate diverse student populations at our colleges and universities. To contribute to the literature on inclusive instruction, our first book, *What Inclusive Instructors Do*, highlighted the voices of college and university instructors. We synthesize their inclusive mindsets, in addition to the instructional principles and practices they use in courses of a variety of disciplines and institution types. In the current book, *Enhancing Inclusive Instruction*, we shift the voices to those of learners. As instructors continue to implement inclusive teaching approaches, the question "Are they making a difference?" is paramount to ask. We believe that a critical approach to answering this question is to invite learners to share: (1) their experiences with instruction that is inclusive, and (2) which teaching practices they perceive as exclusionary, so we in higher education can avoid such pitfalls.

Throughout *Enhancing Inclusive Instruction* we present quotes collected through a study to amplify the voices of the learners and inform various aspects of this book. The students are from diverse backgrounds—first-generation students, neurodivergent students, students with disabilities, students of color, veterans, and more. The learners take courses at a variety of variety of institution types such as community colleges, small private liberal arts institutions, historically Black or minority serving institutions, public universities, private universities, masters colleges or universities. The course modalities they experience are online and in-person. The courses they describe span disciplines. We share the identity information they've disclosed to honor their diversity. While themes do emerge, such information should not, however, be taken out of context and used to make global generalizations about any particular identity, as students' perspectives are complex and can be impacted by any number of variables.

Enhancing Inclusive Instruction also focuses on the outcomes of inclusive teaching practices and instructor tools for monitoring progress toward goals for inclusion. These outcomes can be both instructor-focused, related to one's own pedagogical growth, and student-focused, describing the impacts that the approaches have on their learners. We view reflection as critical for effective teaching. After describing a variety of inclusive teaching practices from the perspectives of students, we discuss the importance of processing what happens in the classroom and student feedback on inclusive teaching practices, which is important for the growth of any instructor. The themes that emerge from our student study speak to a variety of contexts, but there are additional situational factors that are apparent in any classroom such as identity, prior teaching experiences, teaching approaches utilized, comfort level with changing practice, and awareness of diversity issues that enter the classroom. Further, the student makeup of a course, type of course, classroom activities, class size, modality, and other variables are dynamic in any teaching environment, warranting the critical importance of gathering feedback and understanding what works for a particular course, for a particular instructor.

We believe our readers will also benefit from the field notes that we include from our own experiences and the sections that call out specific guidance for instructors from groups historically excluded in academia and educational developers who partner with instructors on their teaching efforts. Our field notes derive from Tracie's experiences as a faculty member, an educational developer who has partnered with numerous instructors and students on inclusive teaching and learning efforts, and a Black female higher educational leader; Derek's as a faculty member, director of his institution's First-Year Seminar program and Center for Student Research and Creative Activity, and White male; and Khadijah's as a faculty member, serial founder of organizations to support historically excluded students in higher education, and a Black woman in STEM.

Also, knowing how much our readers of *What Inclusive Instructors Do* appreciated the reflection questions in that book, we also embed them throughout *Enhancing Inclusive Instruction.*

Specifically, we organize the book as follows:

- Introduction (Chapter 1): The lenses through which we wrote the book as well as general information on the students' perspectives study we conducted
- Part One (Chapters 2, 3, 4): Students' perspectives on inclusive teaching practices that support an inclusive classroom environment (or not) based on our study
- Part Two (Chapters 5, 6, 7): Tools and other methods for obtaining feedback and reflecting on inclusive teaching efforts, and
- Part Three (Chapters 8, 9, 10, 11): Recommendations beyond the course level and for instructors from groups historically excluded, as well as the impacts of generative artificial intelligence on equity

In Part One, we encourage readers to reflect on their inclusive teaching practices and identify any existing alignments as well as instructional opportunities using the themes emerging from the students' perspectives in Chapters 2 through 4. Readers can consider their course contexts when they engage in reflection on feedback presented. In this section we also present common pitfalls of inclusive instruction, the practices that made students in our study feel the most excluded. We reiterate that there is no one-size-fits all approach to inclusive teaching, but there are approaches that students find more effective. Having some guidance by learning what has worked for students as described in the book can be useful information for any instructor.

For Part Two, we advise readers to examine how they currently obtain feedback and reflect on the impacts of their inclusive teaching approaches and opportunities. If there are plans to try new approaches, readers can determine specific ways to monitor and document progress considering the methods and tools presented in this section.

In Chapter 5 we discuss the importance of goal-setting with regards to inclusive teaching approaches. When an instructor is a reflective practitioner, the ongoing monitoring of what is working and what is not with regards to inclusive teaching approaches is critical to identifying areas of focus. We share that reflection is a process and can be diverse with regards to how one carries it out. We also discuss how to maintain a continuous feedback loop on inclusive teaching efforts, how to use the feedback to reflect on teaching practices and iterate, and the importance of making such reflections visible to students as described above and to colleagues where appropriate.

In Chapter 6 we emphasize the importance of inclusive instructors obtaining low-stakes, observational feedback on their instructional efforts to gather a more comprehensive view. There are a variety of forms such observations can take including using established protocols as well as giving general feedback. We highlight a protocol developed by one of the co-authors and collaborators, the Protocol for Advancing Inclusive Teaching Efforts (PAITE), which provides colleagues with data-driven feedback on general efforts on inclusive teaching that can be assessed reliably in a course setting. We also highlight a few other tools, but the list is not meant to be exhaustive.

Chapter 7 specifically focuses on how instructors can determine whether their inclusive teaching approaches are working by focusing on specific outcomes. We encourage instructors to embrace the uniqueness of their contexts and define the most relevant outcomes for their students. For example, common goals are creating environments where students feel a sense of belonging and as if they matter. Direct student outcomes might be assessed by obtaining students' perspectives and indirectly through metrics such as student persistence, reduction of opportunity gaps, and more. However, we also posit that instructor outcomes—mindset, values, implementation of inclusive teaching approaches and more—are also critical and have the potential to directly impact student outcomes.

We have heard from colleagues in various contexts that traditional metrics might not tell the full story of a student's experience, and we see this ourselves. For example, disruption in a student's educational path due to factors such as medical challenges, finances, and more might necessitate the student taking a leave of absence and returning years later; in everyday metrics it would appear as if that student did not persist. Or perhaps skills development is critical for students but not directly assessed. Such factors should be accounted for. We provide a variety of ways to think about monitoring impact in Chapter 7.

While inclusivity is critical in one classroom at a time, dissemination of efforts and more systemic approaches are necessary ingredients for change. While at times it can seem like colleges and universities operate in silos, the learning experiences of students are interconnected across levels: course, departmental, and institutional. In Part Three, Chapter 8, we recommend that readers look beyond their particular courses to consider inclusivity on a broader scale; specifically, how their efforts might fit into department-level inclusivity goals, and how to examine equity and belonging with a broader scope. The inclusivity goals of an individual instructor can ultimately align within the larger mission of a department and institution to support institutional transformation and change.

In Chapter 9 we offer specific guidance to instructors from groups historically excluded in higher education. We see and hear you. Finally, given that we are writing this book during a time when emerging technologies such as generative artificial intelligence continue to impact teaching and learning, we include a discussion of the potential of such technologies in equity work in Chapter 10.

We hope that you appreciate the insights you receive from *Enhancing Inclusive Instruction* to assess your own practices, or to support instructors with whom you partner.

As you take your journey through this book, we hope that it empowers you to:

- Listen—discover what students say inclusive learning means to them through their voices
- Observe—find opportunities to obtain observational feedback on your teaching practices
- Measure—take action to assess meaningful outcomes of your inclusive teaching efforts
- Reflect—determine which teaching approaches are effective for your instructional contexts
- Support—provide structural and other support at the level of the department and institution, and for instructors historically excluded, to advance inclusive teaching and learning more broadly

Applying this framework can help create the perfect storm for enhancing inclusive instruction within our colleges and universities.

1

INTRODUCTION

Guiding Frameworks

Student voices matter. Why, then, does much of the equity work not center them?

Enhancing Inclusive Instruction synthesizes the perspectives of a diverse range of students with regards to how their professors successfully did (or did not) create inclusive courses. The trifecta of student voices, the relevant literature, and field notes can contribute to the personal learning and growth of instructors or those who partner with them. Our authorship team also reflects partnership, consisting of faculty members and an educational developer.

We frame this book around the importance of equity work and fostering belonging in college courses. We view belonging as nuanced and relational, and counter narratives where students from diverse backgrounds must assimilate into dominant cultures within course contexts in order to belong (Graham & Moir, 2022). Instead, the belonging we envision results from equity work that enables students to bring their authentic selves to their courses without negative recourse.

We acknowledge that there are a variety of pathways leading to students' sense of belonging (Hirsch & Clark, 2019). There might be communal influences such as the development of relationships with instructors and their peers; group membership within a class might contribute, as well as being associated with well-respected groups, and having positive day-to-day interactions with members of the classroom community. In the midst of such complexity, the power of the voices of students in this book highlights that there are instructional practices that can foster equity and belonging in course settings. The setup and dynamics of a course environment can play a significant role.

DOI: 10.4324/9781003442929-1

In developing this book we apply several Design Justice Network principles (*Design Justice Network*, n.d.). We center the voices of students directly impacted by classroom teaching, and aim to provide tools for instructors to empower themselves to learn students' perspectives to create more inclusive classrooms. We view students as experts on their own lived experiences with inclusive course environments. We build off of work focused on student co-creation through partnership (Cook-Sather, 2022; 2020). We view engagement in the book as a partnership with the students who contributed their perspectives and with all who read the book. We believe our roles are facilitators in sharing this information, and see this text as a vehicle to disseminate this knowledge to the higher education community. We also acknowledge that the language of inclusion matters and is constantly evolving. After writing this book, various terms may no longer be used or may have different meanings.

We designed this book for those ready to take the next steps in making their environments more inclusive or working with instructors on such practices. Because you are reading this text, you likely want to grow in your knowledge and skills in inclusive instruction. A worthwhile exercise as a reader of this book is to consider where you are with regards to your personal growth and development as an instructor. The diversity interventions—resistance to action model (Thoman et al., 2021) describes a pathway to implementation and was applied to underrepresentation in STEM fields, yet can be considered more broadly to: (a) notice the equity and inclusion problem, (b) interpret the problem as needing immediate action, (c) take responsibility, (d) know how to help, and (e) implement the intervention or teaching practice. This model aligns with our previous study investigating the reasons instructors do not implement inclusive teaching approaches (Addy et al., 2021). We found that awareness could be a challenge—instructors might not realize that there are issues of equity and inclusion in their classrooms or know how to help. We found that instructors might not feel it is their responsibility to incorporate inclusivity principles and practices into their instruction. They might not have sufficient support in place such as professional development that encourages their growth as inclusive instructors.

The EPIC-Implementation model (Exposure, Persuasion, Identification, and Commitment) also describes important steps in faculty adoption of teaching approaches: (a) exposure to the teaching approach, (b) persuasion that the approach is salient, (c) identification as one who implements such approaches, (d) commitment to adoption, and (e) implementation (Aragón et al., 2018). This book was designed to speak to instructors across all levels of adoption of inclusive teaching practices, from those who are developing their awareness of equity and inclusion issues in their courses to those actively engaged in implementation.

Reflection Questions

- Consider the two models presented above (diversity interventions—resistance to action model and EPIC). Where do you see yourself with regards to your adoption of inclusive teaching approaches?
- For which teaching or learning areas are you most interested in hearing students' perspectives?

The Importance of Student Voice

In order to support the advancement of inclusive teaching, throughout this book we focus on the critical importance of student voice in building more inclusive and culturally responsive classrooms in ways that can advance college-wide student success initiatives (Cook-Sather & Des-Ogugua, 2019; Cook-Sather, 2018). As partners within higher education learning environments, students directly experience whether or not a course is equitable or welcoming. However, historically within higher education there are few systemic opportunities to incorporate student voices into the design and enactment of teaching and learning environments. The negative ramifications of excluding and not valuing student voices are many—such as students not persisting in college because of exclusionary practices, protests by groups historically excluded in higher education settings, and increased mental health challenges.

A major way that student voice is solicited within academia is through course evaluations, also called student ratings of instruction. Higher education is at a time of reckoning, as the multiple limitations and challenges of these reviews continue to emerge (Heffernan, 2022). In Tracie's experience, she has observed how an emphasis on course evaluations can result in instructors fearing student voices for a variety of reasons, which is counterproductive. We need to reconsider how we can support teaching in partnership with students. A challenge, however, is that most courses in higher education settings are tied to grades, which results in particular power differentials between students and instructors. Course evaluations also are summative and conducted at the end of the instructional process (i.e., too late) and can play a large role in promotion and tenure decisions. They might not yield feedback that can be used to improve instruction. Anonymity allows for protection of student identity but can also result in hurtful, biased comments. Course evaluations are unidirectional and not designed to facilitate dialogue between students and instructors. While instructors might obtain useful information from course evaluations, such assessments can have serious limitations when used as the sole measure of effective teaching. Course evaluations can be biased, they have not been shown to be effective measures of student learning, and they have been correlated with other factors such as instructor likability (Esarey & Valdes, 2020; Kreitzer & Sweet-Cushman, 2022; Carpenter et al., 2020; Clayson, 2022). Higher education continues to grapple with how to handle course evaluations, but in general, more holistic approaches to evaluating teaching using multiple sources such as student voice, peer review of teaching findings, instructor reflections, and course artifacts can provide a more complete picture of an instructor's teaching practices. In this book we argue that student voice remains critically important to inclusive teaching efforts, and in particular, a variety of formative measures that involve hearing from learners can help build more inclusive courses.

Inclusive instructors can more readily benefit from gathering formative feedback across the duration of a course. With this kind of feedback students can address areas overlooked in the curriculum and pedagogy (Brooman et al., 2015). When an instructor designs a course for the first time or incorporates new content or teaching strategies, inviting students into the process of feedback to learn how it can impact learners is critical.

One of the students we interviewed shared an anecdote from a time when an instructor demonstrated inclusive partnership with students in a STEM laboratory course:

> The professor who was teaching it had taught for a long time, but something that I really respected about them is that they were really focused on continuing to experiment in a good way with how they structured their class, and how they would manage their preps for their class. And one time I came to lab a little bit early, and they were there sort of setting up the lab, and I asked them, "Hey, how is this lab going to work?" And they ended up saying, "Well, I'm trying this for the first time. Do you want to just walk through it and see if it sounds like a good class?" and I was like, "Sure." So they ended up explaining to me like everything that we would do that day, and they would sort of tell me like the pitfalls that they're worried about, and apparently they had done this in a different lab one time. So they like, remember some of the good things and bad things that happened in that lab.
>
> So they were like sort of trying to adjust for my lab, and it was really fun to go through and sort of get a feel for like what that class was about to look like, you know, like the next three hours of my life, like they had been planned by this person, and this person was like telling me the plan beforehand. And then, like genuinely asking me like, "Do you think this is gonna work?" "Do you like this plan?" "Do you think that I should change it in one way or another?" And that was really cool. I feel like that was a pretty inclusive way to like, you know. They knew that I was interested in sort of experimentation in a classroom, and trying to figure out what might work for the students.

> And I think that sort of mindset while that was a very personal experience between me and that Professor, I think that that can apply to any class where I know some people sort of use the word sign posting for this type of behavior where … The instructors can say like what they're going to do before they do it, and like, lay out the plan of the class before the class even starts. So like, "Today we're going to do this, and I'm really hopeful that we can get to this. This is what that's gonna look like," you know, and even maybe suggest some things that they are worried could go wrong, or they're excited to hopefully go right … Everyone is starting this class session together, so it's a nice thing to sort of have that sense of community right off the bat where it's like, "Okay, here's the plan for today. Let's all work together to see if we can get it to go right."
>
> —*A public university student who identifies as White and non-binary*

There is a lot to unpack from this student's reflection. At the forefront is the student's positive view of the instructor's invitation for the student's feedback to improve their teaching as an inclusive practice. Within higher education, the instructor as the sole expert in the classroom remains a prevailing narrative. While critical pedagogical and content expertise often reside within the instructor, a different type of expertise also resides within the student—their perspectives as a learner. This instructor harnessed the student's expertise and interests in an inclusive way that made the student feel invited into the learning experience.

The instructor also made visible their ongoing openness to learning, even as a seasoned instructor, given that they were still experimenting with their teaching. They modeled life-long learning and the student held these actions in high regard. The instructor also demonstrated that student perspectives mattered to them through this informal interaction. Revisiting the mindsets of inclusive instructors described in *What Inclusive Instructors Do*, they were aware of who was in their class and took ownership over their teaching, committing to praxis and intentionality to design a well-structured course for their students.

Additionally, the student viewed their instructor's actions as a model for how to be transparent in teaching with an entire class to build community from the start of a course. The simple act of inviting students into a feedback loop about a modified learning activity was highly regarded as an inclusive action by this student. These are the types of practices that we describe in this book, this time hearing from students and describing tools that instructors can use to obtain feedback on their efforts. One such tool is the Protocol for Advancing Inclusive Teaching Efforts (PAITE), a classroom observation protocol, later described in this book, that provides data-driven feedback on inclusive teaching approaches (Addy et al., 2023).

In the student's perspective shared above, the instructor illustrated such reflective practice. They implemented a revised laboratory exercise and were aware of what went well the first time and what was less than optimal. Their reflections were context-bound, and interconnected to the situational factors of the learning environments in which they taught. As they reflected on the new iteration, they invited the student to share their perspectives on the exercises as a way of gathering more feedback. Simultaneously, we need to emphasize the contextual aspects of this interaction. We do not necessarily suggest that all instructors invite this type of conversation with students. The instructor described had seniority and likely felt a sense of safety in being able to engage in this type of one-on-one discussion with this student. We will share later in the book a variety of methods of generating feedback from students that can be used by instructors across appointment types and rank, e.g., those new to the institution or in their career, adjunct instructors, and instructors from groups historically excluded from the academy.

Like our first book, we use the text as a vehicle to share tools with the community of instructors within higher education across disciplines. These tools encompass student voice, various observational and feedback tools, and more. What we hope for is in the end that instructors bring this information back and apply it in their classrooms, departments, and institutions to create sustained change around inclusive teaching. The idea behind inviting student voices is to use the collective knowledge already present within colleges and universities. We also acknowledge local institutional contexts and the historical, structural, and cultural underpinnings of inclusive teaching practices while simultaneously sharing emergent themes across contexts directly tied to fundamental needs of humanity such as students' sense of belonging and mattering.

As instructors continue to implement inclusive teaching practices, reflecting on the students' themes that are shared in *Enhancing Inclusive Instruction* will continue to be of value. In this book we emphasize these aspects that students value as inclusive, expanding and building upon the knowledge of what is done in course settings. We acknowledge context is critical as well as instructor identity. This book serves as one mechanism to bring learners' perspectives to the forefront of dialogues around inclusive teaching that can be accessible to instructors.

Our Study

In writing this book we drew from a study surveying over 300 college and university students from a variety of institution types taking courses of varying modalities (online, in-person, and hybrid instruction) who shared their perspectives on inclusive learning environments. We used a variety of methods to solicit such feedback through colleges and universities directly, online survey research platforms, student organizations, and other groups. The full survey is available in Appendix I. When the opportunities arose, we also performed student interviews. Students were invited to share their perspectives on what their instructors did that was inclusive as well as any approaches that were not inclusive, with the goals of identifying both practices that students reported being beneficial to their learning, as well as pitfalls for instructors to avoid.

Participants reported describing in-person as well as online instruction. Students could share demographic information such as race and ethnicity as they saw fit. When they reported this information, we included it with their quotes to provide context to their backgrounds. They reported diversity in their gender and sexual identities. Several students were neurodivergent or were students with disabilities. They reported identifying as Black, African-American, White, Latino, Hispanic, American Indian, Asian, and mixed race; 46 percent described themselves as first-generation college students, or learners, neither of whose parents completed a four-year degree; 80 percent reported being full-time students; 5 percent of students identified as being veterans. They indicated that their institutions were in the northeast, south, midwest, and western United States. They identified their institutions as community colleges; small, private liberal arts colleges; historically Black colleges or universities; public universities; private universities; and master's colleges or universities. Student respondents also described a range of courses within STEM disciplines, the humanities, and the social sciences.

After collecting the data, we performed thematic analyses to analyze students' narrative responses according to major themes focused on classroom inclusivity. The findings and student quotes are integrated mostly throughout Chapters 2, 3, and 4 of the book to provide examples of inclusive course design, practices that students perceived as creating welcoming environments, and equitable teaching approaches. We present these findings with the existing literature to provide an even more comprehensive view of students' perspectives on inclusive classrooms.

To obtain a general view of students' experiences within inclusive classrooms, participants were asked to consider all of their college courses and respond to a few preliminary questions focused on inclusivity. We found some notable results worth expounding upon regarding the students' reported experiences in classroom spaces (Table 1.1).

Globally, the lowest scores were reported with regards to instructors knowing about the personal backgrounds of their students and how they implicate their learning in the course. Additionally, fewer students reported that most or all of their instructors directly addressed equity and inclusion concerns in the course. Many of the students reported not feeling valued in most of their courses and not feeling a sense of belonging. A lot of the students in the sample appeared to be operating in many learning spaces where they did not perceive their presence and perspectives to matter.

TABLE 1.1 Students' Reported Experiences with Inclusive Courses

Item	*All or Most (%) (N = 364)*
In how many of your courses did the instructor know your name by the end of the course?	69%
In how many of your courses have you felt that you have had an equal opportunity to succeed compared with other students in the course?	68%
In how many of your courses have you felt able to express your perspectives on the course content/material?	61%
How many of your instructors have successfully created an inclusive learning environment in their classes?	59%
In how many of your courses have you felt a sense of belonging?	58%
In how many of your courses have you felt as if you were a valuable member of the learning community?	59%
In how many of your courses have you felt able to express your perspectives on the course setup and format?	47%
How many of your instructors have directly addressed concepts of inclusion and equity in your classes?	37%
In how many of your courses do you feel your instructor knew about how your personal background might relate to the course?	34%
In how many of your courses do you feel your instructor knew about how your personal background might affect your ability to succeed in the course?	34%

Considering these findings, instructors might wonder, where is the proverbial sweet spot with learning about students and being empathetic while also facilitating an environment with high expectations for their learning? We touched on the topic of getting to know learners in *What Inclusive Instructors Do*, and presented a variety of means to do such even in large courses. Additionally, we acknowledge that the creation of an inclusive classroom is a partnership between both instructors and students, with both playing valuable roles. There is no one-size-fits-all approach to building inclusive learning environments, and different instructors will utilize different approaches. Various course formats will lead to varied approaches.

Another question that might arise is whether all instructors should directly address issues related to topics of diversity, equity, and inclusion. For any courses taken by humans, diversity, equity, and inclusion will remain relevant inclusive of and beyond the course content. A course is a space of learning, and how those interact within the space can implicate any of these principles.

One very comforting observation from the study is that many students in the sample had very positive experiences of their instructors building inclusive classroom environments. As one example, a student who described herself as female, African-American, and neurodivergent (you'll hear more of her thoughts later) indicated that, at the institution she attended which was dedicated to educating a diverse student body, she could not think of any experiences she had had that were not inclusive.

Another student, enrolled at a public university, who self-identified as White, female, with a sensory disability, shared the following with regards to the larger-sized courses she took and how the instructor took time to hold discussions, which stood out in a positive way as not commonplace in traditional lecture courses with large numbers of students.

> [I]t was a big lecture class. So it wasn't like a discussion-based class, so he [the instructor] still created that space for people to do that [discussion] I thought was really good. I think I noticed that more in the big lectures in my smaller classes, more discussion seminars. All of my professors have been great across the discipline. Well, STEM classes have been the bigger ones, but in all my humanities ones, the smaller classes … [N]one of the professors have ever made people feel like whatever they're saying is not valid. So even after creating that encouraging environment to speak out, then making people want to do it again by encouraging whatever they say. So I think that's been really great. Just the environment that my professors have created to make people feel comfortable to speak.

This student's response made it evident that from her perspective there are ways to build more inclusive spaces within larger-sized courses, and when this happens it can be quite noticeable to a student.

This student also described some barriers to her learning because of her disability and how she navigated them through her own initiative and self-advocacy.

> I found that if you disclose to people [your disability], they're very helpful … I do this less so in college, just it's been a little bit different. But I know that in the past talking to friends and having them kind of be my eyes. If there's something that I need to copy down, and them reading it to me or something like that. So, definitely, people are open to help, but it's not immediately evident what is going on with me. So unless I make that step to ask, then people won't reach out because they just won't know.

Reflection Questions

- What most stands out to you with regards to the initial study findings presented in this chapter?
- If you designed survey questions to gather students' perspectives, what questions would you ask?

If inclusive teaching is effective teaching, and a large mission of higher education is to design and enact significant learning experiences, the percentages of students reporting inclusive courses must go up. They also reveal structural factors that impact inclusion.

Conclusion

The findings from our study make evident that there are a number of practices that can be readily identified to support an inclusive classroom environment and not all of them require substantial modification to the course. Some are the small yet powerful pedagogical strategies that any instructor regardless of discipline can apply to a course. Others might take more time to fully integrate, but make a large difference to students. Continue on this journey with us as we start to distill the voices of students in subsequent chapters.

References

Addy, T. M., Reeves, P. M., Dube, D., & Mitchell, K. A. (2021). What really matters for instructors implementing equitable and inclusive teaching approaches. *To Improve the Academy: A Journal of Educational Development*, 40(1), article 1. doi:10.3998/tia.182.

Addy, T., Younas, H., Cetin, P., Cham, F., Rizk, M., Nwankpa, C., & Borzone, M. (2023). The development of the Protocol for Advancing Inclusive Teaching Efforts (PAITE). *Journal of Educational Research and Practice*, 12. doi:10.5590/JERAP.2022.12.0.05.

Aragón, O. R., Eddy, S. L., & Graham, M. J. (2018). Faculty beliefs about intelligence are related to the adoption of active-learning practices. *CBE—Life Sciences Education*, 17(3), article 47. doi:10.1187/cbe.17-05-0084.

Brooman, S., Darwent, S., & Pimor, A. (2015). The student voice in higher education curriculum design: Is there value in listening? *Innovations in Education and Teaching International*, 52(6), 663–674. doi:10.1080/14703297.2014.910128.

Carpenter, S. K., Witherby, A. E., & Tauber, S. K. (2020). On students' (mis)judgments of learning and teaching effectiveness. *Journal of Applied Research in Memory and Cognition*, 9(2), 137–151. doi:10.1016/j.jarmac.2019.12.009.

Clayson, D. (2022). The student evaluation of teaching and likability: What the evaluations actually measure. *Assessment & Evaluation in Higher Education*, 47(2), 313–326, doi:10.1080/02602938.2021.1909702.

Cook-Sather, A. (2018). Listening to equity-seeking perspectives: How students' experiences of pedagogical partnership can inform wider discussions of student success. *Higher Education Research and Development*, 37(5), 923–936.

Cook-Sather, A. (2020). Respecting voices: How the co-creation of teaching and learning can support academic staff, underrepresented students, and equitable practices. *Higher Education*, 79(5), 885–901.

Cook-Sather, A. (2022). *Co-Creating Equitable Teaching and Learning: Structuring Student Voice into Higher Education*. Cambridge: Harvard Education Press.

Cook-Sather, A., & Des-Ogugua, C. (2019). Lessons we still need to learn on creating more inclusive and responsive classrooms: Recommendations from one student-faculty partnership programme. *International Journal of Inclusive Education*, 23(6), 594–608.

Design Justice Network. (n.d.). *Design Justice Network*. Retrieved December 23, 2022, from https://designjustice.org.

Esarey, J., & Valdes, N. (2020). Unbiased, reliable, and valid student evaluations can still be unfair. *Assessment & Evaluation in Higher Education*, 45(8), 1106–1120. doi:10.1080/02602938.2020.1724875.

Graham, C., & Moir, Z. (2022). Belonging to the university or being in the world: From belonging to relational being. *Journal of University Teaching & Learning Practice*, 19(4). https://ro.uow.edu.au/jutlp/vol19/iss4/04.

Heffernan, T. (2022). Sexism, racism, prejudice, and bias: A literature review and synthesis of research surrounding student evaluations of courses and teaching. *Assessment & Evaluation in Higher Education*, 47(1), 144–154. doi:10.1080/02602938.2021.1888075.

Hirsch, J. L., & Clark, M. S. (2019). Multiple paths to belonging that we should study together. *Perspectives on Psychological Science*, 14(2), 238–255. doi:10.1177/1745691618803629.

Kreitzer, R. J., & Sweet-Cushman, J. (2022). Evaluating student evaluations of teaching: A review of measurement and equity bias in SETs and recommendations for ethical reform. *Journal of Academic Ethics*, 20(1), 73–84. doi:10.1007/s10805-021-09400-w.

Thoman, D. B., Yap, M.-J., Herrera, F. A., & Smith, J. L. (2021). Diversity interventions in the classroom: From resistance to action. *CBE—Life Sciences Education*, 20(4), ar52. doi:10.1187/cbe.20-07-0143.

PART I

Students' Perspectives

2

HOW MY INSTRUCTORS DESIGN INCLUSIVE COURSES

> "[T]he instructor thought it was very important to include everyone and created an environment that made it easy and less stressful to learn."
>
> —*A private university student who identifies as a straight Polish female*

This chapter centers students' perspectives on inclusive course design based on responses from hundreds of students around the country who shared what inclusive course design approaches most resonated with them. Their input is valuable for instructors. Having a firm grasp on inclusive course design principles and practices, and knowing strategies that support a diversity of students, can inform teaching and learning for instructors while also acknowledging and addressing students' individual accessibility needs. Here we emphasize key themes identified through content analysis of student surveys and interview responses where students were asked to provide reflections on their instructors' inclusive course design efficacy, highlighting practices and pitfalls. We have further supported student voices with expert voices from the educational literature and our own real-world instructional experiences. The student quote above exemplified how inclusive teaching is not making course material easy but rather creating environments where students feel comfortable learning.

The Themes

Seven key themes emerged when we analyzed students' collective responses on how their instructors did or did not succeed in designing inclusive courses. Their instructors' course designs:

DOI: 10.4324/9781003442929-3

- Maximized student engagement from the first assignment and throughout the course
- Included course policies, activities, and assignments that respectfully considered students' time
- Involved structures that were easy to follow and designed for student success
- Personalized the course for individual students, acknowledging mental health status, disability, neurodivergence, and socioeconomic status
- Encouraged students to provide feedback on instruction
- Used diverse course materials that valued real-world student experiences
- Accounted for the type of course delivery (in-person, hybrid, or online)

These themes emerged from the responses of students that varied by institution type, across geographic regions, visible and invisible demographics, major and discipline, class year, full-time or part-time enrollment, and veteran status. The power of these themes arising amidst the diversity of students demonstrated that there are shared fundamental needs that they believed to help them be successful learners. Sometimes these themes appeared when the students described learning experiences that worked well. In other instances, students highlighted how the lack of inclusive course design hindered their learning. In general, when an instructor designed inclusively, with intention to who may be in the room, it benefited the greatest proportion of students.

Reflection Questions

- Do any of these themes surprise you? If so, which ones?
- Which, if any, of these themes have students commented upon in your courses? Was the feedback positive or negative?
- How could you go about gathering student voices to identify relevant themes that apply to your own inclusive course design planning?

Maximized Student Engagement from the First Assignment and throughout the Course

First Assignment

> *The first day of class I like when a professor asks us to email them about who we are, makes me feel like I am being seen.*
>
> *—A public university student who identifies as White, non-binary, and lesbian*

I'm taking a sociology of death and dying course and the first assignment was asking us to introduce ourselves with an obituary.
—A small, private liberal arts college student who identifies as Caucasian, non-binary, and lesbian

Students highlighted the importance of the first assignment. Several students believed that inclusive course design includes a first assignment that has a high degree of student engagement and requires little new content mastery, rather, relying on existing student knowledge. Positive feedback from successfully completing a first assignment can trigger both short-term and long-term positive emotions in students. Students have reported a successful first assignment is critical to increasing self-efficacy, motivation, and ultimately future student engagement (Kahu et al., 2019). One important consideration is that student engagement is not always positive and subject to fluctuations and cycles. As the course progresses, content and later assignments can get more challenging and negate the positive emotions facilitated by a successful first assignment. These difficulties may trigger strong negative emotions and reduce students' self-efficacy later in the course. A common first assignment Khadijah has used in her classroom to maximize student engagement is "What's your origin story in three chapters (past, present, and future)?" as it relates to the course topic. Sometimes this is an oral presentation and at other times it is a written assignment. Students routinely say how they appreciate the opportunity to share about their personal backgrounds and what first got them interested in the discipline, their motivation for taking the class now, and how they believe their newfound knowledge will help them accomplish future professional and personal goals.

Throughout the Course

Created [an] opportunity to connect with other classmates.
—A public university student who identifies as White, male, and straight

Peer Teaching and Peer Review

The professor had the students teach different subject material, which got everyone involved in the learning.
—A public university student who is a first-generation college student and identifies as a heterosexual Hispanic male

Discussions on readings and peer reviews.
—A community college student who self-identifies as a pansexual White female

Another way students recognized effective inclusive course design, which maximized their engagement, was peer teaching and peer review throughout the course. Their instructors planned peer teaching activities where students learned in groups by teaching others. Peer teaching requires student "interactivity," where teachers contribute their own information to their learners, and involves interdependence, where students participate as both teachers and learners (Rusli et al., 2021). Peer teaching allows students to be actively engaged with one another and the learning process.

Peer review activities can hone communication, critical thinking, collaboration/teamwork, and awareness skills (Wu et al., 2014; Suñol et al., 2016) and is one approach to keep students learning and involved. As a part of the peer review process, students use metacognition. Metacognition is thinking about how one thinks. Specifically, it refers to the processes used to plan, monitor, and assess our own understanding and performance. Metacognition includes being critically aware of one's thinking and learning. This facilitates a collaborative exchange of ideas and feedback among students by creating a space for dialogue where students better understand current standards and produce better work in the future (Yucel et al., 2014). Students' participation in peer review is likely to create a more engaged and cohesive learning community. One pitfall of peer review is that it can require a significant time investment. To combat this, astute inclusive course design can allow for peer review to be used for discrete course elements, such as assignments, assessments, teaching and learning activities, and content. For example, student A can use a grading rubric to provide peer review of Student B's written report or final portfolios before Student B submits the assignment or assessment to their instructor. Additionally students may need to be coached on how to provide productive feedback.

Group Work

Physics/in-person/labs required group work.

—A public university student who identifies as Caucasian and Native American racially but does not identify his Native heritage on any documents, is male, straight, and between the ages of 25 and 34

Group work activities that involved collaborating ideas and perspectives.

—A small, private liberal arts college student identifies as heterosexual and White but did not supply a gender identity

We often did group work and were encouraged to speak to new people and share ideas.

—A private university student who identifies as a first-generation college student and identifies as a straight Caucasian female

Most of the assignments or activities were designed to include everyone and so the class can work together.
—A private university student who identifies as a straight Asian female

Last semester my teacher ha[d] us do many group activities that encouraged us to all make friends.
—A private university student who identifies as a first-generation White female

The labs included working with your classmates to ensure that you are getting to know new people and learning in a new environment.
—A private university student who identifies as a straight Latina/White female

Made random seating to force us to talk to others.
—A private university student who is a first-generation student and identifies as a straight White male

Group work is often used throughout higher education as an active learning strategy that promotes deeper learning and teamwork. Numerous students in our study appreciated when inclusive course design included group work throughout the course because it maximized student engagement, as illustrated in the preceding quotes. Furthermore, culturally diverse groups are known to help prepare college and university students for a multicultural and global society (Poort et al., 2020). Therefore, maximizing student engagement through group work can help realize these goals. Recent work has used student voices to explore how trust in the group, cultural diversity in the group, and group formation contribute to student engagement in group work (Poort et al., 2020).

Trust among group members is known to be crucial for group functionality and performance. Surveys of 1,025 bachelor's students from six universities identified students' trust in the group as the strongest positive predictor of behavioral and cognitive engagement (Poort et al., 2020). Greater perceived cultural diversity also promoted behavioral and cognitive engagement, but to a lesser degree when compared with trust. A higher perception of cultural diversity increases idea exchange, evaluation, and integration and promotes deeper learning. Culturally homogeneous groups tend to have ideas and perspectives that are more similar. Whether students could choose their group members did not significantly affect student engagement.

Khadijah uses instructor tools, like the Who's in Class? form and Comprehensive Assessment of Team Member Effectiveness (CATME), to assemble and manage diverse groups without outnumbering historically excluded students in her classroom (Addy et al., 2021; Layton et al., 2010; Dasgupta et al., 2015). For example, the CATME Team-Maker feature allows instructors to only use criteria that are important to them. Team-

Maker provides a list of criteria from which instructors can choose when forming teams. These are presented to students in a Team-Maker Survey. Instructors can also write in their own questions. Research has found some criteria (e.g., gender, race, ethnicity) to be important to student learning in groups (Layton et al., 2010). CATME can also be used for peer review and to structure group roles. This is important as outnumbering historically excluded students in small group settings can have a great impact on underrepresented student persistence (Dasgupta et al., 2015).

Group work also comes with pitfalls. Designing courses inclusively with culturally diverse groups means that some students can face challenges, such as different cultural and communication styles, language differences, and feelings of anxiety. By contrast, students in Poort et. al.'s study indicated that the overall effect of cultural diversity on cognitive engagement was positive (Poort et al., 2020). Another pitfall concerns the needs of neurodivergent students.

Instructors should also design group work experiences that take into account how neurodiverse students in their courses can experience such learning activities. The documentary film *Autism Goes to College* (2019) features five diverse students on the autism spectrum disorder (ASD) and takes us into their lives and classrooms to show us how they are making college work. Many autistic students in higher education report having challenges with group work (Hillier et al., 2017). If a student discloses they have ASD, instructors can help design more inclusive environments for them by individually asking them about their thoughts and experiences on group work, and what can best support them in accomplishing the learning goals. Alternatives might be considered if group work proves to be too challenging. Instructors can have similar conversations with students with attention deficit hyperactivity disorder (ADHD). They may find group work is a preferred mode of learning and have insights into what helps them learn in such environments. Tracie has had the experience of students with ADHD privately approaching her about learning concerns, particularly for longer courses like three-hour laboratories. She witnessed positive outcomes when a student discovered that engaging in hands-on group work activities for the course worked well for them. They told Tracie at the end of the course that they never felt their ADHD to be a barrier to their success in that class.

During one of the study interviews, a student who was neurodiverse shared their experiences with inclusive group work:

> *Yeah, I think the dynamic of the group is definitely important, and whether or not it feels like a sort of inclusive space, like if one person in the group is zooming ahead on all the work and kind of leaving the other people in the dust that does not necessarily feel like you're all on the same page. But when everyone is kind of working together to help each other,*

> *figure out the problems, or even if they finish their problem first, they just check in like. What did you guys get? Do you have any questions? I didn't understand this XYZ. Just kind of listening to each other more, and actually taking the time to check in with each other as you're doing the work rather than just doing it on your own, checking the answers and then being like, okay, we [agree,] that was like so-called group work.*
>
> *—A small, private liberal arts college student, who identifies as a White female and has an unspecified disability*

Group work has undergone innovations in higher education to meet current sociocultural norms. Students have found multiple methods of communicating and successfully completing group work assignments, even when not meeting in person (McKinney & Cook, 2018). Cellphones, in particular, have become a popular method of collaboration through social media and messaging apps. Video Conferencing sites and apps provide learners with opportunities to see one another as they complete the work, perhaps in contradiction to the idea that group work can only happen in shared physical spaces. The virtual spaces students occupy create another mode of engagement that increases student accountability and participation in its disavowal of the belief that learning can only take place in the physical classroom. This is especially true when the group consists of individuals without close proximity to one another.

Another pitfall to consider when inclusively designing group work is the emergence of "free-riders" and "social loafers" (McKinney & Cook, 2018). Group agreements can be a useful tool for every student involved. The idea is for group members to co-create their own ground rules for how to work together effectively and respectfully, and to discuss actions that the team will take if there is a problem. Disruptive, ineffective, and unsuccessful group work is the result of a plethora of factors that can be mitigated through thoughtful, structured inclusive course design. For example, specifying roles for each member allows students to take responsibility for portions of the assignment they feel best suits their expertise and comfortability. McKinney and Cook explain that the absence of defined roles may leave certain group members lacking confidence or interest, causing them to withdraw from the work altogether; doing so invites other group members to make assumptions about the degree of investment the free-riding student has to the assignment, often causing animosity toward that student. Students might overlook the emotional or mental challenges a group member might be experiencing when they have discomfort with their role.

This is not to say that all free-riding students lack a defined role and do not participate to the fullest extent possible. Some students may depend too heavily on the rest of the group to complete the work. Designing group assignments that result in all members receiving one grade can unintentionally produce free-riders. While the intent of inclusive course design is to encourage equitable participation and accountability, group assignments can sometimes instigate a contrary outcome. Disinvested or self-conscious students tend to be more willing to play the background if they are convinced the rest of the group will earn a good grade, giving the free-rider perceived permission to not engage (McKinney & Cook, 2018).

The same can be said of free-riders within multicultural group dynamics, where specific approaches to group dynamics inform the level of engagement students have with one another. As previously mentioned, issues like language barriers and how difficult the task or assignment may be, among other factors, play a part in encouraging a student's active participation in the group (McKinney & Cook, 2018). For instance, some international students may gravitate toward hierarchical group dynamics due to cultural respect for guidance and structure. It is not unusual for these students to seek one specific leader who will ideally create ordered interactions and assign responsibilities because compromise is preferred to direct confrontation. These students may perceive critiques of the work being produced as disrespectful and may go along with the rest of the group members, even if they see fault in the work being created (McKinney & Cook, 2018).

The student quoted above also noted during the interview the importance of in-class group work in which their professor actively engaged with groups to support inclusivity by supporting learners and keeping them on track and accountable:

> *I definitely think it's up to professors there, and walking around the classroom and checking in on what you're doing, so that you have to be doing what you're supposed to be doing, or else.*
>
> *—A small, private liberal arts college student, identifies as a White female and has an unspecified disability*

Reflection Questions

- How can you, or do you, design first course assignments that allow your students to engage with you and their peers?
- In what ways do you maximize student engagement throughout your course?
- What are the most likely student engagement pitfalls you may need to avoid?
- If you currently, or in the future, integrate group work in your courses, how can you design it so that it is more inclusive from the start?

Included Course Policies, Activities, and Assignments that Respectfully Considered Students' Time

Allows for Self-Pacing and Provides Open Access to the Syllabus, Course Materials, and Assignments

I go to [institution name redacted] where it is all self-paced. I think the instructors have designed each of the courses in a way that makes self-pacing possible.

—A public university student who identifies as a heterosexual White female between the ages of 45 and 54

Syllabus

Providing [the] syllabus beforehand.

—A small, private liberal arts college student who identifies as a straight South Asian male

Course materials

[T]he instructor made sure that all the readings and lecture materials were available since the beginning of the semester and that we could work on it anytime that we're free. This reduces the stress of having to complete the work on weeks/days that we're not free.

—A private university student who identifies as a straight African and Asian female

Assignments

[O]pened all assignments from the beginning of the course with suggested due dates so that students could work at their own pace.

—A public university student who is a first-generation college student and identifies as a straight White female

All assignments were 0s until graded, which allows working at your own pace.

—A small, private liberal arts college student who identifies as a straight White male

One professor ... asked us about the schedule and rate of assignments.

—A private university student who identifyies as a bisexual White female

> *[M]y professor notified us of assignments well before due dates to allow students to have as much time as possible and with several acceptable formats to turn assignments in.*
>
> *—A small, private liberal arts college student who identifies as a straight White female*

Higher education courses can be a source of student anxiety about assignments and grades, and self-pacing with can be a tool to circumvent it. Several of our study respondents commented on how effective inclusive course design clearly explains self-pacing on the syllabus and then utilizes self-pacing in the course materials and assignments to reduce student anxiety. Assignments that allow for students to work at their own pace with a suggested and final deadline can effectively take away the anxiety some students feel at having to submit work at the same time as peers. Coupled with multiple-attempt assignments, this may alleviate the stress of feeling one's work has to be perfect on the first try. Recent research has shown students given self-paced assignments provided increased student confidence over the course of an academic term (Bell, 2023). Using pre- and post-surveys, the Westside Test Anxiety Scale showed the use of self-paced, multiple-attempt assignments reduced students' perceived anxiety. Student comments were largely positive and grades strongly correlated with high scores. A pitfall to consider is that negative correlations are observed between course grades and late module attempts and submissions. This is due to academically weaker students having a harmful association with student procrastination and course performance.

Overall, clear evidence exists regarding the effectiveness of self-paced, multiple-attempt assessment in reducing the stress and anxiety students may feel when having to complete challenging assignments (Bell, 2023). Including self-pacing strategies in inclusive course design is important in strengthening a student's perception of their academic selves and their intellectual capabilities. It also allows them to see the ways in which they have grown over the course of an academic term, and reinforces the concept of growth mindset, that intelligence is not fixed, as well as formative assessment, that multiple low-stakes assessments (e.g., multiple attempt) can support students in achieving learning outcomes through practice.

Uses Flexible Deadlines

> *Flexible deadlines for assignments.*
>
> *—A public university student who identifies as bisexual White female*

> *There are no hard deadlines.*
>
> *—A private university student who identifies as asexual, agender, and White*

Giving extra time for homework and exams.
—A community college student who identifies as a heterosexual Caucasian female over 55 years old

This teacher made their Canvas page very easy to access and find all the information that I needed. Also I felt that the time to complete assignments was structured very well.
—A public university student who identifies as a bisexual White woman

[M]y instructor designed the course in a way that everything was not rushed through and we had enough time to go over the concepts and understand them.
—A private university student who identifies as a Hispanic and White female

During this course our instructor made sure to give us enough time to complete assignments while also helping teach us about important things before they were needed.
—Student has not identified the type of institution they are enrolled in and identifies as a White male

My writing professor is extremely thoughtful and always makes sure everyone knows what they are doing and always understands things happen and deadline extension.
—A small, private liberal arts college student who identifies as a White male

Understanding how full our schedules are and giving us extra time to complete.
—A small, private liberal arts college student who identifies as a straight Latina female

Numerous study participants recounted the importance of having flexible deadlines as a marker of inclusive course design. Deadlines have the benefit of providing structure for the instructor and learners to maintain a uniform pace and collective progression through course materials. Deadlines can also, however, make assumptions about the extracurricular lives of the students in any particular class. While deadlines can be helpful, they can miss the individual out-of-class priorities and experiences learners have. All students do not have the same barriers to accomplishing work by the predetermined dates throughout the term. Students with full-time employment, children, or caretakers for others, have medical issues that require constant treatment etc. may struggle with competing priorities, forcing them to choose between turning assignments in by the deadline or attending to their other equally important imperatives.

Flexible deadlines, however, take into account the whole person and acknowledge the realities of a person's life outside of school. Flexible deadlines are an inherent component in inclusive course design since a greater degree of flexibility regarding submission dates recognizes the individual nature of students' life circumstances. As such, moving away from rigid deadlines allows for greater participation and engagement by students with the added benefit of the student creating quality work without being under the duress deadlines bring with them. Furthermore, flexible deadlines give students more agency in how and when they meet their learning goal. Extensions, as a prime example, are useful in alleviating the stress students can feel when completing their work.

Extensions are defined as "proactive" when built into the course assessment structure in advance during course design planning and available to all students. For example, every assignment may have a deadline and extension date. Students can therefore use extensions for as many assignments as they desire without penalty. Students are not required to request the extension, self-disclose any reason(s) for the extension, or notify their instructor they are using an extension. When used effectively, extensions are not abused and only requested out of absolute necessity (Hills & Peacock, 2022). As a measure of inclusive course design, proactive extensions encourage an increase in the quality of the work a student does, increase equity and inclusivity, and make students more responsible for managing their own course loads and time, operating as self-pacing, self-regulated learners (Hills & Peacock, 2022). Inclusive course design also emphasizes areas where students commonly struggle and can provide support. For example, as the course progresses, content tends to become more challenging. Instructors can provide a suggested priority deadline and extension date to help students manage their time for assignments and assessments that deal with difficult topics later in the course.

Examples of how to provide flexible deadlines while still upholding expectations for individual students and teams are context-dependent. In a STEM laboratory course, this might include providing students with an opportunity to repeat particular experiments or re-analyze already collected data in a new way (in line with the scientific process) before submitting a high-stakes final laboratory report by a set deadline and/or standard extension date (typically one week later). For a team in a lecture-based course, this may facilitate iterative peer feedback on a low-stakes group presentation with an extension date (3–5 days) with students who have very different schedules. All deadlines and proactive extensions should be clearly described in the syllabus at the beginning of the course and on the learning management system website, if applicable. Overall, extensions are more commonly used for team assessments when compared with individual assignments (60 percent vs. 30 percent) (Hills & Peacock, 2022). Students are not the only ones who can benefit from proactive extensions. Instructors employing proactive deadlines as a component of their inclusive course design saw the benefits by spreading out the time instructors have to grade assignments, as well as not feeling as if they have to judge the legitimacy of a student's request for extra time in completing their work. This approach reinforces the notion that students should be active participants and managers of their academic careers (Hills & Peacock, 2022).

Build in Brain Breaks

> *Structured the (online) class session with breaks built-in.*
>
> —*A small, private liberal arts college student who identifies as agender, pansexual, and White*

Using brain breaks is an inclusive design approach that acknowledges the way that the brain works to improve attention and learning. Recent work has advocated for instructors of adult students to shift from thinking about learning as an exclusively mental effort, and appreciate how they can improve their students' knowledge and skills through physical movement (Hrach, 2021). Brain break strategies can include movement breaks (e.g., stretching, yoga, jumping jacks, or dancing) or mental breaks (deep breathing, mindfulness, creative art activity, or playing music or a game). A recent study has shown that taking short breaks may help our brains learn new skills (Buch et al., 2021). Brain activity was mapped in healthy volunteers who were learning something new. During a rest phase, the brain rapidly and repeatedly replayed faster versions of the activity seen while they practiced. The more a volunteer replayed the activity, the better they performed during later practice sessions. This suggested that the breaks improved learning and memories (Buch et al., 2021). The improved learning may be due to the "spacing effect" (Vlach et al., 2008). Breaking learning up into several short chunks of time is better than cramming learning into one large block.

When planning brain breaks, the time duration of the class is an important consideration for the instructor. A general rule is to plan a quick and easy 3–5-minute activity for every 20–30 minutes of learning. Undergraduate and graduate students sustain attention to a taxing cognitive task for approximately 20–30 minutes (Lim et al., 2010; Lim et al., 2013). After that time, researchers have found blood flow decreased to regions of the brain involved in cognitive vigilance, leading to slower reaction times and greater mental fatigue (Lim et al., 2010). When focusing on a learning task, our brains devote more processing resources to areas that improve our performance. Mental fatigue might be a signal that we are expending too much energy relative to the benefit from staying on task. As a result, the brain withdraws these resources. In fact, theta brain waves (which indicate mental fatigue) increase during bouts of sustained attention (e.g., up to 65 minutes) but decrease during 5-minute breaks every 30 minutes (Lim et al., 2013). Therefore, a 50-minute class is expected to have fewer and shorter brain breaks than a 3-hour seminar. Brain breaks (also known as screen breaks) are particularly advantageous for synchronous online courses since these students have fewer opportunities to take breaks on their own like their counterparts in asynchronous courses.

Reflection Questions

- Are you able to provide a syllabus (full or abbreviated) of the course before it starts to your students? If not, is there information you might be able to share beyond the course title and description?
- Could it benefit your students to make all of your course materials and assignments available at the beginning of the course?
- Do you build flexible deadlines and extensions into your courses? If so, does the type of assignment or assessment influence your deadline policy?
- Are you able to incorporate breaks into your courses? Are these short breaks during a class session or entire class periods? Are they movement breaks, mental breaks, or both?

Involved Structures that Were Easy to Follow and Designed For Student Success

The Syllabus Clearly Explains the Course Structure

> *Great syllabus and was organized.*
>
> —*A community college student who identifies as a Filipino male*

> *Course was organized and clearly followed the syllabus.*
>
> —*A small, private liberal arts student who is a first-generation college student and identifies as a straight female of Asian and White descent*

> *Following the syllabus was great.*
>
> —*A community college student who is a first-generation college student and identifies as a straight White female*

> *They set [a] good syllabus.*
>
> —*A community college student is a first-generation college student and identifies as a bisexual White female between the ages of 25 and 34*

They provided the students with a syllabus that contains all the due dates and expectations for the course.

—A private university student who is a first-generation college student and identifies as a White female

The syllabus was neat and due dates were clearly shown which made it easy to prepare for the semester.

—A private university student who is straight and White

The Course Set-Up/Structure/Organization Facilitates Student Success

They made the set-up easy so I could complete the task properly.

—A community college student who identifies as a pansexual Black female between the ages of 25 and 34

My … class was well set-up to succeed and easy to understand. Plus, there [were] plenty of help topics available.

—A community college student who is a first-generation college student and identifies as a gay White male between the ages of 25 and 34

Asked students how they wish the course could be set up.

—A private university student who is a first-generation college student and identifies as a straight Caucasian female

[M]y teacher always had a set structure… and it was highly beneficial in my ability to learn.

—A public university student who identifies as a White female

It's organized the same for all students.

—A community college student who identifies as a White female

Numerous students in our study commented on the importance of the syllabus clearly explaining the course structure, and how the organization made their success easier. An inclusive course design perspective can be adopted to create an inclusive syllabus. Helmer (2021) describes six principles of inclusive syllabus design (ISD): 1) learning-focused; 2) organized around big questions and themes; 3) integrates Universal Design for Learning (UDL) principles; 4) rhetoric and tone include inclusive and motivating language; 5) contains supportive course policies; 6) embeds an accessible design. Some of our respondents who reflected on the syllabus being clear were first-generation college students, highlighting its importance for all learners. Using ISD principles to develop a transparent syllabus is particularly important for this student demographic given that they may have fewer family college supports. However, it is important to note that every syllabus, even an inclusive syllabus, has an associated hidden curriculum as there are unwritten mores, rules, values, norms, messages, and implicit biases that instructors may inadvertently communicate. For example, Khadijah routinely uses ISD practices 1, 2, and 5. She makes her syllabus learning-focused by centering set professional and personal course themes/goals for each student cohort, in addition to course learning objectives. In the body of the syllabus, she makes sure to spell out acronyms, explain that the essential office hours she facilitates are also to form positive instructor–student relationships, her preferred email etiquette from students, and how she prefers students to address her. This knowledge supports all students in successfully navigating the course.

Reflection Questions

- Which, if any, inclusive syllabus design principles do you use in your syllabus? Are there additional ones that you might be able to use?

Personalized the Course for Individual Students, Acknowledging Mental Health Status, Disability, Neurodivergence, and Socioeconomic Status

Sees Each Individual Student While Including All Individual Student Needs

> *They did not have a specific plan for all of us to be the same. They took time and made us each individual plans.*
>
> *—A private university student who identifies as a heterosexual White female between the ages of 35 and 44*

> *It catered to my needs.*
>
> *—A public university student who identifies as a bisexual White male between the ages of 35 and 44*

> *We were able to teach how [we] as individuals learned and post it to help out someone who might not understand in the way it was taught.*
>
> *—A community college student who is a first-generation college student and identifies as a heterosexual female of American Indian/White descent between the ages of 35 and 44*

> *This professor had a certain amount of daily assignments and quizzes that would be "dropped" at the end of the semester. This showed that she understood*

that we are individuals and have busy lives outside of school, and gave us a degree of accountability and responsibility over our learning.

—A private university student who identifies as a heterosexual White female

Professors were lenient and understanding with personal experiences that students had that affected school work.

—A public university student who identifies as a straight White male

Individual Student Preferences: Assignments and Exams

The professor gave the option to either present the final project or submit a long form essay on the topic to cater to students with anxieties in presenting or those who struggle to write analyses and decide which they would be more successful in.

—A public university student who identifies as White, non-binary, and queer

[P]rojects and assignments were flexible, meaning that you had a choice in how you wanted to format your work or complete the assignment.

—A private university student who identifies as a straight White female

[W]e were given very general questions for the essays. We were given the freedom to choose anything that interests us.

—A small, private liberal arts college student who identifies as a straight African American/Hispanic female

[C]hoice of a final exam format (take home essay or in person verbal exam).

—A private university student who identifies as a straight Caucasian female

According to the 2017 US Department of Education National Education Technology Plan, the definition of personalized learning is:

> Personalized learning refers to instruction in which the pace of learning and the instructional approach are optimized for the needs of each learner. Learning objectives, instructional approaches, and instructional content (and its sequencing) all may vary based on learner needs. In addition, learning activities are meaningful and relevant to learners, driven by their interests, and often self-initiated.
>
> *(U.S. Department of Education, 2017, p. 1)*

The student respondents appreciated when instructors attended to individual learning needs and when they had some agency or choice in assessments. The essential function of individualized personalized learning is to engage students in taking ownership over their learning by focusing on their individual strengths, aptitudes, and interests (Hughey, 2020). When students are able to chart their own academic paths they tend to have a greater investment in their scholastic success. Rather than instructors dictating to students what they will learn and the methods through which they will gain mastery of particular subject matter, individualized personalized learning tends to student needs and preferences.

Major structural challenges limiting more personalized learning in higher education are that not all class sizes are small, course context matters, and some instructors have very high teaching loads and competing obligations. Instructors must consider the strategies that would be most appropriate for their situations.

Includes Everyone

> *Making sure we are all included.*
>
> *—A community college student who is a first-generation college student and identifies as a straight White male between the ages of 45 and 54*

> *Include[d] everyone.*
>
> *—A private university student who is a first-generation White female*

> *None were excluded.*
>
> *—A community college student who identifies as a heterosexual, White non-Hispanic male between the ages of 25 and 34*

> *During Biology the teacher had us do review days during class which involved the whole class.*
>
> *—A private university student who is a first-generation college student and identifies as a heterosexual Hispanic female*

Although individual students comprise a classroom, the needs of all must simultaneously be considered when designing inclusive courses. In our study, we saw this was vital for first-generation college student respondents. The majority of students who mentioned the importance of everyone being included were first-generation college students, whether they attended community colleges or private universities. This is important, because the interest of these students enhances the learning environment and allows their voices to be acknowledged in contributions to the entire classroom (Hughey, 2020).

The students in our study who saw "including everyone" as important varied by age, gender, and race. It is important to recognize that even the most inclusive instructor might not have familiarity with every student demographic. This requires you as an instructor to acknowledge this and do the work to inform yourself about particular groups through formal or informal mechanisms.

For example, increased awareness around religious diversity could be considered when planning courses. Instructors should take into account how adherence to certain religious holidays may impact a student's ability to fully participate in a class session or complete assignments.

Including statements about a student's inability to attend class, participate in the learning environment, or complete assignments due to religious observances connotes a sensitivity to the needs of students beyond the classroom. This strategy is important because it does not penalize a student for being unable to fully engage because of religious responsibilities; nor does it make the student feel like they have to choose between their participation in religious services and meeting their academic requirements. Instructors can plan in advance for these considerations by looking at the school's academic calendar for dates religious holidays fall on (Hughey, 2020).

Recent diversity, equity, and inclusion (DEI) efforts have foregrounded religious diversity on higher education campuses. The Interfaith, Spiritual, Religious, and Secular (INSPIRES) Campus Climate Index is a tool that scores colleges and universities on their levels of religious DEI based on extensive faith-related resource surveys from 185 public, private, and religiously affiliated institutions (Mayhew et al., n.d.). Instructors can consult their institution's INSPIRES score, if available, to better course plan for what type of religious diversity could be present in their student population. Students in our study attended institutions in the United States, which is a religiously plural society. Consequently, this means there are religious majorities and minorities. Instructors need to educate themselves on the various minority traditions to ensure those students are also included. There are a variety of courses, curricula, and tools to help increase religious DEI awareness (Wallace, 2023).

Considers All Student Accessibility Needs

Mental Health Status

Changed syllabus based on the mental health of the students.

—A small, private liberal arts college student who identifies as a non-binary Asian lesbian

I just remember the teacher being very flexible [with] submissions as long as you let her in with what was happening. And I really appreciated that because I knew friends in the class who were able to get extensions when they needed, because they let her know ahead of time, and they worked it out ... we have other classes. We have mental health to take into consideration. So I really appreciated that.

—A public research university student who is a straight White female

One of my professors uses ungrading, a system in which students present the grade they think they deserve at the end of the course. This class is very important to me, but with no tests and an ungrading system I am able to get through it without immense amounts of stress and pressure.

—A small, private liberal arts college student who identifies as a straight White woman

My science teacher set up the course using ungrading and then asked for our thoughts and feelings on this.

—A small, private liberal arts college student who identifies as a bisexual White female

Student mental health is a pressing concern for colleges and universities around the country. Exacerbated by the COVID-19 pandemic, growing numbers of students have experienced mental health challenges and well-being issues. It is estimated that approximately a third of American university students meet the criteria for a clinically significant mental health issue (Lister & McFarlane, 2021). There are both individual and structural barriers to mental well-being. A certain level of stress is the norm in academic settings; however, higher education systems, structures, and study practices can trigger mental health episodes. One student in our study mentioned the importance of accounting for mental health status by changing the syllabus. Most research on how to better support student well-being is student-focused, such as enhancing student resilience, enabling mental health-related support mechanisms, and promoting self-care (Lister & McFarlane, 2021). By contrast, a willingness to change the syllabus, or designing the course in a way that accommodates mental health status, is a change to a higher education structural practice that creates a learning environment which promotes student well-being.

Other student respondents indicated the strategy of ungrading as effective in alleviating some of the stress and mental pressure they felt at the prospect of exams and graded assignments by the instructor. Ungrading in an umbrella term for a variety of grading methods that aim to focus more on learning than on grades. For example, through some ungrading practices students, through thoughtful and honest reflection, might evaluate their success and grade themselves in a course based on their perceptions of their engagement with the learning process. In other words, students learn how to evaluate their development in a particular class based on personal reflection and assessment of their progress and understanding of the course's subject matter (Guberman, 2021). Inherent in this type of learning-focused grading is the willingness for students to fail. In fact, students may greatly benefit from instructors who emphasize ungrading as a more appropriate way of evaluation based on the principle that failure and laboring through assignments are fundamental to deepening one's conversance with a subject and should be embraced, rather than viewed as a marker of incompetence.

Ungrading certainly has its challenges. Pitfalls include not being fully transparent and clear with students how ungrading methods are different from traditional grading, reinforcing them throughout the course, and discussing with students how such approaches can be beneficial and support their learning. It can also be a learning curve for the instructor to implement ungrading successfully throughout an entire course. However, inclusive course design is amenable to using ungrading for a particular assignment or unit. According to a research study conducted in an online synchronous course by Gorichanaz (2022), the eight respondents (six information systems majors, one information technology major, and one business major; two women and six men) were overall agreeable to the method. Respondents reported a greater level of comfort with being wrong. One participant even confessed that rather than making him feel like each answer given needed to be correct, being wrong has its benefits, as it allows students to learn from their errors. The satisfaction that comes with being wrong but knowing why one was wrong encourages deeper, more sustained engagement with the instructor and the material. Ungrading also gives learners experience with assessing themselves and growing from self-evaluation. Another student respondent remarked that the exercise of ungrading and self-evaluation gave them a sense of success, rather than failure, due to the act of constant self-reflections on their work.

Learning Disabilities

> *Having all the assignments in one place and all learning materials online made it easier for students with learning disabilities to follow the class.*
>
> *—A small, private liberal arts college student who identifies as an asexual White woman*

Visual Disabilities

> *For a college marching band course, we had a blind student join. The primary instructor took great care to ensure he had readable music (inverted colors—white text on black page).*
>
> *—A public university student who identifies as a bisexual White cis-male*

Physical Disabilities

There was a student in a wheelchair in science. We all sat in a different seat every day.

—A community college student who is as a first-generation college student and identifies as a heterosexual White woman between the ages of 25 and 34

Sensory Disabilities

We had a lot of readings, and one of them was unavailable in a format that I needed. Instead of making me go out and continuously search for it to figure it out, my professor actually recorded herself reading each of the chapters for me, and shared it with me. And then there was this one time that she wasn't going to be able to do it, and so she arranged for her husband to do it.

—A public research university student who identifies as a straight White female

Yes, just getting things in different formats is challenging, because I think a lot of professors assume that those alternate formats make it the same for me, just like "Oh, get her the formats, and then it's just like all the other students." But that's not the case. Those digital formats are the only way that I can even access the material. Then it still takes a bunch of extra work to actually complete it. One of my psychology professors saw me. We had talked at the beginning of the semester, [and] sorted [it] out. How are we gonna work through the semester together? And I told her how we would do it. … then she saw me manipulating the screen once. How I have to do it to read, and she was like "This is the work that you have to do? Oh, no. Like we're going to not make you have to do this much work. We're going to figure out another way. I didn't realize. … seeing this is eye opening to me. So we're gonna reduce your work even more, because this is still too much. So that was just a great moment … it really took seeing it for herself to really understand what it's like on my side.

—A public research university student who identifies as a straight White female

Neurodivergence

This past semester one of my courses … was designed to give students a bunch of different opportunities to do well on assessments and assignments, so that it wasn't all riding on a few big assignments, which I think was really helpful for those who maybe get overwhelmed with that kind of idea, that a test tests knowledge, and that's it. If you don't do well, you don't do well. … in this particular course there [were] a lot of opportunities to do other things that would go towards your grade and different completion of assignments. So I thought that was a good design.

—A public research university student who identifies as a straight White female

As evident through the quotes presented thus far, several of the students in our study had a disability or were neurodivergent. Their disabilities were both visible and invisible, and provided critical considerations for course planning. For these students, it was critical that the course design included class materials that were accessible. Equally important was embedding student choice in the assignment and assessment design. One student commented on how inclusive course design sometimes only partially supported their learning needs, and they were oftentimes left with the burden to fill in the gaps. For example, providing course readings in varied formats is important. A one-size-fits-all approach is insufficient and requires students to search for the appropriate format. Instructors should consider this in course design. This either requires the instructor to provide an alternative and appropriate format (e.g., reading the chapter themselves) or becoming more knowledgeable and understanding of assistive technology or accessibility features in technology (He et al., 2022).

Socioeconomic Status

Provide free literature instead of [making] students buy unnecessary books that are very expensive.

—A small, private liberal arts college student who identifies as a straight White male

The course allowed students of all financial backgrounds to succeed, even though some of the equipment being used was very expensive.

—Student chose not to share demographic information

Socioeconomic status can shape a student's experience in higher education. Even when students receive financial assistance, it does not always cover all of their educational expenses. Our student respondents highlighted an appreciation for inclusive course design that was welcoming to students from various socioeconomic statuses. The Open Educational Resources (OER) movement supports equity and flexibility in college and university classrooms. It is grounded in the human right to access high-quality education. This provides free or low-cost course materials to all students, regardless of financial background. In Khadijah's course, texts are often very costly. She reconciles the current edition with past editions on the syllabus, and provides OER to supplement content that may be lacking in older versions. She also does not require publisher learning aids, but rather provides all students with the additional learning aids she created. Students can always exercise the option to purchase commercially available materials. Inclusive course design should offer students flexibility, variety, and choice in course materials (Devlin & McKay, 2016).

Reflection Questions

- In what ways do you incorporate individual student needs and preferences into your course design while making space for all students?
- How do you educate yourself on student demographic attributes in which you may be unfamiliar?
- How do you account for a variety of student accessibility needs, such as mental health, visible and invisible disabilities, neurodivergence, and diverse socioeconomic status, while designing your courses?

Encourages Student Feedback

> *Always ask for input from everyone in class.*
>
> *—A community college student who is a first-generation, heterosexual White female, aged 55+*

> *My instructor decided to let us all give our own views on one of our projects which was pretty cool.*
>
> *—A private university, first-generation college student who identifies as a heterosexual Black female aged between 25 and 34*

> *Several of my instructors have reached out to us as a class and inquired as to our opinions and suggestions as far as change is concerned.*
>
> *—A public university student who is a White male between the ages of 45 and 54*

Using student feedback in course design fosters a more inclusive learning community. Our student respondents commented on how their opinions, suggestions, and views can be incorporated into the course design in a prospective manner (e.g., a project). Student feedback can also lead to retrospective course design and a review of effective strategies that promote inclusive learning environments for future iterations of a course. Weekly journal reflections from 65 students over 10 weeks revealed the importance of embedding meaningful interactions and carefully scaffolded motivation, engagement, and management strategies in an online course (Speiser et al., 2022). A tree model was used to describe a process-oriented approach to fostering an inclusive learning community that highlights conditions and practices necessary for a transformative learning experience in remote contexts. The model is based on a "learning tree." The "roots" represent instructors, students, and course structure. Careful cultivation is reflected in course planning (Speiser et al., 2022),

Some students were above the age of 25 years. Student feedback from these individuals is important as they may have more diverse life experiences than their classroom counterparts. For example, they may live off-campus or be older adult learners who are returning to school to earn certifications or degrees (Rao, 2013). For the older adult learners discussed here, they may experience challenges, such as ambiguity and uncertainty about expectations, isolation and lack of community, and technology challenges (Rao, 2013). Designing course elements that encourage student feedback can help support learners in this demographic by alleviating fears, building community, and offering technological primers. Additional discussion on when, how, and why to collect and utilize student feedback will occur in Chapters 3 and 4, as well.

Reflection Question

- Do you build in opportunities for students to provide feedback on the overall course design or specific elements (like projects) at the beginning of the course?

Used Diverse Course Materials that Valued Real-World Student Experiences

Diverse Course Materials

Diverse Scholars

> *In my English course the instructor included teachings based on people of different races and people who have disabilities. This allowed students to make connections or learn about something outside of what they're accustomed to.*
> *—A private university student who identifies as a straight Black female*

> *Content includes many different peoples lives and their perspectives as reading material.*
> *—A public university student who identifies as an aromantic/asexual White woman*

> *My teacher … included assignments and discussions of the contributions of diverse scholars by including individuals from a range of cultures, races, genders, or sexual orientations to convey that everyone can be successful.*
> *—A public university student who is a first-generation college student and identifies as a heterosexual Puerto Rican female, aged between 35 and 44*

Acknowledging things like colonization.

—A small, private liberal arts college student who identifies as a bisexual White female

Included male and female writers.

—A public university student who identifies as a bisexual Caucasian female

In our study, historically excluded students based on race (e.g., Black and Puerto Rican) and sexual orientation (e.g., aromantic/asexual and bisexual) shared that using diverse scholars was a sign of good inclusive course design. Particularly, diverse scholars being used and respected as legitimate sources of critique or knowledge resonated with them. They commented on the importance of multiple identities and communities being represented, including things you can see (like race and gender), attributes that are latent (like culture and sexual orientation), and things that can be both visible or invisible (like disabilities). Such framed content can help Black, Indigenous, persons of color (BIPOC), female, and LGBTQIA+ students improve learning outcomes (Livezey, 2021). Incorporating diverse scholars can de-emphasize Eurocentric representations. For example, one of our students mentioned the importance of acknowledging things like colonization. Considering diversity in course design is a critical pedagogical practice.

Diverse Course Content

Diverse selection of reading material.

—Student chose not to share demographic information

[D]esigned with a mix of readings, assignments and tests, which I appreciated.

—A small, private liberal arts college student who identifies as a bisexual White female

[C]ompletely open-to-discussion posts that aren't dedicated to any one question or questions.

—A community college student who identifies as a straight White male

All teachers had open discussion time of a given topic at least once.

—A small, private liberal arts college student who identifies as an asexual White/Jewish male

Communications class regarding inclusiveness within written texts, such as children's books and the examples of inclusiveness. Sometimes we had a worksheet to fill out with answers, sometimes it was essays.

—A public university, first-generation college student who identifies as a bisexual Caucasian, aged between 25 and 34

I had a professor give public exams, giving us the exam beforehand to review and ask questions about beforehand. Please look this up if you haven't heard about it, it was awesome! The exam was still very challenging, but there were no surprises, and I felt like I was given a fair shot at studying for it.

—A public university student who identifies as a White non-binary pansexual

As mentioned previously in this chapter, students in our study appreciated student choice in assignments and exams. Several students also mentioned variety in assignments and assessment methods overall throughout the course design, even if choices are not possible or limited. Offering assessment variety can support students in the following key ways: 1) students can have a deeper understanding of select topics or concepts instead of simply memorizing for an exam, thus moving higher on Bloom's taxonomy; 2) students can apply knowledge in authentic learning and assessment activities to develop the skills necessary to work in their future career or discipline; and 3) students have diverse abilities, backgrounds, and interests, so assessment diversity puts all students on a level playing field in terms of showcasing their knowledge and actions.

Real-World Student Experiences

Where I'm from it's predominantly a French-speaking country. And one of my college professors went to my hometown and knows so much about the culture there.

—A public university, first-generation college student who identifies as a straight Black female aged between 25 and 34

In a class about the history of sex in America, my professor designated a day each week (we only met three days each week) to only have a group discussion about the readings and how they relate to our own experiences.

—A public university student who identifies as a White, non-binary, and pansexual

Relating the concept to real life experience.

—A community college student who identifies as a White male between the ages of 25 and 34

Authentic learning is a teaching and learning philosophy that connects learning with real-world student experiences. Our students appreciated when inclusive course design facilitated authentic learning (1) by connecting course content to their real-world problems, situations, and experiences; (2) by providing opportunities for them to make their own connection between their real life and learning so that it is personally meaningful; and (3) when it is reflected in the learning tasks. This also involves disciplinary practices so students can be situated and immersed in real-world situations typically found in their professional careers (Abramenka-Lachheb & De Siqueira, 2022). Authentic assessment is an extension of authentic learning (Abramenka-Lachheb & De Siqueira, 2022). An authentic assessment evaluates if the student can successfully transfer the knowledge and skills gained in the classroom to various real-world contexts, scenarios, and situations beyond the classroom. Authentic assessments can include a variety of types, including discussions, simulations, role-plays, projects, and debates. All authentic assessments can be redesigned using diversity lenses as a tool. For example, using real-world student experiences in the course design appealed to our student participants with a diversity of identities, such as Black, non-binary, pansexual, and non-traditional ages.

Reflection Questions

- How can, or do, you consider diverse scholars in your course materials?
- What strategies do you use, or have you used, to add variety to instructional materials, assignments, and assessment tools?
- John Dewey's Constructivist Learning Theory is based on each student's own perspective and real-world experiences. In what ways do you scaffold your course's learning outcomes based on students' lived experiences?

Accounted for the Type of Course Delivery (In-Person, Hybrid, Online)

In-Person

> *Allowed online options.*
>
> *—A public university student who identifies as a straight White female*

Hybrid

> *When there is an exam assigned, class is optional that week. The professor understands that even though we picked a Hybrid course, we might need that specific time to get the exam done.*
>
> *—A community college student who identifies as White, non-binary, pansexual*

I think the online courses are very equally accessible for people who have a hard time having transportation.

—A community college student who identifies as White, non-binary, bisexual, aged between 25 and 34

Online

[T]he teacher invited students to come be with her during class on campus as well if they wanted.

—A community college student who identifies as a mixed race, asexual female, between the ages of 25 and 34

The final inclusive course design theme that emerged from our study accounted for the type of course delivery. Whether in-person, hybrid, or online, students mentioned the instructor's attention to the course delivery type was important. In a post-pandemic landscape, some instructors are hybridizing their in-person courses (Widjaja et al., 2023). Maximizing learning outcomes in both in-person and online modes, while facilitating concurrent delivery, has emerged as a key priority. Instructors also adapted an optional hybrid approach where students primarily attend in-person classes but are offered an online alternative if they are isolating due to health-related issues (Widjaja et al., 2023). The converse is also true. Sometimes online classes can have optional or encouraged in-person course elements. For example, Khadijah has held essential in-person office hours to meet with online students at the beginning of a course.

Options in hybrid course delivery models (e.g., hyflex, blended) were also mentioned by our study respondents. In particular, one student appreciated class being optional if an exam was assigned that week. Another appreciated how the hybrid format met their particular transportation needs. Inclusive course design recognizes transportation can be a barrier for some students, including those who live in rural and remote areas. Hyflex learning presents the components of hybrid in a flexible course structure that gives students the option of attending sessions in the classroom, participating online, or doing both. For example, one student in a completely online course liked the option of meeting with the instructor while they taught the class in-person on campus. This may be desirable for students with disabilities or neurodivergent students as additional support. Blended learning is another course delivery type where students learn online as well as through in-person instruction. Independent of hybrid course delivery, and as emphasized earlier in this chapter, students want course policies designed to allow for flexibility.

Reflection Questions

- Are there options you can provide students who cannot attend a class session in-person? What are they?

- How can you structure the course in a way that maximizes access to hybrid class sessions, whether in-person or online?
- How can you give in-person students online options, or online students opportunities to engage with you in-person?

Conclusion

When centering student voices on inclusive course design, seven robust key themes emerged. These were important for a variety of student demographics. Interestingly, student choice, student options, and instructor flexibility were cross-cutting, and permeated many of the themes. What was abundantly clear was students wanted to be intentionally and actively included, as well as considered for their individual needs and not treated as a collective.

References

Abramenka-Lachheb, V., & De Siqueira, A. (2022). Authentic assessments through the lenses of diversity, equity, inclusion and justice in a fully online course. *Journal of Teaching and Learning with Technology*, 11(1). doi:10.14434/jotlt.v11i1.34591.

Addy, T. M., Mitchell, K. A., & Dube, D. (2021). A tool to advance inclusive teaching efforts: The "who's in class?" form. *Journal of Microbiology Biology Education*, 22(3). doi:10.1128/jmbe.00183-21.

Autism Goes to College (2019). [documentary] dir. E. Linthorst. Available at: https://www.autismgoestocollege.org/

Bell, E. C. (2023). Self-pacing and multiple-attempt assessment to address student anxiety in pharmacy calculations. *Discover Education*, 2(1). doi:10.1007/s44217-023-00032-3.

Buch, E. R., Claudino, L., Quentin, R., Bönstrup, M., & Cohen, L. G. (2021). Consolidation of human skill linked to waking hippocampo-neocortical replay. *Cell Reports*, 35(10), 109193. doi:10.1016/j.celrep.2021.109193.

Dasgupta, N., Scircle, M. M., & Hunsinger, M. (2015). Female peers in small work groups enhance women's motivation, verbal participation, and career aspirations in engineering. *Proceedings of the National Academy of Sciences of the United States of America*, 112(16), 4988–4993. doi:10.1073/pnas.1422822112.

Devlin, M., & McKay, J. (2016). Teaching students using technology: Facilitating success for students from low socioeconomic status backgrounds in Australian universities. *Australasian Journal of Educational Technology*, 32(1). doi:10.14742/ajet.2053.

Gorichanaz, T. (2022). "it made me feel like it was okay to be wrong": Student experiences with Ungrading. *Active Learning in Higher Education*, 146978742210936. doi:10.1177/14697874221093640.

Guberman, D. (2021). Student perceptions of an online ungraded course. *Teaching & Learning Inquiry*, 9(1), 86–98. doi:10.20343/teachlearninqu.9.1.8.

He, W., Zha, S., Watson, S., & He, Y. (2022). Teaching tip: Promoting inclusive online learning for students with disabilities in information systems courses. *Journal of Information Systems Education*, 33(1), 7–14. https://jise.org/Volume33/n1/JISE2022v33n1pp7 14.html.

Helmer, K. (2021). Six Principles of an Inclusive Syllabus Design. In R. Kumar & B. Refaei (Eds.), *Equity and Inclusion in Higher Education: Strategies for Teaching* (pp. 19–28), Cincinnati, OH: University of Cincinnati Press.

Hillier, A., Goldstein, J., Murphy, D., Trietsch, R., Keeves, J., Mendes, E., & Queenan, A. (2017). Supporting university students with autism spectrum disorder. *Autism*, 22(1), 20–28. doi:10.1177/1362361317699584.

Hills, M., & Peacock, K. (2022). Replacing power with flexible structure: Implementing flexible deadlines to improve student learning experiences. *Teaching and Learning Inquiry*, 10. doi:10.20343/teachlearninqu.10.26.

Hrach, S. (2021). *Minding bodies: How physical space, sensation, and movement affect learning*. Morgantown, WV: West Virginia University Press.

Hughey, J. (2020). Individual personalized learning. *Educational Considerations*, 46 (2). doi:10.4148/0146-9282.2237.

Kahu, E. R., Picton, C., & Nelson, K. (2019). Pathways to engagement: A longitudinal study of the first-year student experience in the educational interface. *Higher Education*, 79(4), 657–673. doi:10.1007/s10734-019-00429-w.

Layton, R. A., Loughry, M. L., Ohland, M. W., & Ricco, G. D. (2010). Design and validation of a web-based system for assigning members to teams using instructor-specified criteria. *Advances in Engineering Education*, 2(1), 1–28. https://files.eric.ed.gov/fulltext/EJ1076132.pdf.

Lim, J., Quevenco, F.-C., & Kwok, K. (2013). EEG alpha activity is associated with individual differences in post-break improvement. *NeuroImage*, 76, 81–89. doi:10.1016/j.neuroimage.2013.03.018.

Lim, J., Wu, W., Wang, J., Detre, J. A., Dinges, D. F., & Rao, H. (2010). Imaging Brain Fatigue from sustained mental workload: An ASL perfusion study of the time-on-task effect. *NeuroImage*, 49(4), 3426–3435. doi:10.1016/j.neuroimage.2009.11.020.

Lister, K., & McFarlane, R. (2021). Designing for wellbeing: An inclusive learning design approach with student mental health vignettes. *Open Praxis*, 13(2), 184. doi:10.5944/openpraxis.13.2.126.

Livezey, M. R. (2021). Using diverse, equitable, and inclusive course content to improve outcomes in a chemistry course for nonmajors. *Journal of Chemical Education*, 99(1), 346–352. doi:10.1021/acs.jchemed.1c00433.

Mayhew, M. J., Ray, W., Adamson Flesher, M., & Rockenbach, A. N. (n.d.). Inspires index. *Inspires Index*. https://inspiresindex.org/.

McKinney, P., & Cook, C. (2018). Student conceptions of group work: Visual Research into LIS student group work using the draw-and-write technique. *Journal of Education for Library and Information Science*, 59(4), 206–227. doi:10.3138/jelis.59.4.2018-0011.

Poort, I., Jansen, E., & Hofman, A. (2020). Does the group matter? Effects of trust, cultural diversity, and group formation on engagement in group work in Higher Education. *Higher Education Research & Development*, 41(2), 511–526. doi:10.1080/07294360.2020.1839024.

Rao, K. (2013). Universal instructional design of online courses: Strategies to support non-traditional learners in postsecondary environments. In S. Burgstahler (Ed.), *Universal design in higher education: promising practices*. Seattle: DO-IT, University of Washington. Retrieved from www.uw.edu/doit/UDHEpromising-practices/uid_online.html.

Rusli, M., Degeng, N.S., Setyosari, P., & Sulton (2021). Peer teaching: Students teaching students to increase academic performance. *Teaching Theology & Religion*, 24, 17–27. doi:10.1111/teth.12549.

Speiser, R., Chen-Wu, H., & Lee, J.S. (2022). Developing an "Inclusive learning tree": Reflections on promoting a sense of community in remote instruction. *Journal of Educators Online*, 19(2). doi:10.9743/jeo.2022.19.2.11.

Suñol, J. J., Arbat, G., Pujol, J., Feliu, L., Fraguell, R. M. & Planas-Lladó, A. (2016). Peer and self-assessment applied to oral presentations from a multidisciplinary perspective. *Assessment & Evaluation in Higher Education*, 41(4), 622–637. doi:10.1080/02602938.2015.1037720.

U.S. Department of Education. (2017). *Reimagining the role of technology in education: 2017 National Education Technology Plan Update*. Office of Educational Technology. https://tech.ed.gov/netp/learning/.

Vlach, H. A., Sandhofer, C. M., & Kornell, N. (2008). The spacing effect in children's memory and category induction. *Cognition*, 109(1), 163–167. doi:10.1016/j.cognition.2008.07.013.

Wallace, B. (2023, April 12). Improving religious diversity and inclusion in higher ed. *HigherEdJobs*. https://www.higheredjobs.com/Articles/articleDisplay.cfm?ID=3409&Title=Improving%20Religious%20Diversity%20and%20Inclusion%20in%20Higher%20Ed

Widjaja, M., Kim, R. Y., & Donovan, C. (2023). Hybridized face-to-face and online laboratory content in the time of COVID-19. *Biochemistry and Molecular Biology Education*, 51(3), 327–328. doi:10.1002/bmb.21714.

Wu, C., Chanda, E., & Willison, J. (2014) Implementation and outcomes of online self and peer assessment on group based honours research projects. *Assessment & Evaluation in Higher Education*, 39(1), 21–37. doi:10.1080/02602938.2013.779634.

Yucel, R., Bird, F. L., Young, J., & Blanksby, T. (2014). The road to self-assessment: exemplar marking before peer review develops first-year students' capacity to judge the quality of a scientific report. *Assessment & Evaluation in Higher Education*, 39(8), 971–986. doi:10.1080/02602938.2014.880400.

3

HOW MY INSTRUCTORS MAKE ME FEEL WELCOME

> "[T]o feel relaxed and engaged, it's imperative that they're safe and secure ... Teachers can go one step further by adding more elements and making simple changes to a classroom to make it more welcoming."
>
> —*A public university student who identifies as a White heterosexual male between the ages of 35 and 44*

This chapter uses our national survey data to summarize students' perspectives on how their instructors make them feel welcome. Similar to the themes that emerged in Chapter 2, students valued when instructors welcomed all students while simultaneously appreciating their individuality. The instructor's personality, communication style, respect for student diversity, ability to help everyone participate, and care behaviors all contribute to a welcoming atmosphere and promote a sense of student belonging. Based on student experiences, here we also highlight intentional and unintentional instructor practices and behaviors that lead to students feeling unwelcome. We provide evidence-based research and personal experiences that echo student sentiments.

The Themes

Four key themes emerged when analyzing students' responses to questions focused on creating a welcoming environment. Their instructors:

- Welcomed all students
- Acknowledged and respected student differences
- Intentionally fostered equitable participation by students
- Integrated relationship-building as a core component of their courses

DOI: 10.4324/9781003442929-4

These themes all center on "professor immediacy." Professor immediacy can be defined as the availability of an instructor to the students, as well as any welcoming behaviors. Instructors who practice immediacy behaviors tend to create classroom environments that foster positive feelings, are encouraging, and lead to increased confidence and the development of expectations for success in students (Liu, 2021). Put another way, how an instructor communicates with their students will dictate the degree to which a student feels competent in their abilities and how likely they are to believe they will be successful. When done well, professor immediacy increases the closeness a student has with their instructor through verbal affirmation and non-verbal language (Liu, 2021). The closeness and affirmation students feel can have a profound impact on a student's desire to engage in the educational process and feel connected to the community. The said behaviors can be demonstrated verbally and non-verbally.

Verbal immediacy can be described as simply the act of an instructor verbally communicating with students in a way that demonstrates respect for the inherent differences and equal personhood of the student and instructor. Calling a student by their name, providing students equitable opportunities to contribute verbally to class discussions and lessons, getting to class early and staying late after class to speak to students about assignments or extra-curricular activities to build relationships are a few of the ways one might verbally communicate in positive ways with students (Liu, 2021). Other examples of verbal immediacy behaviors that instructors can use are sharing personal stories and experiences, praising students' effort and work, and the use of humor (Estepp & Roberts, 2015). A positive consequence of intentional and directed verbal immediacy is the strengthening of pleasure or displeasure students feel for instructors and tends to develop the rapport between instructor and student the quickest (Akif Sözer, 2019). When students have positive experiences with verbal immediacy behaviors, they experience higher levels of cognitive-affective learning, motivation, and a greater desire to actively engage in the class (Akif Sözer, 2019).

Non-verbal immediacy, on the other hand, is demonstrated by the subtle things instructors do physically to demonstrate a welcoming environment. These can include behaviors or body languages, such as gestures, physical presentation (how an instructor is dressed), facial expressions, and body movements, that relay an instructor's warm invitation to the classroom community (Akif Sözer, 2019). Where verbal intimacy may sound like telling a student "good job," non-verbal intimacy may relay the same message through a smile, a thumbs up, and a facial expression.

Reflection Question

- What are verbal and non-verbal ways that you make your students feel welcome?

Welcomed All Students

Always Has a Welcoming Attitude

They made sure to come to class with a welcoming attitude.
—A private university student who identifies as a straight White male

[M]y professor [brought] the best attitude to class throughout the semester.
—Student chose not to share demographic information

The teacher was able to give off happy and welcoming energy at all times, which helped students be able to express how they feel.
—A private university student who identifies as a straight, White Hispanic female

The professor was very warm and welcome and talked to every student in the class. I felt welcome in that room and everyone had equal opportunity.
—A private university student who identifies as a first-generation, straight Caucasian female

[W]elcoming personality and good natured.
—A public university student who identifies as a straight White female

[M]y instructor was always very welcoming and she always tried her best to accommodate everyone's academic needs.
—A private university student who identifies as a female of Hispanic and White descendancy

Friendly, knowledgeable, and welcomed opinions [and] expressions.
—A public university student who identifies as a first-generation, heterosexual White male

The professor always has a smile on his/her face and is always positive.
—A public university student who identifies as a straight Black male

The teacher is always nice and never gets angry.
—A private university student who identifies as a White male

A key professor immediacy behavior described by students in the study was a welcoming attitude. According to our study respondents, this can take on verbal (warmly talked to every student) and non-verbal (friendly smile) forms. These interactions not only welcome all students, but they include historically excluded populations who are at risk of feeling isolated, which improves student achievement for the entire class. Often higher education research focuses on microaggressions and how they negatively impact students feeling included. By contrast, microaffirmations are small actions that can make students feel welcome, valued, and encouraged (Pittinsky, 2016). When instructors always have a welcoming attitude, they can better microaffirm their students and promote a supportive environment.

Tells Jokes

> *My teacher tells us jokes, to try to get us to talk to each other as classmates.*
>
> *—A community college student who identifies as first-generation and Black*

Many instructors use humor in the college and university classroom. Advocates for using humor suggest it can have a positive effect on the students and learning environments (Nienaber et al., 2019). Students tend to positively evaluate professors who incorporate humor. Interestingly, increased use of humor has also been associated with increased professor immediacy (Gorham & Christophel, 1990; Wanzer et al., 2006). Instructor humor positively related to students' perceptions that the instructor had a positive attitude toward them (Wilson & Taylor, 2001).

Although there is robust evidence that says humor can positively reinforce a welcome footprint, it is important to note that it can also be negative. Some students in our national study felt disrespected and offended by jokes.

> *Cracking jokes is a great thing to do, but it needs to be done carefully. I had a professor joke about the class in a "meta" way, about his own teaching style and whether it works or not … it was pretty cringey and made [me] feel disrespected as a student.*
>
> *—A public university student who identifies as a White non-binary pansexual*

> *Openly talks about politics and his political views—makes jokes about mental health.*
>
> *—A public university student who identifies as a bisexual Caucasian female*

Humor can be used in two forms, affiliative or aggressive. Affiliative humor is defined as "an essentially non-hostile, tolerant form of humor that is affirming of others and presumably enhances interpersonal attraction and cohesion" (Martin et al., 2003). On the other hand, aggressive humor includes sarcasm and using humor to "ridicule and manipulate others" (Martin et al., 2003). In our study, one student commented that the instructor used course-related and non-course-related humor. The literature shows humor in the classroom should be course-related when it comes to supporting students' sense of belonging (St-Amand et al., 2023). Other recent research that centers students' voices has shown they are more likely to have positive emotional well-being and feel comfortable with an instructor who uses affiliative humor as opposed to hostile humor or no humor at all (Nienaber et al., 2019; Tsukawaki & Imura, 2020).

Uses Clear Communication

> *Communication with inclusive tones. She would use our culture and cultural background to connect with us. She did this by asking questions and was sincere about wanting to learn.*
>
> *—A public university student who identifies as a first-generation college student and is a bisexual Caucasian female between the ages of 25 and 34*

> *They created a more welcome and personal environment, opening up lines of communication.*
>
> *—A private university student who identifies as a straight White female*

> *Made sure everyone knew how to contact the professor and that they were communicating expectations, assignments, due dates, projects etc on a weekly or as necessary basis.*
>
> *—A public university student who identifies as a straight White female and first-generation college student*

Our students said clear communication is key to ensuring that they feel welcome in a learning space. Synchronous online teaching communities have always been a good example of using clear communication and technology to maintain teacher immediacy behaviors (Belt & Lowenthal, 2022). As higher education dealt with the fallout of the COVID-19 pandemic, embracing technology to facilitate clear communication and a welcoming environment became essential to those who regularly taught in-person (Belt & Lowenthal, 2022). Particularly for these instructors, remote learning acutely endangered professor immediacy behaviors.

Today, some of the same professor immediacy behaviors that were practiced in-person can easily be done with in-person classes with remote options, hybrid and hyFlex, and synchronous and asynchronous online classes. One student in our study stated a verbal immediacy behavior was clearly communicating how to contact the instructor. For example, in-person courses traditionally have in-person office hours. Courses that incorporate some form of an online element can use technology to host virtual in-person office hours.

Similarly, instructors teaching in-person courses use nonverbal immediacy behaviors to communicate they are welcoming students, like giving a thumbs up or clapping. The same thing can be accomplished when going from in-person to remote online classes by using thumbs up and clapping emoji reactions. Khadijah promotes her students' sense of belonging by inviting them to change their digital thumbs up skin tone if they wish to reflect their own complexion. Another in-person to remote nonverbal immediacy behavior that translated by course modality is the welcome email. One student respondent shared the importance of professors clearly communicating expectations. Instructors can provide an introduction to themselves and the course, as well as detailed expectations for classroom decorum and etiquette, and academic goals. How the email is constructed can mean the difference between a disinvested student and one who feels invited to engage in what will happen in the course. The use of emojis in emails can have a general positive outcome, as the use of these animated shapes and symbols projects the perception of immediacy from a caring and welcoming instructor (Vareberg, et al., 2022). A pitfall is the overuse of emojis in emails can also have the opposite effect. Some students reported that too many or overly frequent use of emojis can call into question the competence on the part of the instructor (Vareberg et al., 2022).

In-person instruction regularly uses confirming communication. Confirming communication can consist of recognition (verbal or nonverbal), acknowledgement (usually verbal), or endorsement (usually a behavior) (Adler et al., 2013). Verbal recognition uses verbal communication to recognize and address the student. Nonverbal recognition of students often includes making eye contact, turning to face them, or physical touch. Acknowledgement means directly acknowledging a student's statement, request, or feelings, or asking them for clarification. Endorsement is the strongest level of confirming communication because it supports student experiences. This may mean agreements with judgments and feelings or offering compliments.

Confirming climates occur when we receive messages that show we are valued from those with whom we have a relationship. A welcoming classroom is a confirming climate where instructors show they value students through clear communication. When exploring how students assessed their emotional outcomes in relationship to the presence or absence of confirming communication by their professor, the principal findings were that students expressed higher levels of emotional interest in the course and also felt a greater degree of emotional support from the instructor when the professor used confirming methods of communication (Goldman & Goodboy, 2014).

Obviously, there are some challenges associated with relaying the three types of confirming communication in online classes. For example, nonverbal recognition through eye contact in-person is much easier with students in the same physical classroom. This is difficult to accomplish online if the instructor's camera is on a different screen from the shared screen used to deliver the course content. In this case, a professor might position their camera to imitate direct and in-person eye contact with students.

Students also commented that a lack of communication contributed to them feeling unwelcome. The absence of a warm and welcoming environment can have significant negative impacts on a student's perception of their inclusion in a classroom. Some respondents expressed a lack of investment when instructors did not utilize clear or confirming communication, stating they felt disconnected from the other class members, unclear about lecture material, and how to best communicate with the instructor.

> *The lack of communication left the class in the dark on most topics taught and gave a very "do your work and leave" feeling.*
>
> *—A community college student who is first-generation and identifies as a straight White female between the ages of 25 and 34*

> *They don't allow for facilitated interaction and learning, [and] have roadblocks in communication they don't address.*
>
> *—A public university student who identifies as a first-generation college student and is a bisexual Caucasian female between the ages of 25 and 34*

> *Didn't tell us how to communicate with him and his email that was in the syllabus was difficult to get a response from him (took a long time to answer).*
>
> *—A public university student who identifies as a first-generation college student and is a straight White female*

Reflection Questions

- What verbal and non-verbal cues do you use to project a good attitude?
- How do cultural views of good and bad attitudes from an instructor and student perspective operate in your classroom?
- Do you use humor in your classroom? If so, do you use affiliative or aggressive humor and how can you be sure?
- When you opt to use humor, how do you account for mixed student perceptions in the same class (i.e., some view joke(s) as affiliative and others view joke(s) as aggressive)?
- What verbal and nonverbal immediacy behaviors do you use to make your students feel included?
- How have you effectively used recognition, acknowledgement, and endorsement to communicate clearly and make students feel welcome?

Acknowledged and Respected Student Differences

Understands the Power of Learning Every Student's Name

Learns Names

> *[M]ade it a point to know everyone's name within the first couple days of class in a pretty big class.*
>
> *—A community college student who identifies as an asexual mixed female between the ages of 25 and 34*

> *Always greeted us by our names.*
>
> *—A private university student who identifies as a lesbian White female*

> *[W]armly greeting me and others by name.*
>
> *—A private university student who identifies as a straight Caucasian female*

> *Makes sure to speak to you by name.*
>
> *—A community college student who identifies as first-generation college student and is a heterosexual White female*

One of the most robust themes we observed in our study was the power of learning every student's name in the class. Many students commented on how they value this behavior. One student remarked how the welcome footprint was more evident when this was done in the first few days of class. Several strategies can be used on the first day of class to help instructors and students learn names (e.g., name tents, annotated class roster, seating chart, photos, mnemonics, student introductions) (Winter, 1992). Learning student names has been widely accepted as an inclusive teaching practice that builds community, helps students feel more comfortable, and increases student satisfaction with a course (Cooper et al., 2017; Glenz, 2014; Murdoch et al., 2018). Through student surveys and semistructured interviews, Cooper and colleagues investigated the importance of instructors knowing their names. They found 78 percent of students perceived that an instructor of the course knew their names (mostly through the use of name tents) even though instructors only knew 53 percent of names (Cooper et al., 2017). This finding indicated that instructors do not have to know student names in order for students to perceive that their names are known and benefit from this welcoming practice.

As important as using students' names is, one pitfall to be aware of is the cultural implications and conventions name usage has. A given name is the legal first name given to a student by their parents. Calling students by their given name, for instance, will look different depending on the student's cultural background. For example, Korean names tend to be written as surnames first and then the given name. Being conversant with various naming conventions can create stronger instructor–student relationships. When instructors use students' names, given names specifically, it communicates the instructor's intention to strengthen the bond. Doing so may imply a greater concern for and interest in the student as a person (Murdoch et al., 2018). This strengthening can look like a student's comfort level in seeking outside class help, confidence to speak with the instructor about non-course-related matters, and a greater investment in the classroom (Cooper et al., 2017).

Failure to resolve the topic of learning names can make students feel alienated or unacknowledged. Respondents to our survey commented that instructors not learning or remembering their names made them feel unwelcome and excluded.

> *Maybe not remembering our names [affected] us in the way that it felt like we weren't included fully.*
>
> *—A private university student who identifies as a first-generation college student and is a White female*

> *This teacher still was messing up my name by the very last quiz we had in that class.*
>
> *—A private university student who identifies as a straight White female*

> *[Didn't] care to know our names.*
>
> *—A private university student who identifies as a lesbian White female*

> *[N]ot trying to know our names.*
>
> *—A small, private liberal arts college student who identifies as a heterosexual Asian female*

> *[T]eacher not even knowing his students by name.*
>
> *—A small, private liberal arts college student who identifies as straight and White*

> *I don't think he remembered any of our names.*
>
> *—A small, liberal arts college student who identifies as a first-generation college student and is a straight female*

Says Names Correctly and Uses Chosen Names

> *[M]aking sure they pronounce my name right.*
>
> *—A small, private liberal arts college student who identifies as a White female*

My professor did not use my chosen name.

—A small, liberal arts college student who identifies as a Black and White male

Two students commented that their instructor not only mispronounced their name; they did not say their chosen name at all. A recent study has posited that there are racial undertones to mispronouncing student names and these incidents can be classified as racial microaggressions because they are "subtle daily insults that, as a form of racism, support a racial and cultural hierarchy of minority inferiority" (Kohli & Solórzano, 2023). The Santa Clara County Office of Education and National Association for Bilingual Education co-sponsor the "My Name, My Identity" campaign, which encourages students to feel a sense of pride about their name and patiently correct people who mispronounce it (2016). K-12 and higher education instructors can "Take the Pledge" to respect student names, and the website provides resources to assist with proper name pronunciation. To avoid ambiguity around chosen and given names, instructors can implement their own preferred name policy, or use one already instituted by their college or university, to inclusively address students.

As a student, Khadijah was well acquainted with instructors mispronouncing her given name. As an instructor, she works to ensure her students avoid having the same negative sense of belonging. In her classroom, some students opt to use an "English" name or shortened nickname if their given name is not easy to pronounce for others. On the first day of class she verbally acknowledges that names are important aspects of cultural identity and heritage, and encourages students to use their given names. On name tents she asks them to write the phonetic spelling of their name, as well as models welcoming practices by asking students to correct her in front of the class if she mispronounces their name during any class session. This simple practice honors all student names, whether given or chosen.

Understands the Power of Learning Every Student's Pronouns

Asks Students for Their Pronouns

Asked pronouns.

—A small, private liberal arts college student who identifies as a Caucasian, non-binary lesbian

Introductions included pronouns.

—A private university student who identifies as a first-generation college student and queer, non-binary Guyanese Indian

[M]ade a game so everyone knew each other's ... pronouns by the end of class.
—A public university student who identifies as queer/bisexual Hispanic female

Respects Students Changing Their Pronouns

One of the more well-respected staff members consistently showed she was willing to accept and support ensemble members who wished to change ... pronouns.
—A public university student who is a first-generation college student and identifies as a White, bisexual cis male

As important as using students' names is, it is not the only way to acknowledge a student's identity. When instructors intentionally work to incorporate as many identities in the room as possible, it demonstrates respect for students. Using pronouns is a way to affirm a student's self-identified gender. On the other hand, misgendering students could be marginalizing while implying a student's stated identity is unimportant. Specifically, misgendering by instructors was a common stressor for non-binary students in a higher education classroom (Goldberg et al., 2019).

The Trevor Project's 2021 National Survey on LGBTQ Youth Mental Health examines the effect that not acknowledging pronouns has on non-binary youth between the ages of 13 and 24, which includes the age range of traditional undergraduate students. Recent data show when "no one" respected non-binary youth pronouns, there was an increase of more than 2.5 times in suicide rates (27 percent attempted suicide in the past year). The suicide attempt rate dropped as acceptance of pronouns increased from "a lot" of people respecting their pronouns (15 percent) to all or most people respecting their pronouns (10 percent) (The Trevor Project, 2021). Pronoun language can be liberating or oppressive. Misgendered students may find it difficult to feel safe enough to learn. Instructors can instigate a greater sense of belonging for all students in general, and welcome LGBTQ youth in particular, by spending time learning students' pronouns.

Allows Students to Introduce Themselves

[S]tudents were asked to introduce and tell something about themselves such as educational goals and/or where you come from.
—A community college student who is a first-generation college student and identifies as an African American female, aged 55+

[H]e let us introduce ourselves if we wanted to and made us feel comfortable talking in the class.
—A public university student who identifies as a pansexual African American female

Have everyone introduce themselves from the onset and explain a little about each [other].

—A public university student who is a first-generation college student and identifies as a heterosexual Hispanic male between the ages of 25 and 34

Introduced [their]self and [the] entire class.

—A private university student who identifies as a heterosexual White female between the ages of 25 and 34

Introduce ourselves, going in groups introducing each other.

—Respondent is a first-generation college student who identifies as a heterosexual White and Hispanic female

When students have a positive sense of belonging, they feel like they can relate to others in the classroom community (McMillan & Chavis, 1986; Strayhorn, 2019). Classrooms, like all communities, satisfy four criteria; membership, influence, integration and fulfillment of needs, and shared emotional connection (McMillan & Chavis, 1986). From a higher education perspective, membership is defined as a student's shared sense of personal relatedness or a sense of belonging. Influence would be the student's need to believe their individual identities matter and make a difference to the class. The integration and fulfillment of needs element is the feeling that a student's needs will be met by the resources received by being a part of the class. The final element is shared emotional connection, which is the commitment and belief that students have shared and will share history, common places, time together, and similar experiences. Several students who completed our surveys shared the importance of instructor–student and student–student introductions to facilitate welcoming and belonging through membership and shared emotional connection (e.g., educational goals and where you come from).

Not having everyone introduce themselves ... was boring and ineffective and didn't provide for a good learning environment.

—A public university student who identifies as a heterosexual Hispanic male between the ages of 25 and 34

[He] did not try to introduce himself or ourselves. This was not effective because I did not feel comfortable in the class and always felt down and not confident in the content.

—A private university student who is first-generation and identifies as a heterosexual Hispanic female

When instructors did not spend time on introductions, several students commented this was ineffective in making them feel welcomed. Two Hispanic students (Spanish-speaking persons with ancestry from a country whose primary language is Spanish, regardless of race) in our study felt the classroom environment was unwelcoming without an instructor-facilitated introduction. Research has shown Hispanic students' perceptions of a hostile classroom climate directly affected their sense of belonging (Strayhorn, 2019). Other work with Latino students (persons with origins from anywhere in Latin America—Mexico, South and Central America—and the Caribbean, regardless of race) revealed interactions with diverse peers affected a sense of belonging, suggesting peer–peer introductions may support Latino students' belonging (Strayhorn, 2008).

Acknowledges and Responds to Student Differences

Provides International Examples for More Diverse and Global Perspectives

> *[The] teacher used numerous examples of international affairs, and helped the international students in that class to understand words and phrases they did not know.*
>
> *—A small, private liberal arts student who identifies as a straight White male*

> *[S]ome of my classes teach people about different racial backgrounds so it's very welcoming to all sorts of people. They were [effective] because it makes me feel more comfortable talking to that teacher since most people view my country as poor when it's not the truth. [I] feel like we could talk about different countries more in good light and what happened to them because some [countries were] colonized and left to be poor.*
>
> *—A public university student and a first-generation college student who identifies as a straight Black female*

In recent years there has been a growing number of international students on college and university campuses (Dove & Bryant, 2016). Our students commented on instructional practices catered to this student demographic. In particular, two students mentioned that instructors made international students feel welcome through acculturation to American colloquialisms and idioms and by taking an interest in their home country. Thus, classroom climates can be more welcoming spaces to international students depending on instructors' cultural competence. Cultural competence in education has been defined as "the ability to successfully teach students who come from different cultures other than your own" (Diller & Moule, 2005). Cultural competence is vital for instructors because it requires that they relate to students from other cultures to be effective (Diller & Moule, 2005; Dove & Bryant, 2016).

Various assessments of cultural competence exist, like the Intercultural Sensitivity Scale (ISS) and Intercultural Development Inventory (IDI) (Nieto & Zoller Booth, 2009; Hammer, 2011). The ISS effectively measures cultural awareness, with cultural sensitivity scores ranging from 24 as the lowest and 120 as the highest (Nieto & Zoller Booth, 2009). The Student Cultural Awareness Inventory (SCAI) has 12 additional questions related to cultural sensitivity in educational settings. When analyzing the instructors' responses to the ISS and the SCAI, three significant correlations were observed. First, SCAI item C7 (it is important for teachers to understand the challenges of getting a degree in a second language) had a moderate positive relationship to the total ISS score (R = 0.529, P = 0.002). The second significant correlation, and moderate positive relationship, was found between SCAI item C8 (I think it is essential for teachers to help international students to feel welcome in this culture) and total ISS score (R = 0.518, P = 0.002). Finally, a third significant and positive correlation was found between SCAI item C9 (it is important to focus on creating an engaging environment when teaching ESL students) and the total ISS score (R = 0.389, P = 0.023). In sum, instructors with higher levels of intercultural sensitivity are more likely to help international students feel accepted (Nieto & Zoller Booth, 2009). Some instructor perspectives reinforced our students' sentiments: "learning a new onset of English, all the colloquialisms, and idioms take a long time. And then there are dialects as well," and

> When I have a student in my class, I develop an interest in where they are from, what they are thinking, what their philosophies are, and their ways of life. Then I listen to the news and I happen to hear a certain country mentioned. If I know somebody from there, automatically that becomes interesting to me. What happens there is no longer a faraway place, which I have no connection with ... So it's that personal engagement that helps a great deal ... This is what matters.
>
> *(Nieto & Zoller Booth, 2009)*

One student who responded to our national survey shared that students in their class received penalties for not using American spelling or terminology and that the instructor exclusively used examples specific to the United States. In contrast to the instructors mentioned above, this suggested these instructors had lower levels of intercultural sensitivity.

> *[S]tudents were penalised for not using American spelling or terminology. Included grammar questions with US-specific examples. Made a big deal of questions that demonstrated a student's lacking knowledge of American history.*
>
> *—A small, liberal arts college student who identifies as an agender White pansexual*

Other research has further supported this student's voice. For example, a male student from China stated, "an educator is meant to teach students from a universal viewpoint and not from a limited viewpoint that has not been expanded beyond one country" (Nieto & Zoller Booth, 2009). A female student from Puerto Rico suggested, "Teachers should be trained on different cultures and have a more broad perspective about international students' cultures" (Nieto & Zoller Booth, 2009). An instructor can actively pursue culturally relevant information such as reading books about different cultures and the way academic expectations in those cultures may differ from academic expectations in the current culture (Nieto & Zoller Booth, 2009). Instructors should also be mindful of domestic student and international student interactions. A recent study has investigated domestic students' prejudice against international students. The results suggested that colleges and universities may lower prejudice against international students by boosting university identity and increasing high-quality interaction between international and domestic students (Quinton, 2019). In fact, qualitative research on international students' expectations and perceptions of the American higher education system report a desire to build relationships with domestic students but consider it unlikely (Tang et al., 2018). Other international students have suggested instructors and peers can be more inclusive and welcoming by exercising more patience with international students (Yan & Pei, 2018).

Welcomes Students with Disabilities

> *[M]aking class inclusive for people like me who have mental/emotional disabilities.*
>
> *—A public university student who identifies as a bisexual White female*

> *Having different modes of engagement, help students with learning disabilities or even students who don't like speaking up in a crowd the chance to contribute to the class.*
>
> *—A private university student who is a first-generation college student and identifies as a straight African and Asian female*

Similar to the inclusive course design and accessibility points brought up in Chapter 2, instructors should be mindful to welcome students with a variety of disabilities. Students in our study mentioned the importance of being welcomed and affirmed in their mental, emotional, and learning disabilities. One study found that "for students with disabilities, more emphasis is placed on accommodations, access, and support services without sufficient attention to the social aspect of the student experience" (Fleming et al., 2017). That is why a positive and inclusive classroom environment is essential for students with disabilities. In a study of 268 students and 76 faculty members at a small liberal arts college, participants were asked to respond to statements about students with disabilities. Students and faculty had very different impressions of how students with disabilities were treated in classrooms, with faculty indicating a more favorable perception of how students with disabilities were treated than the students surveyed (Baker et al., 2012).

Instructors can begin the work of developing a welcoming environment for students before a course starts by educating themselves on important issues impacting students with disabilities.

Students with disabilities expressed that while they were reluctant to share their disability status, they had a deep desire for instructors to participate in regular professional development and educate themselves on effective practices for making students with disabilities feel welcome and that they belong in the classroom (Baker et al., 2012). For example, dispelling myths about disabilities, letting students share their personal experiences with a visible or invisible disability, or talking about the experiences of people they know personally with a disability. An instructor who demonstrates verbal and nonverbal confirming communication can shift a classroom environment toward supporting students with disabilities. Doing so would create spaces where they develop a sense of belonging with their peers without a disability (Fleming et al., 2017). Being sensitive to the social challenges students with disabilities face can assist the instructor in being attentive and addressing specific student needs (Fleming et al., 2017).

> *Was mean and made fun of students' learning disabilities.*
>
> *—A private university student who identifies as a first-generation college student and is a queer, non-binary Guyanese Indian*

> *[My] professor had a bag with each student's name and would pull a name out to make that student answer a question on the spot. [It] didn't help that I wasn't very confident in that subject. I felt like my disability was holding me back a lot more.*
>
> *—A small, private liberal arts college student who identifies as an asexual White female*

> *For students who may have health issues, learning disabilities or take care of family members with health issues, this makes it difficult to find encouragement to participate.*
>
> *—A community college student who identifies as a straight White female between the ages of 25 and 34*

Neglecting to use verbal and nonverbal confirming communication can lead to further isolating students with disabilities. One respondent in our survey stated their instructor made jokes about students who have disabilities. This is the kind of attitude that disrupts and perhaps even destroys a student's belief that they belong in the classroom. Other study respondents indicated some instructors created a negative environment that does not acknowledge students with learning disabilities.

Pays Attention to Religious Diversity Amongst Students

> *[M]aking students of all faiths and beliefs take a "religion in the [plural] world" class but then proceed to only talk about Christianity and only mention Islam and Judaism along the way, [leaving] out all other religions and beliefs … not paying attention to the individualism of the students.*
>
> *—A small, private liberal arts college student who identifies as a straight White male*

As mentioned in Chapter 2, a student commented that instructors should acknowledge diverse religious backgrounds amongst the student body. Earlier in this chapter we discussed microaffirmations. These small gestures can be used to promote equity, help cater to student differences, and enable positive outcomes through small acts of active listening that encourage feelings of inclusion and shared cultural intimacy (Boyce-Rosen & Mecadon-Mann, 2023). They can be intersectional and are beneficial to a wide range of populations, including international students, students with disabilities, students from diverse religious backgrounds, and any other demographic.

Reflection Questions

- How do you learn, and properly pronounce, your students' names?
- How do you handle letting students disclose their pronouns?
- Do you think instructor–student or student–student introductions are better at promoting welcoming through membership and shared emotional connection?
- What strategies do you use to ensure students with disabilities feel like a part of the classroom community?

Intentionally Fostered Equitable Participation by Students

Fosters a Respectful Classroom Environment for All Students Regardless of Background

> *Stating what are the main principles for a class environment, how we should respect and address each other and be mindful that everyone is from a different background.*
>
> *—A private university student who identifies as a first-generation college student who is a straight African and Asian female*

Consistently encouraged class etiquette and treated all opinions as valuable [and] encouraged a respectful learning environment.

—A community college student who is a first-generation college student who identifies as a pansexual White female

My … teacher made sure everyone's beliefs were respected [and] … talked about respect on the first day of classes.

—A small, liberal arts college student who identifies as a bisexual White female

Respects all races.

—A community college student who identifies as a straight White male between the ages of 35 and 44

[E]veryone's opinions and voices were heard and valued by the professor and your peers. All of these approaches were effective because they were eye opening and left a mark on your mind. Other students engaged more than I thought and you were able to retain others' opinions in a respectful way and learn new things about your peers.

—A private university student who identifies as a straight White female

Students from a variety of backgrounds shared with us how important it was for their instructors to foster a respectful classroom in order for them to feel welcomed and included. When students perceive that they are respected by their instructors, there are positive consequences for the quality of instructor–student relationships (Thompson, 2018). A foundational respect-producing behavior is listening. This factor clearly emerged in our research when students mentioned the importance of being heard and valued by their instructors. Respectful and caring instructor–student and student–student relationships also result in improved academic performance (Thompson, 2018). Respect begets respect and respect is due to everyone (Goodman, 2009). Mutually respectful engagements between instructors and students can lead to shared decision-making as an expression of hearing from the other (Thompson, 2018). One example of fostering a respectful classroom is the co-creation and use of classroom guidelines and agreements, and modeling of civil behavior by the instructor.

Another way to foster respect and show care amongst students is to provide trigger warnings. Trigger warnings are statements that respect variable student experiences and alert them to the fact that they may be exposed to potentially distressing material (Faulkner et al., 2020). The controversy over trigger warnings in university classrooms has sometimes been viewed as an issue of academic freedom while ignoring the social justice rationale and how it related to students' sense of belonging and well-being (Spencer & Kulbaga, 2018). Academic spaces are never devoid of the complex social experiences students have. Trigger warnings help to broaden academic speech, while maintaining respect in the classroom, since this requires all students in the space to affirm their agency and take ownership over their intellectual, emotional, and physical boundaries.

> *One of the teachers kept making fun of our president at the time and was disrespectful towards the LGBTQ community.*
>
> *—A community college student who is a first-generation college student and identifies as a bisexual White female between the ages of 25 and 34*

> *[They] let people talk about random topics that had nothing to do with the course content. they disrespected everyone involved.*
>
> *—A small, private liberal arts college student who identifies as a Caucasian, non-binary lesbian*

> *[Having] both teachers and so-called mentors make embarrassing comments about my career goals or my age, in front of other students.*
>
> *—A community college student who identifies as a heterosexual female, aged 55+*

> *[D]id not treat the class with respect.*
>
> *—A private university student who is a first-generation college student and identifies as a straight White male*

> *[N]on-privately dealt with student issues.*
>
> *—A community college student who is a first-generation college student and identifies as a pansexual White female*

Some of our student respondents highlighted times when instructors did not respect the classroom environment and it made them feel unwelcomed. In other words, their instructors exhibited faculty incivility (FI). FI is defined as any behavior disrupting learning or maintaining a positive classroom environment (Alt et al., 2022; Mohammadipour et al., 2018). FI can manifest in different ways, such as having little interaction with students or being aloof when interacting with them. Students experiencing FI behaviors feel stressed, undervalued, and helpless, and this negatively affects their self-esteem (Mohammadipour et al., 2018). Faculty can use the Perceived Faculty Incivility Scale (PFIS) to determine the prevalence of FI from their students' perspective (Alt et al., 2022). The PFIS was designed to measure the frequency of active and passive faculty incivility occurrences. Students experience more FI behaviors in in-person settings than in online courses. From students' perspective, online learning strategies diminish active FI instances (Alt et al., 2022). There are 24 PFIS items and some aligned with FI behaviors described by our students, including mentioning discriminative ideas (making fun of political affiliation and the current President), disrespecting others (making disparaging remarks about student career goals), and being impolite to others (embarrassing students in front of the class and non-privately).

Ensures as Many Students Participate as Possible

> *[T]o create a welcoming environment throughout the course my … instructor included movement. [I]t was a very different approach to a class but because everyone was participating, we slowly became comfortable with one another and doing things we thought as strange.*
>
> *—Student chose not to share demographic information*

> *[The] teacher liked interacting with [the] class and making sure as many people participated that were willing to.*
>
> *—A public university student who identifies as a straight Mexican and White male between the ages of 25 and 34*

> *[A]llows people to participate as much or as little as they are personally comfortable with.*
>
> *—Student chose not to share demographic information*

> *I felt like I could not ask a question because they would make me feel stupid and call people out for not knowing certain things. They were not effective because I always dreaded going to the class and felt secluded.*
>
> *—A small, private liberal arts college student who identifies as a White female*

> *I had a … professor who made students feel stupid when asking questions and expected us to complete the lab in 3–4h but instead, it took everyone 10h and we could not speak up without feeling inferior. They were not effective because every student's background is not taken into consideration. Also, by not making everyone comfortable to ask questions, the class is not being seen as a learning environment."*
>
> *—A private university student who is a first-generation college student and identifies as a straight African and Asian female*

> *Instructor regularly chastised students for asking "wrong" questions, and seemed surprised when, very quickly, few students wanted to participate in in-class discussions … Because they shut down student agency and often included instructors power tripping over a class of college freshmen and sophomores.*
>
> *—A public university student who is a first-generation college student and identifies as a White bisexual cis male*

[T]ried to force people to participate not in a productive way [that] made me feel on edge when in class.

—A private university student who identifies as a heterosexual Caucasian female

My ... professor had a few students who were always included in activities and discussions. It made others feel invisible. I felt like I didn't belong and my voice or opinion had no value.

—A public university student who is a first-generation graduate student and identifies as a heterosexual Puerto Rican female

Student participation is an equity issue. Without fair and active participation, learning cannot occur. Equitable participation is the idea that the instructor has taken steps to intentionally plan to help every student participate. Many of the students in our survey mentioned these steps made them feel welcome. Several of our survey respondents shared that sometimes asking questions, mandatory participation, and playing favorites did not lead to students feeling welcomed or free to participate equitably. Chapter 4 focuses on how these same strategies can be used to conduct class inclusively.

Reflection Questions

- Can you use classroom agreements and trigger warnings to encourage respect in your classroom and equitable participation by all of your students? If not, what other strategies do you employ?
- How can you discourage faculty–student and student–student incivility and promote welcoming in your classroom?
- In what ways can you ensure you are encouraging equitable participation and not prioritizing certain students' contributions over others?

Integrated Relationship-Building as a Core Component of Their Courses

Uses Encouragement, Friendliness, Transparency, and Safety as Relationship-Building Tools

Encouragement

[C]reated a warm and welcoming environment by encouraging us to speak to her if we had any questions and to come to her office hours.

—A public university student who is a first-generation graduate student and identifies as a White female

The teacher was very encouraging, sweet, and helpful to everyone in class.
—A private university student who is a first-generation college student and identifies as a straight Caucasian female

Encouraging students to be able to freely express opinions ... to give people like myself (an older senior citizen student) the same chance to succeed as younger students.
—A community college student who identifies as a heterosexual Caucasian female

[T]he professor is always glad to hear what you have to say and encourages raising your hand to say anything.
—A public university student who identifies as a straight Caucasian male

Friendliness

[Talked] to me like [I] was a friend. They made me feel welcome and [wanted] to go to class.
—A private university student who is a first-generation college student and identifies as a straight White male

She made it known she wanted us to succeed and was almost like a friend that was always there to help.
—A private university student who identifies as a heterosexual White female

Transparency

[T]he professor welcomed the class with an introduction to herself including that she makes mistakes as well.
—Respondent attends a community college and identifies as a straight White female between the ages of 25 and 34

[T]he Professor told something about herself and her background.
—A community college student who is a first-generation college student and identifies as an African American female, aged 55+

Makes Students Feel Safe

Repeatedly stated this is a safe space for all to share their opinions [on people], race and poverty.
—A public university student who identifies as a bisexual Caucasian female

They made me feel safe to ask questions.
—A public university student who identifies as a bisexual White woman

Some students indicated their instructors made them feel uncomfortable to reach out to and made them feel unsafe.

[M]ade students uncomfortable and nervous to reach out.
—A small, private liberal college student who uses she/her pronouns and identifies as straight and Caucasian

Students felt unsafe and not comfortable to communicate with the professor, therefore being unable to learn.
—A private university student who is a first-generation college student and identifies as queer, nonbinary Guyanese Indian

Our students highlighted the importance of encouragement, friendliness, transparency, and feeling of safety to building positive relationships based on care. The relationship between instructor and student is pivotal in how teacher and student experience their participation in higher education because student absenteeism, scholastic learning, and classroom management are all impacted by the vitality of the relationship. While student–teacher relationships have been traditionally thought of in terms of immediacy or distance, new approaches have started to recognize the increasing significance of emotions and power dynamics in teacher–student relationships. A new theoretical model (student–teacher affective relationships) proposes three necessary dimensions in creating a theory about establishing effective student–teacher relationships: affection or warmth, attachment and safety; and assertion and power. Using the Classroom Affective Relationships Inventory (CARI) with data from 851 students, this three-dimensional model was tested and the data support the implementation of this multidimensional model in fostering successful student–teacher relationships. The development of this multidimensional theoretical model, along with the development of an instrument to evaluate the usefulness of these dimensions, could produce a significant step forward in the instructor–student relationship and its ability to create welcoming classroom environments. (Tormey, 2021)

Promotes Proactively Reaching Out to Help Students

Proactively Reaches Out to Students to Provide Extra Help

My … professor always found ways to make us feel welcomed in her class by providing candy and even providing us with office hours and reaching out with those students [who] seemed to be struggling more.
—A private university student who is a first-generation college student and identifies as a homosexual Hispanic/Latina female

Made sure to always check in and provide time outside of class for students to reach out for support, and ensure well-being.

—A private university student who is a first-generation college student and identifies as a heterosexual White (Bosnian) female

[M]y professors always tried reaching out to the students.

—A private university student who identifies as a straight Asian female

They are always there to give extra help.

—A public university student who identifies as a White female between 35 and 44 years old

Routinely offered up extra help in-person, online, as well as giving students other resources for help.

—Student chose not to share demographic information

Encourages Students to Proactively Reach Out to the Instructor for Extra Help

Reminded people to reach out to them and let them know what they struggled most with so the teacher could better cater to their needs.

—A community college student who identifies as a White female

In all of the classes I am in this spring semester I have felt welcomed. [Each] of my teachers have made it easy for me to feel comfortable asking questions and or reaching out.

—A private university student who identifies as a straight White female

[M]ade students feel comfortable reaching out for help instead of ashamed.

—A small, private liberal college student who uses she/her pronouns, and identifies as straight and Caucasian

Proactively reaching out to students provides them with support. Students remarked that they perceived and received ample support from instructors. The literature suggests that perceived and received support (the idea that support is available when needed) is associated with more positive feelings and less negative feelings and improves support perceptions (Faulkner et al., 2020). Instructors who communicate availability of support to their students can have a powerful impact on students' learning and their psychological well-being, which promotes a welcoming environment.

Has Empathy for Students Due to Unforeseen Circumstances

> *Professor was welcoming and understanding about absences and late work.*
> *—A small, private liberal arts college student who is a first-generation college student and identifies as a straight female*

Employment Conflicts

> *[T]old [the] teacher I would be around 5 minutes late to most classes due to work. They would not allow me to enter even 1 minute after class started and would not accept any assignments if I was even 10 seconds late. Needed to contact head of department to have a chance to succeed.*
> *—A public university student who identifies as a straight Mexican and White male between the ages of 25 and 34*

Emergency

> *[My] professor made a comment [that] he doesn't accept late work or make-up days, even if it was an emergency situation.*
> *—A community college student who identifies as a straight White female between the ages of 25 and 34*

Empathy is an emotion that motivates someone to act when they see another in distress. It usually involves listening, asking questions, and proposing solutions (Munoz et al., 2022). Instructors should work to build flexibility into their course policies and manage expectations in a compassionate and empathetic way. As mentioned in Chapter 2, inclusive course design allows for flexible deadlines. Some students have commitments outside of the classroom, like full-time employment, that impact their time and are beyond their control. Students in our study said flexible deadlines made them feel welcomed. Others commented that an unwillingness to accept late entry to class or assignments did not make them feel welcomed. Faculty with high levels of empathy can reduce additional student barriers, which often work to threaten a positive sense of belonging (Munoz et al., 2022). In fact, instructor empathy played a key role in positively impacting student satisfaction and well-being while reducing students' sources of concerns such as household conflict, lack of wi-fi reliability, lack of access to a constant computer, and financial and food insecurity (Munoz et al., 2022).

Reflection Questions

- In what ways can you convey care to your students to build positive relationships?

- How have you been proactive in reaching out to your students who need academic assistance?
- What have you done to show empathy and flexibility with assignment due dates and lateness to/absence from class?

Conclusion

This chapter addressed numerous practices that instructors can use to welcome every student. Professor immediacy, using affiliative humor and not aggressive humor, and confirming communication were key from a student perspective. Students appreciated when instructors learned their names and pronouns, responded to student differences, and ensured equitable and respectful participation by all. Students also felt relationship-building was demonstrated through instructor encouragement, friendliness, transparency, ensuring safety, proactively reaching out to students, and empathy. Several of the welcoming themes students identified in this chapter can be monitored and improved upon by instructors using the Protocol for Advancing Inclusive Teaching Efforts (PAITE) tool introduced in Chapter 1 and further described in Chapter 6 (Addy et al., 2022). It can provide inclusive instructors with formative feedback on observable inclusive teaching practices regarding community standards, relationship building, equitable participation, and diverse examples.

References

Addy, T., Younas, H., Cetin, P., Cham, F., Rizk, M., Nwankpa, C., & Borzone, M. (2022). The development of the Protocol for Advancing Inclusive Teaching Efforts (PAITE). *Journal of Educational Research and Practice*, 12. doi:10.5590/JERAP.2022.12.0.05.

Adler, R. B., Rosenfeld, L. B., & Proctor, R. F. (2013). Chapter 10: Communication Climate. In *Interplay: The process of interpersonal communication* (pp. 310–347). Oxford: Oxford University Press.

Akif Sözer, M. (2019). Effective teacher immediacy behaviors based on students' perceptions. *Universal Journal of Educational Research*, 7(2), 387–393. doi:10.13189/ujer.2019.070211.

Alt, D., Itzkovich, Y., & Naamati-Schneider, L. (2022). Students' emotional well-being, and perceived faculty incivility and just behavior before and during COVID-19. *Frontiers in Psychology*, 13. doi:10.3389/fpsyg.2022.849489.

Baker, K. Q., Boland, K., & Nowik, C. M. (2012). A campus survey of faculty and student perceptions of persons with disabilities. *Journal of Postsecondary Education and Disability*, 25(4), 309–329.

Belt, E. S., & Lowenthal, P. R. (2022). Synchronous video-based communication and online learning: An exploration of instructors' perceptions and experiences. *Education and Information Technologies*, 28(5), 4941–4964. doi:10.1007/s10639-022-11360-6.

Boyce-Rosen, N., & Mecadon-Mann, M. (2023). Microaffirmations: Small gestures toward equity and advocacy. *Professional School Counseling*, 27(1a). doi:10.1177/2156759x231160722.

Cooper, K. M., Haney, B., Krieg, A., & Brownell, S. E. (2017). What's in a name? the importance of students perceiving that an instructor knows their names in a high-enrollment biology classroom. *CBE—Life Sciences Education*, 16(1). doi:10.1187/cbe.16-08-0265.

Diller, J., & Moule, J. (2005). *Cultural competence*. Portland, OR: Book News.

Dove, L. R., & Bryant, N. P. (2016). Law in translation: Challenges and opportunities in teaching international students in Business Law and Legal Environment Courses. *Journal of Legal Studies Education*, 33(2), 263–291. doi:10.1111/jlse.12048.

Estepp, C. M., & Roberts, T. G. (2015). Teacher immediacy and professor/student rapport as predictors of motivation and engagement. *NACTA Journal*, 59(2), 155–163. https://www.jstor.org/stable/nactajournal.59.2.155.

Faulkner, S. L., Watson, W. K., Pollino, M. A., & Shetterly, J. R. (2020). "Treat me like a person, rather than another number": University student perceptions of inclusive classroom practices. *Communication Education*, 70(1), 92–111. doi:10.1080/03634523.2020.1812680.

Fleming, A. R., Oertle, K. M., Plotner, A. J., & Hakun, J. G. (2017). Influence of social factors on student satisfaction among college students with disabilities. *Journal of College Student Development*, 58(2), 215–228. doi:10.1353/csd.2017.0016.

Glenz T. (2014). The importance of learning students' names. *Journal of Best Teaching Practices*, 1(1), 21–22. http://teachingonpurpose.org/wp-content/uploads/2015/01/JoBTP-vol.-1-issue-1.pdf.

Goldberg, A. E., Kuvalanka, K., & Dickey, L. (2019). Transgender graduate students' experiences in higher education: A mixed-methods exploratory study. *Journal of Diversity in Higher Education*, 12(1), 38–51. doi:10.1037/dhe0000074.

Goldman, Z. W., & Goodboy, A. K. (2014). Making students feel better: Examining the relationships between teacher confirmation and college students' emotional outcomes. *Communication Education*, 63(3), 259–277. doi:10.1080/03634523.2014.920091.

Goodman, J. F. (2009). Respect-due and respect-earned: negotiating student–teacher relationships. *Ethics and Education*, 4(1), 3–17, doi:10.1080/17449640902781356.

Gorham, J., & Christophel, D. M. (1990). The relationship of teachers' use of humor in the classroom to immediacy and student learning. *Communication Education*, 39(1), 46–62. doi:10.1080/03634529009378786.

Hammer, M. R. (2011). Additional cross-cultural validity testing of the Intercultural Development Inventory. *International Journal of Intercultural Relations*, 35(4), 474–487. doi:10.1016/j.ijintrel.2011.02.014.

Kohli, R., & Solórzano, D. G. (2012). Teachers, please learn our names!: Racial microagressions and the K-12 classroom. *Race Ethnicity and Education*, 15(4), 441–462. doi:10.1080/13613324.2012.674026.

Liu, W. (2021). Does teacher immediacy affect students? A systematic review of the association between teacher verbal and non-verbal immediacy and student motivation. *Frontiers in Psychology*, 12. doi:10.3389/fpsyg.2021.713978.

Martin, R. A., Puhlik-Doris, P., Larsen, G., Gray, J., & Weir, K. (2003). Individual differences in the uses of humor and their relation to psychology well-being:

Development of the Humor Styles Questionnaire. *Journal of Research in Personality*, 37, 48–75. doi:10.1016/s0092-6566(02)00534-2.

McMillan, D. W., & Chavis, D. M. (1986). Sense of community: A definition and theory. *Journal of Community Psychology*, 14(1), 6–23. doi:10.1002/1520-6629(198601)14:1<6::aid-jcop2290140103>3.0.co;2-i.

Mohammadipour, M., Hasanvand, S., Goudarzi, F., Ebrahimzadeh, F., & Pournia, Y. (2018). The level and frequency of faculty incivility as perceived by nursing students of Lorestan University of Medical Sciences. *Journal of Medicine and Life*, 11(4), 334–342. doi:10.25122/jml-2018-0055.

Munoz, L., Fergurson, J. R., Harris, E. G., & Fleming, D. (2022). Does empathy matter? An exploratory study of class-transition satisfaction in unplanned course interruptions. *Journal of Marketing Education*, 44(2), 217–234. doi:10.1177/02734753211073891.

Murdoch, Y. D., Hyejung, L., & Kang, A. (2018). Learning students' given names benefits EMI classes. *English in Education*, 52(3), 225–247. doi:10.1080/04250494.2018.1509673.

Nienaber, K., Abrams, G., & Segrist, D. (2019). The funny thing is, instructor humor style affects likelihood of student engagement. *Journal of the Scholarship of Teaching and Learning*, 19(5). doi:10.14434/josotl.v19i5.24296.

Nieto, C., & Zoller Booth, M. (2009). Cultural competence. *Journal of Studies in International Education*, 14(4), 406–425. doi:10.1177/1028315309337929.

Pittinsky, T. L. (2016). Backtalk: Why overlook microaffirmations? *Phi Delta Kappan*, 98(2), 80–80. doi:10.1177/0031721716671918.

Quinton, W. J. (2019). Unwelcome on campus? predictors of prejudice against international students. *Journal of Diversity in Higher Education*, 12(2), 156–169. doi:10.1037/dhe0000091.

Santa Clara County Office of Education and National Association for Bilingual Education. (2016). *The My Name, My Identity Campaign*. https://www.mynamemyidentity.org/.

Spencer, L. G., & Kulbaga, T. A. (2018). Trigger warnings as respect for student boundaries in university classrooms. *Journal of Curriculum and Pedagogy*, 15(1), 106–122. doi:10.1080/15505170.2018.1438936.

St-Amand, J., Smith, J., & Goulet, M. (2023). Is teacher humor an asset in classroom management? Examining its association with students' well-being, sense of school belonging, and engagement. *Current Psychology*. doi:10.1007/s12144-023-04481-9.

Strayhorn, T. L. (2008). Sentido de Pertenencia: A hierarchical analysis predicting sense of belonging among Latino college students. *Journal of Hispanic Higher Education*, 7(4), 301–320. doi:10.1177/1538192708320474.

Strayhorn, T. L. (2019). *College students' sense of belonging: A key to educational success for all students*. London and New York: Routledge.

Tang, X., Collier, D., & Witt, A. (2018). Qualitative study on Chinese students' perception of U.S. university life. *Journal of International Students*, 8(1). doi:10.32674/jis.v8i1.158.

The Trevor Project. (2021). *2021 National Survey on LGBTQ Youth Mental Health*. West Hollywood, California: The Trevor Project. https://www.thetrevorproject.org/survey-2021/.

Thompson, C. S. (2018). The construct of "respect" in teacher-student relationships: Exploring dimensions of ethics of care and sustainable. *Journal of Leadership Education*, 17(3), 42–60. doi:10.12806/v17/i3/r3.

Tormey, R. (2021). Rethinking student-teacher relationships in higher education: A multidimensional approach. *Higher Education*, 82(5), 993–1011. doi:10.1007/s10734-021-00711-w.

Tsukawaki, R., & Imura, T. (2020). Students' perception of teachers' humor predicts their mental health. *Psychological Reports*, 125(1), 98–109. doi:10.1177/0033294120972631.

Vareberg, K. R., Vogt, O., & Berndt, M. (2022). Putting your best face forward: How instructor emoji use influences students' impressions of credibility, immediacy, and liking. *Education and Information Technologies*, 28(5), 6075–6092. doi:10.1007/s10639-022-11421-w.

Wanzer, M. B., Frymier, A. B., Wojtaszczyk, A. M., & Smith, T. (2006). Appropriate and inappropriate uses of humor by teachers. *Communication Education*, 55, 178–196. doi:10.1080/03634520600566132.

Wilson, J. H., & Taylor, K. W. (2001). Professor immediacy as behaviors associated with liking students. *Teaching of Psychology*, 28(2), 136–138.

Winter, J. K. (1992). Learn students' names during the first class. *The Bulletin of the Association for Business Communication*, 55(3), 61–62. doi:10.1177/108056999205500318.

Yan, L. (Wendy), & Pei, S. (Linda). (2018). "Home away from home"? How international students handle difficult and negative experiences in American Higher Education. *Journal of International Students*, 8(1). doi:10.32674/jis.v8i1.174.

4

HOW MY INSTRUCTORS CONDUCT CLASS INCLUSIVELY

> "Having a wide range of opportunities, both for students to demonstrate that they understand the material that they're getting out of the class, and also a wide range of ways that the materials [are] being presented to students is really helpful in creating this kind of overall inclusive atmosphere in a classroom."
>
> —*A small, private liberal arts college student who identifies as White, female, and having an unspecified disability*

In Chapters 2 and 3 you heard from students about what instructors did to design inclusive courses and make them feel welcome within those courses, as well as teaching practices that did not work as well for certain students. In this chapter, we share and expound upon the perspectives of students on effective and inclusive endeavors within the class time itself, geared toward meeting the particular learning objectives of that specific course. We highlight common themes that emerged from the student survey and interview responses when they were asked to provide examples of when their instructors "did something well" or "have not done well" with regards to inclusive teaching in daily class activities. We identify specific points of progress and pitfalls, and supplement this information with the educational literature and our personal experiences.

The Themes

Four major themes emerged when synthesizing student responses on how their instructors did or did not succeed in conducting their classes inclusively:

DOI: 10.4324/9781003442929-5

- Using varied approaches to learning were beneficial for many students
- Incorporating student voices was critical
- Instructor time awareness and management mattered for course activities, and
- There was not one "right" way to conduct a class, but there were "better" ways to do so

Each of these themes emerged in the responses of numerous students, across educational settings and student demographics and identities, though approached in different ways and at times focusing on different aspects of the theme. Sometimes these themes appeared when the students were relating experiences that worked well, and other times they were noted in situations that did not go well. However, when analyzed holistically, replies came back to these same themes. That is not to say that there weren't other important responses that fell outside of these themes, but just that their repeated appearance potentially indicates shared criteria for what responses considered successful inclusive teaching.

Reflection Questions

- If you have taught previously, have you seen any of these major themes appear in the feedback you have received from students, either through course evaluations or via other means?
- If so, were they provided as examples of successes or opportunities for growth in your teaching?

Utilizing Varying Approaches to Learning Can Be Beneficial

There are a variety of different ways in which teaching and learning can be approached, including both aspects of instruction and assessment. Focusing on instruction, these include various forms of lecturing, active learning, group work, discussions, and more. For assessment, variety can present itself in terms of the format of the assessment, whether it is a small assignment, an exam, a paper, a presentation, or otherwise, to the relative grade importance of a particular assessment, to how the students then interact (or not) with that assessment after its completion. These different approaches have their own strengths and limitations, and when choosing which means to utilize in a particular course, careful consideration should be given to the goals of the course and which means of instruction or assessment is best able to help the students achieve those goals. In our previous book, *What Inclusive Instructors Do*, we detail a number of different approaches that instructors utilized with perceived success, with examples of how they can be and have been implemented, and evidence from the literature supporting these approaches where available. What really came out through listening to students in this study was that students felt that variety, and even choice, in their learning were key aspects of courses they found to be inclusive. This aligns closely with concepts of Universal Design for Learning (UDL) (*UDL: The UDL Guidelines*, n.d.) and can be seen in the following quotes, where the students brought up the concept of using varied approaches specifically as something they found beneficial:

> *[Classes] that I've taken have been multimodal learning … we always have some sort of activity, whether it be hands-on or online. So it's not just written and verbal, it's also tactile learning, which is really good for me.*
>
> *—A private university student who identifies as African American, female, 25–34 years old, and neurodivergent*

> *Be … inclusive, especially to different types of learning. We split the class up by doing both group work and lecture from the professor. So we usually talk about some sort of concept, practice it in the group work in small groups within the class, get to balance ideas off of each other, and then kind of come back together as a whole class and review the group work, and that provides the opportunity to kind of both be an active listener, but also participating in the discussion and whatever it is you're working on. That also doesn't necessarily put pressure on students who aren't comfortable with the topic. So it allows the opportunity for people to work together in order to find the solutions, or to better understand the concepts, rather than just being lectured at and expecting them to understand what the professor is saying.*
>
> *—A small, private liberal arts college student who identifies as White, female, and having an unspecified disability*

Reflection Questions

- Would you consider your current course(s) varied in terms of teaching approaches? Why or why not?
- Would you consider your current course(s) varied in terms of assessment? Why or why not?

Teaching Approaches

The core idea behind using a variety of approaches learning is that students are provided with learning environments where instruction is presented in more than one sensory mode or pedagogical form (Bouchey et al., 2021; Sankey et al., 2010). This not only allows an individual student to encounter the instructional elements in multiple ways, deepening their understanding, but also provides opportunities for different students to utilize the means that are most effective for them (Rose & Meyer, 2002). Ideally, each critical concept of a course would be explored in multiple modes, however issues of available course time may make this impractical in certain cases. Regardless, opportunity presents itself over the breadth of an entire class to vary the pedagogical approaches across the course content, and our student responses indicated the importance of this as well, both in their learning and their sense of personal value.

> *[The instructor] varied the daily structure of the class so that we did not repeat the same activities every day (like lecture and then examples), but instead had a variety of activities to keep us interested and unexpecting of what the daily class session would turn out like. A lot of varied, dynamic, and fresh approaches to learning prevents students from getting bored or skipping class [because] they think they know what will happen.*
>
> *—A public university student who identifies as White, female, and first-generation*

> *No group activities or review where we are open to ask questions. [The instructors] make us feel like we are just attending a class and never been seen, only graded. Like all we are worth is our effort and hard work, rather than valuable human beings.*
>
> *—A public university student who identifies as White and non-binary gendered*

Below are some examples of how our students viewed their experiences with various forms of instruction, both positively and negatively.

Lecture

The didactic, instructor-centered lecture format has long been the predominant mode of instruction in higher education, in part because of its ability to efficiently disseminate information to a potentially large audience leaning on the content expertise of the lecturer (Freeman et al., 2014). Further, the lecturer may serve as a "role model" for student learning, and students develop listening and note-taking skills (Regmi, 2012). However, the effectiveness of this pedagogical choice in developing deep understanding and disciplinary skill has been under debate for the better part of the last 50 years (Bligh, 1998; Knight & Wood, 2005; Roettger et al. 2007; Loughlin & Lindberg-Sand, 2023). To this end, there has been a push to move to more active learning approaches, or at least to incorporate these approaches, as well as to revamp how "lecturing" is done (*Effective Lectures*, n.d.; Tronchoni et al., 2022).

Our student respondents had both positive and negative experiences with the lecture format, which appeared connected to different aspects of those lectures.

Positive experiences included:

> *There are PowerPoint slides ... but there's also talking and explaining what's on each of the slides, what everything means, and sometimes where the image is found in a book or where we can find additional material online.*
>
> *—A private university student who identifies as African American, female, 25–34 years old, and neurodivergent*

> *They provided us with lectures formatted in a way that makes sense to our learning.*
>
> *—A private university student who identifies as White/European, female, and first-generation*

> *[The instructor] gave clear notes on what to learn, what was important and [was] not important.*
>
> *—A small, private liberal arts college student who identifies as Asian/White, female, and first-generation*

> *Professor always wears a microphone and (tries very diligently) to keep it on and charged.*
>
> *—A community college student who identifies as White and non-binary gendered*

Negative experiences included:

> *[There was] no class engagement. Three-hour lectures with no break, too much content ... [and the instructor] did not acknowledge students with attention disorders.*
>
> *—A public university student who identifies as Caucasian/Native American, male, and 25–34 years old*

> *[The class was] only lectures.*
>
> *—A small, private liberal arts college student who identifies as White and male*

> *When students are just sitting down and listening to a lecture instead of actually finding ways to engage in course materials, I feel like we are not really retaining the important information and just showing up to class just to show up.*
>
> *—A private university student who identifies as a Hispanic/Latina, homosexual, female, and first-generation*

The instructor would just lecture and/or cruise the material with poor question answering.

—A community college student who identifies as Asian, male, and first-generation

The quotes above are representative of others from the study, and indicate that features of lectures that make them more inclusive include aspects of organization and clarity, as also alluded to in previous chapters. When instructors were clear about the learning expectations, the format was logical, time was taken to expand on the meaning of topics, and could be well heard (or otherwise received), many students found lecturing an effective learning approach for them. Characteristics of goal setting and clarity in format are attributes found in the UDL framework (*UDL: The UDL Guidelines*, n.d.). Further, it makes logical sense that, if a lecture is to be effective, it needs to be clearly received by the student audience. This is true for all students, but even more poignant when considering a learning community that includes individuals for whom the course is not in their most-fluent language or those with hearing disabilities (Alsalamah, 2020; Kent et al., 2018; Mayer, 2014). Especially in large classrooms, the use of a microphone may overcome volume barriers within the space. Moreover, speech recognition and transcribing methods are becoming more widely available. In synchronous online courses, where live virtual meetings occur between the instructor and students, many of the virtual meeting platforms have the ability to caption the meeting in real time, while creating a complete transcript that can be accessed (and edited for clarity if needed) later. Similar captioning tools can be used even during in-person courses and projected in real time, and when recording lectures of asynchronous viewing, in online or in-person courses. While initial studies examining the efficacy of captioning on student performance across disciplines has varied and more research is needed (Allen & Katz, 2011; Ranchal et al., 2013; Ritzhaupt et al., 2015), student perceptions on the inclusion of captioning has been almost universally positive in the studies conducted to date (Dommett et al., 2022; Kent et al., 2018; Tisdell & Loch, 2017).

Alternatively, pitfalls for utilizing the lecture method as an inclusive teaching tool were the courses and instructors that relied solely on lecturing as the means of teaching, moved too quickly through the lecture content, lectured for too long in a single session, and did not find ways to engage the audience. Indeed, published literature supports the concept that students in courses which rely too heavily on lectures are less successful than those that incorporate other pedagogies like active learning (Freeman et al., 2014). So how can these pitfalls be avoided? While it is widely quoted that student attention span for lectures lasts less than 30 minutes, specific evidence for the exact time frame varies (Bradbury, 2016; Wilson & Korn, 2007). Rather, there is likely a wide range in student attention spans, which are dependent only partially on the student, but more commonly based on the instructor and the teaching format itself. Lectures can go on for too long without interruption, alteration, or a break. The concept of "lecture bursts" or "microlecturing," as noted in earlier chapters, has become more prominent, where the lecture portion of a class lasts for a shorter period of time (5, 10, and 15 minutes are common durations), preceding a break, an activity, or other means of instruction. While published studies examining the effects of "lecture burst" pedagogy are limited, there are initial studies which show that students perceive improvement in their physical, mental, and cognitive condition simply by incorporating breaks during a standard lecture session (Paulus et al., 2021; Timmer et al., 2020). Mechanisms by which student engagement can be incorporated into lectures will be discussed further when the theme of incorporating student voices is addressed.

Reflection Questions

- If you utilize lecturing in your courses, how much do you focus on the organization and clarity of those lectures? Is there something that you could add to your lectures to enhance these features?
- If you teach through lecturing, in which of your courses do you use it most? What approximate percentage of the course time is lecture-based? Considering the information above, do you believe that to be appropriate?
- If you do not utilize lecturing, is there a course where it might be beneficial? How could you implement it in an inclusive manner?

Discussion

A contrast to the traditional didactic lecture, where the instructor does the majority of the speaking, is discussion-based learning. When using this approach, the instructor may frame and even guide the conversation; it is the students who are contributing most of the dialogue. The historical precedent for discussion-based learning goes back to Socrates and beyond, with roots across global cultures (Ying, 2020). In modern day, discussions can occur meaningfully both in a physical classroom, or, as is becoming more and more common, in online courses using written discussion boards (Bender, 2012; Herman & Nilson, 2018; Smith et al., 2003). Some of the goals of discussion-based learning are to enhance students' critical thinking about a topic, reduce the instructor–student power differential in the classroom, allow for the incorporation of a variety of student voices and perspectives (a topic that will be further addressed later in the chapter), and build communication skills (Brookfield & Preskill, 1999; Christensen & Others, 1991). Students in our survey acknowledged some of these benefits when speaking about what their instructors did well related to inclusivity:

In a discussion-based class heavily focused on social issues, it's great when a teacher treats every idea as valid and lets the students guide the discussion, letting us respond to other students' questions

—A small, private liberal arts college student who identifies as White, female, and asexual

Encouraged students to make space for the voices and perspectives of others and moderated discussions with attention to who was talking, for how long, and who wasn't speaking as much, and inviting them to contribute if they wished.

—A small, private liberal arts college student who identifies as White, agendered, and pansexual

One of my [instructors] always asks "who hasn't spoken all semester/this week" as we're a big class and he wants everyone to have a chance to share at least once. [This] made people feel like they had a place and something they felt like they could talk about. We all likely have wildly different lives to each other, but we become able to ... talk about it.

—A public university student who identifies as White, female, and asexual

Some of the student responses also gave insight into what they perceived as a constructive means for incorporating discussions into their courses, as well as ways that were potentially detrimental. In an interview, one student spoke deeply about the importance of setting the expectations and community standards in discussions early.

This professor, from day one, was really good about setting the ground rules for our discussion, which were simple ground rules, like, we need to be respectful of what other people are going to say in this class, and we should all be willing to debate with each other over these topics. But we need to understand that these are sensitive topics to many people, and we might come out feeling different ways about them.

This student went on to then speak about the role the instructor took in the discussion itself, saying:

Another thing I really respected about that instructor is that they really were, from the very beginning, willing to include themselves into the discussion as an equal discussion member, and they would debate with us if we brought something up that they disagreed with, they would very happily join in and disagree or agree with us, but in a very respectful way. And that was really nice, because I think a lot of times instructors will feel like they can't join in ... that's not their role. I think that by sort of showing us

> *through their actions that this instructor is a part of our class, just like any of us, and can join into the discussion if they feel like they have something important to say, that was really nice to see.*
>
> *—A public university student who identifies as White, non-binary gendered, and pansexual*

Meanwhile, other students spoke to aspects of discussion-based learning that they did not find inclusive:

> *[The instructor] relied on most outspoken students for class discussions, didn't encourage others to speak up.*
>
> *—A community college student who identifies as White, female, pansexual, and first-generation*

> *In [a] religion [course], I feel that the topics can be too much sometimes and we usually talk in groups, but a lot of the topics can be sensitive for some people. These approaches were not effective because it can make students feel out of place.*
>
> *—A private university student who identifies as Caucasian, female, and first-generation*

Within these quotes, we can see the importance of creating a space for discussion that is clearly defined, where the roles for students and the instructor are apparent, and the concept of respect for alternative viewpoints is paramount. This can be especially important in situations where there are topics that could be sensitive in nature. While guidelines can be crafted by the instructor, the co-creation of those expectations with students can both be inherently more inclusive and give students more investment in following the created guidelines (Bovill, 2020). Further, after creating the guidelines for the discussion, allowing room to practice implementing them as well as the foundational discussion skills of questioning, listening, and responding, is useful in developing quality discussion-based learning (Garrett, 2020). We also see in these student quotes how the instructor, while guiding a discussion, can also act as a member of the discussion, and both model appropriate discussion behavior and communication skills, and provide their perspectives. Being involved in this way allows for potential redirection or pivoting the conversation when needed, whether that be due to the sensitive nature of the topic and observed discomfort in members of the classroom, or the need to incorporate students beyond those who might be dominating the conversation. As noted earlier, these approaches are common not only to real-time, face-to-face or virtual discussions, but also to asynchronous discussion boards occurring in online courses. In some ways, having clear guidelines for discussions from the onset of a course may be even more critical in asynchronous courses, as the instructor may not be directly present when the dialogue is occurring and able to immediately respond or redirect when necessary. While the guidelines will hopefully limit the occurrences when redirection or remediation is needed, it is important that the instructor does actively monitor the discussions and respond in an appropriate manner when required. This will help maintain the culture of respect and accountability to the guidelines that have been created.

Reflection Question

- What specifically could you do to make discussions in your in-person or online courses more inclusive?

Active Learning

Active learning is an inherently learner-centered practice where students are asked to be involved more directly in the learning process than just as listeners and recorders. This can range from teaching methods like the discussions noted above, to case studies, problem-based learning (PBL), process-oriented guided inquiry learning (POGIL), and more. A number of these approaches were described, and their efficacy in supporting learning and closing achievement gaps evidenced, in our previous book, *What Inclusive Instructors Do*, so they will not be repeated here. These active learning approaches can be implemented in manners whereby students work independently, in pairs, or as groups; and, interestingly, each of these scenarios was communicated by students surveyed and interviewed in our study in ways that their instructors were successful and unsuccessful in providing inclusive experiences for these students.

In situations where students were asked to work independently, aspects that made the experience more inclusive included the instructor actively engaging with the students, and the students progressing in their independent work in a way that considered their desires.

> *[The] lab instructor went from table to table to help students if they needed. Very hands on. The teachers went out of their way to make sure every student felt supported.*
>
> *—A community college student who identifies as mixed ethnicity, female, asexual, and 25–34 years old*

> *The professor always walks around and gives positive feedback, but also respects students who like to keep their art to themselves until they're ready.*
>
> *—A community college student who identifies as White, female, and 25–34 years old*

However, a student who has challenges related to executive functioning, such as planning, organizing, and managing time and space, noted the barriers that independent work created for her.

> *[In the class, students had to] work by yourself. It was not designed for people with EF [executive function disorders].*
>
> *—A private university student who identifies as White, agendered, and asexual*

These comments show that while some view independent work as inclusive, others, such as some students who are neurodivergent, may see independent work as exclusionary to them (Clouder et al., 2020). This further indicates the importance for instructors to know the students in their courses, and consider their needs in the day-to-day activities of the course.

Regarding paired work, again student feedback on classroom experience can provide insight into tactics that students view as more or less inclusive. Positive experiences included the following:

> *They paired us up but they made us pair each other.*
>
> *—A community college student who identifies as White, male, homosexual, 35–44 years old, and first-generation*

> *We were allowed to choose our partner.*
>
> *—A public university student who identifies as Caucasian/Native American, male, and 25–34 years old*

Those with paired-work experiences that they did not find inclusive stated:

> *I was forced to work with a partner, but neither of us talked. Having people randomly work together creates a sense of awkwardness and unknown. This makes students less inclined to work with one another.*
>
> *—A small, private liberal arts college student who identifies as White/Black and male*

> *Partnering up for class activities is less than ideal. But that's just because of the people we have in that class. I am much, much older than a lot of the people here, so I also am on a different emotional level. So it bothers me more than it might bother other people.*
>
> *—A private university student who identifies as African American, female, 25–34 years old, and neurodivergent*

In these quotes, students indicate that having some control over who they are paired with may increase their feelings of belonging and comfort in the learning environment. However, as noted in the final student quote, some students may prefer not to work with partners in general, or in a particular class community where they feel uniquely different from their peers. In this case, the student noted an age difference between her and her classmates, however the same concept could be applied to race, gender, sexual orientation, sociopolitical status, or any other number of visible or invisible identities. An instructor having more knowledge about their student population may help avoid a situation like this, but perhaps an even more effective means to navigate these situations is by, where possible, allowing for student choice not only on what partner they work with on a project, but if they work with a partner on a project. This is evidenced in another student's response to what their instructor did to make the class inclusive, when they stated:

> *Giving us the choice to work with or without partners.*
>
> *—A small, liberal arts college student who identifies as White, female, and bisexual*

Interestingly, peer review, a process discussed in Chapter 2, was a specific topic that came up in multiple student responses here as well, both as something that students felt was inclusive and something they felt was not inclusive. One student said:

> *We did a lot of peer reviews which engaged all students and we were able to help others with their writing.*
>
> *—A private university student who identifies as Caucasian, female, and first-generation*

Alternatively, another stated:

> *I do not want to peer review, okay. Some kids do not know how to write and I don't want them criticizing my work.*
>
> *—A public university student who identifies as White, female, and bisexual*

Published data does indicate the value of peer review for student learning, and in general finds peer review to be a positive experience, which mimics the fact that in our student response data there were more responses that noted peer review as an inclusive practice than not. However, the second student's comment alludes to a challenge that can be faced in peer review of students at different stages of developing their understanding of a topic and their writing skills (Mulder et al., 2014; Nicol et al., 2014; Serrano-Aguilera et al., 2021). Methods that can be used to address these challenges in situations where peer review is utilized in a class include: explaining the goals of peer review as a process that benefits both the reviewer and reviewee, clarifying the expectations of the process, the use of structured review forms, the potential incorporation of "expert" reviewers in addition to the student reviewers, and many of the features discussed in Chapters 2 and 3 of this book, which describe how to develop a culture of inclusivity within the classroom (Mulder et al., 2014, Boardman et al., 2023). In Derek's courses, he finds having each student conduct and receive confidential reviews from multiple students, rather than just a single peer, can also help minimize some of the challenges indicated.

Small group work is often looked at as a mechanism to enhance student engagement in large courses, giving students some of the benefits of leveraging their peers' understanding, skills, and perspectives, while also providing the opportunity for their own understanding, skills, and perspectives to be utilized in accomplishing a common goal. There are many variations on how small group work can be implemented, from cooperative and collaborative learning, to problem-based and team-based learning, and others (Davidson et al., 2014). A large number of our student respondents noted group work from the prompt of daily class activities that they found to be inclusive, including comments such as:

> *Our professor spent at least one day a week where we would break up into groups and do posters to explain the different topics we were learning about. This allowed us to get to know each other as well as learn from our peers.*
> *—A private university student who identifies as Latina/White and female*

> *Allowing group work. It makes the class more engaging and gives students the opportunity to engage themselves in the content.*
> *—A small, private liberal arts college student who identifies as White and male*

However, there were also students who had experiences with group work that they did not consider inclusive:

> *Having us work with unreal, abrupt, and disrespectful students not seeing there is toxic energy.*
> *—A part-time community college student who identifies as Black and first-generation*

These differences in experience highlight the importance of the instructor's role in overseeing the group activities and being able to respond to situations that are not working effectively in real time, similarly to what was noted in the conversation on discussions. A different student who had similar experiences provided some insight on how the instructor could both prevent and navigate such situations:

[Setting clear] boundaries, communication and then reassignment.
—A private university student who identifies as African American, female, 25–34 years old, and neurodivergent

In their interview, this student further expounded upon how setting initial guidelines and boundaries for group work was important, both in the class as a whole and between members of each group. When issues arise, students should be able to communicate with each other, and if appropriate, with the instructor. Following this, if the issues cannot be resolved, then considering options for having the students join other groups may be beneficial. While this could be challenging in a situation where groups have been formed intentionally, or work has already begun, this flexibility within courses is a key component to maintaining equity, and will be discussed later in the chapter.

Within responses that noted the positive impact of group work, were comments that spoke specifically to means of group formation. These included:

[The instructor] has different cards that assign us to groups daily so we can learn from each other and help one another.
—A community college student who identifies as White/Hispanic, female, and 25–34 years old

Allowing students to have a say in the formation of their small discussion groups for the semester.
—A private university student who identifies as Caucasian and female

Meanwhile, another student, who identified as having a vision-related disability, stated challenges she had with certain means of group formation.

I think there are a few activities that are supposed to be fun, but assume a certain ability that I don't have visually. Something like counting off [to then] find your group, are actually very overwhelming and not fun for me .... In my anthropology class we had to get in order, or group ourselves by the color that we were wearing on our shirts.
—A student with a sensory disability who identifies as White and female

The student describes how she would have to rely on a friend in the class to help her get to the proper group, and how that could be challenging in certain situations. This demonstrates how the diverse needs of a class' student population can in some cases take a process or activity that was intended to be inclusive, and in fact make it an obstacle for certain students. In the case of this student, she noted how she appreciated when her instructors were aware of what group she was in, and then instead of having her go to a specific meeting place in or out of the classroom, have her group mates come to her. In this instance, the student was comfortable with this being announced directly in the class; however, in some cases a student may not feel as comfortable having a similar acknowledgement in front of their peers, so a more subtle approach involving a discussion in advance with the student or pre-planning group locations would be warranted. To this end, providing opportunities for students to share information with you as their instructors that may impact their comfort, sense of belonging, and ability to succeed in the class can be vital to ensuring a broadly inclusive course.

Reflection Questions

- Consider an activity you have had students work on in your course (or if you have not done this, create a hypothetical activity).
  a Was it structured as an independent, paired, or small group assignment?
  b What barriers could that structure present to a learner, considering the neurodiversity found in student populations?
  c How could you design the activity to mitigate this barrier(s) without sacrificing the student's ability to achieve the desired learning outcomes?

Assessments

Whether through traditional letter grades, numerical rubrics, mastery-based mechanisms, or even forms of ungrading (as mentioned in Chapter 2), assessment is a key component in the majority of college courses. Assessments can be categorized as formative, to monitor and support student learning commonly as it is developing, or summative, to evaluate student learning generally after the learning was intended to occur. However, there can certainly be cases that blur these lines, instances where one or the other is preferred, and times when both can be implemented (Glazer, 2014; Ismail et al., 2022; Morris et al., 2021; Yüksel & Gündüz, 2017). Assessments can come in many forms such as examinations, presentations, written pieces, performances, projects, or other mechanisms for displaying one's understanding and skill. While in some cases the manner of assessment is directly aligned with learning objectives for the course, in other instances it is simply a means of evaluating the student's learning and it may not necessarily matter in which way the student demonstrates that they have successfully met the learning objective. Arguably the core concept that students spoke to, when addressing aspects of inclusivity related to assessments, was not one particular type of assessment versus another, but rather the allowance for student choice in the means by which they displayed their mastery. Each of the comments below came from students identifying aspects of courses they took that they perceived to be inclusive.

> *Letting students choose a written or oral assignment, depending on which was more comfortable for them. [This gave] people like myself (an older senior citizen student) the same chance to succeed as younger students.*
>
> *—A part-time student community college student who identifies as Caucasian, female, and 55+ years old*

> *The teacher would not care what format we chose to do our assignments and participate in taking class notes about discussions, or in filling out papers for the class; as long as we completed our work in an efficient way for us.*
>
> *—A private university student who identifies as White and female*

> *In a seminar English class, a professor would come up with fun ways to process the readings as a group. We put one of the characters on trial and decided if she was innocent or guilty (an intense debate!) and we completed open-ended "response" projects to share with the class that prompted discussion. One student recorded a dance that represented a character's development over the course of the book.*
>
> *—A public university student who identifies as White, non-binary gendered, and pansexual*

In his courses, Derek has made an attempt to be both more varied in his assessments and, where possible, provide options for student choice in how they are assessed. As an example, in a first-year seminar course that he teaches, students explore the human condition through various artifacts including science fiction literature, historical events with sociopolitical context, music, film, and more. Initially, part of the course asked students to write a single paper that melded their understanding of these various artifacts and how they informed the student's own definition of what it meant to be human. While in a number of ways this process worked well, in the papers Derek saw how the writing skills of some students interfered with their ability to showcase what seemed to be interesting ideas and deep critical thinking on the topic. While Derek believes written communication to be a critical skill for college students to develop, it was not necessarily the main learning goal of this class or this assignment, as he was more interested in their ability to think critically and develop communication skills in a variety of manners. As such, he modified this portion of the class to replace the paper, and instead have a series of shorter reflections throughout the semester using a web-based tool known as Padlet, where students post digital "sticky notes" on a digital class "white board."

The first assignment asked the student to write their reflection; the second asked them provide either a drawing or a haiku; the third asked them to create a meme using an image from the Internet; the fourth asked them to record a short video of themselves talking about their ideas; and the fifth was a free-choice reflection using any of the past means or a new mechanism of their choosing. At the end of the course, the merging of these various artifacts and the students' thinking around them still occurred, but in a fully open-format project, where Derek was happy to give some potential suggestions, but allowed the students to decide how, ultimately, they wanted to showcase their critical thinking on the topic. The students could work independently, in pairs, or in small groups, and they could create a written piece, an art piece, a baked good, a performance, or anything else they decided, so long as they could justify how it met the learning goals of the assignment. Student feedback, through course evaluations, anecdotally in conversations, and his own observation of the process and outcomes, was all quite positive about this implementation and is something Derek hopes to build on in the future, and take into some other courses where appropriate.

Specifically related to examination-based assessment, one of the students interviewed in our study spoke to a mechanism that they found to be particularly inclusive; what they referred to as an "open exam." The student describes it, and their feelings around the format, as such:

> *The exam itself was open … two weeks before the final exam in this class [the instructor] literally gave us a copy of what the exam would look like. They printed out the exam, and they gave it to us and said, "This is what your final looks like. You will have … five days to let me know if you find any issues with this exam, and I will um adjust it accordingly." And then, four or five days before the final exam, we'll have a review session where we're all literally holding the final exam in our hands and talking about what each question is. And I think that sounds super crazy and radical. It definitely did to me the first time I heard it. But believe me, when I say that was the best exam I've ever taken, and not because it was super easy, because it was [actually] super hard. That exam was just as hard as any other exam I've ever taken in college, but I knew what was on it. I knew what it was going to be, so it was not stressful for me thinking about …. It allowed me to actually review the things that are most important to the class from my instructor's point of view. When you do things like having an open exam, not only does it often help the students who have accommodations for their mental health issues, because it offers them more flexibility in how they study or how they take the exam. But then it also benefits everyone else like the people who maybe don't identify as having a specific accommodation. They're still going to have a more pleasant exam experience.*
>
> *—A public university student who identifies as White, non-binary gendered, and pansexual*

The "open exam" is one way to think about potentially making assessment more inclusive, though it admittedly will not likely work in all courses and in all situations. Another topic that was brought up in the student survey responses that relates to this idea of examinations is where a student identified "pop quizzes" as something that they found to not be inclusive, noting what they perceived as a high failure rate. The concept of "pop" (unannounced) quizzes is an interesting one, with supporters and detractors on each side of the issue. The idea behind pop quizzes is that they are a means to assess student knowledge at a given time that provides insight into if and how well the students are engaging with the material (commonly out of class) without being foretold that a quiz was coming and they should appropriately prepare. The thought is that if it is known that pop quizzes may occur within a course, it will be motivation for students to be "kept on their toes" and stay on top of their studies.

Indeed, there are some studies which indicate that pop quizzes can lead to positive performance results in certain courses (Cicirello, 2009; Kamuche, 2007; Willyard, 2010). However, in a number of ways, pop quizzes seem to be almost the opposite of the "open exam" described above. And conducting an online search of "pop quizzes" will yield a large number of opinion articles, from students and instructors alike, expressing negative aspects of pop quizzes, questioning their true efficacy, how they do not allow for students to set their own pace and process for learning, and the added stress they place on students. Further, it is not difficult to imagine a scenario where the unexpected arrival of a quiz may have a negative impact on an individual who is neurodivergent, who thrives in situations where there is more structure and routine.

To counter this, some instructors have found creative ways to leverage the potential benefits of unannounced quizzes, while minimizing some of the disadvantages, including using ungraded pop quizzes, either anonymous or not, or pop quizzes that allow students to earn bonus points (Agrawal et al., 2021; Carter & Gentry, 2000; Khanna, 2015). One particularly interesting study examined a Psychology course of 140 students, who either had graded pop quizzes, ungraded pop quizzes, or no quizzes, and compared their final exam scores. The students with the ungraded pop quizzes performed the best of all groups, and also felt positive about having the quizzes as part of their course (Khanna, 2015). This potentially shows a pathway for instructors who are interested in leveraging the advantages of pop quizzes, while also doing so in an inclusive manner that mitigates some of the potential disadvantages.

Reflection Questions

- Consider a course you have taught or are planning to teach.
    a. What format of assessments did, or will, you include?

  b If there are only one or two forms of assessment, is there an opportunity to include a broader variety of ways students demonstrate their learning?
  c For any one particular assessment, is there an opportunity to provide the students with choice, to select the format that they prefer to demonstrate their learning?

- What are your personal thoughts around the idea of pop quizzes?

Incorporating Student Voices Is Critical

The second major theme that came from student responses about ways that their instructors were or were not successful in creating inclusive class sessions was the importance of students not just being passive members of the class during a given day, but their knowledge, perspectives, ideas, questions, and opinions being incorporated as a core characteristic of the course. This can be seen in some of the student comments made around aspects of courses that were not perceived as inclusive, including:

> *It was [the instructor's] way or the highway.*
>
> *—A community college student who identifies as White and male*

> *[The instructor] didn't ask for us to participate.*
>
> *—A public university student who identifies as White, male, and 35–44 years old*

> *[The instructor was] just continuously lecturing without getting everyone involved.*
>
> *—A public university student who identifies as Hispanic, male, and 25–34 years old*

Alternatively, involving the students in the course, especially through diverse means, was seen as an inclusive practice:

> *In my business writing course, my professor makes sure he includes everyone while he is teaching so he could gauge every individual's progress.*
>
> *—A community college student who identifies as American Indian/White, female, and 35–44 years old*

> *[The instructor] ensured that students were able to engage in a way that felt comfortable to them, which meant that participation could be the times you raised your hand, your questions, and also written reflections on classes and forum posts. It ensured that students who found it harder to*

concentrate in real-time had the opportunity to express their thoughts without feeling pressured to speak in class for the sake of speaking.

—A small, private liberal arts college student who identifies as White, agendered, and pansexual

If not getting students involved and incorporating their voices within a class session can lead to it not being perceived by the students as an inclusive space, then what are specific means to incorporate student voices and how can they best be implemented? Students spoke to a variety of options, including whole group discussions, which was described in the "Teaching Approaches" section, but also more specifically around ways to procure student questions and how to ask questions of the students, both with and without the use of technology.

Procuring Student Questions

Providing space and opportunity for students to ask questions, to help clarify or extend the course content, was seen as an inclusive practice.

In my history class we were encouraged to ask questions about the content or if we were confused.

—A private university student who identifies as White, female, and first-generation

[The instructor] allow[ed] students to ask questions [to] make sure everyone is up to speed.

—A small, private liberal arts college student who identifies as White, male, and 35–44 years old

Everyone was given the right to ask questions or interrupt in my psychology class.

—A private university student who identifies as Asian and female

In my chemistry class last semester my professor would make sure everyone's questions were answered before moving on to another topic and did not exclude anyone.

—A private university student who identifies as White, female, and first-generation

However, as discussed more holistically in Chapter 3 about how to create a welcoming environment, the tone by which those questions from students were received and responded to also influenced the student perception on whether the practice was inclusive or not. For example:

> *[The] professor made every question asked seem like a good question.*
>
> *—A small, private liberal arts college student who identifies as Caucasian and female*

While students who felt demeaned, embarrassed, or unsafe in asking questions noted these as practices that were not inclusive.

> *[The instructor] just boringly lectured and kind of demeaned students for asking questions.*
>
> *—A small, private liberal arts college student who identifies as White, male, and first-generation*

> *Being made to feel embarrassed by teachers if I didn't agree with their point of view, in front of the class. They made me feel somewhat humiliated and not really interested in asking more questions. When I spoke to one teacher about this, she seemed very dismissive of my feelings.*
>
> *—A part-time community college student who identifies as Caucasian, female, and 55+ years old*

There are some specific avenues for acquiring questions from students in an inclusive manner. Sometimes this can be as simple as changing the phrasing by which questions are requested. Rather than asking questions like "Does this make sense?" or "Any questions?", which have an implication that it should make sense and someone asking a question is falling behind, altering the prompt to "What questions do you have?" can frame the moment in such a way that there is an expectation that there will be questions at that point, and you as the instructor just want to find out what they are. However, this still does require students to identify themselves as having a question.

Other classroom assessment techniques can remove this barrier, by allowing students to ask their questions anonymously (Angelo & Cross, 1993). This could include "Muddiest Point" activities where students write down their questions on paper or index cards, which then can be reviewed either in class or out of class by the instructor and responded to. This can also be done in a more technologically advanced manner, by having anonymous surveys built into your class's learning management system, using Q&A (question and answer) features on freely available online tools where students can use devices like smartphones, tablets, and laptops to share their questions. In asynchronous online courses, many of these same tools can be used. Alternatively, in Derek's online teaching where discussion boards serve as a main interaction point of the class, students not only respond to instructor-created questions, but also are required to ask a question of their own. These student-created questions can either be geared at clarifying a challenging topic they are examining or extending the conversation in a meaningful way. While student peers are often tasked with responding to these questions directly, it also lets Derek as the instructor have a better picture of challenging concepts and learn about the interests of the students in the class related to their weekly topics.

Reflection Questions

- Do you directly invite student questions in your classes? What language do you use, and what implications might that language have?
- What is a way that you could request questions from your students in your particular class that could increase the number of questions you receive while decreasing the anxiety some students might feel in asking those questions?

Asking Students Questions

In addition to collecting questions from students, it is a common practice in college classrooms for instructors to ask questions of the students in the class, as either a formative assessment tool or just to assess student understanding of a particular topic. Students shared their thoughts on what worked, including involving all students and not just a subset, and providing positive feedback.

> *[The instructor] was inclusive by not selecting favorites, and asked all of us questions.*
>
> *—A public university student who identifies as Caucasian, female, bisexual, first-generation, and 25–34 years old*

> *The teachers gave us compliments and good feedback when we [provided] a good response.*
>
> *—A small, private liberal arts college student who identifies as White and male*

Meanwhile, some of these same concepts can be seen in the features of courses that were not considered inclusive by students, including calling on specific students and then reacting negatively if the student answers were incorrect.

> *Calling on students and mak[ing] them feel stupid.*
>
> *—A small, private liberal arts college student who identifies as White, male, and 35–44 years old*

My management professor gives everyone popcorn questions about the chapter and is extremely rude to those who do not know the answer.

—A small, private liberal arts college student who identifies as White and male

"Cold-calling," the practice of calling on students directly without warning, also sometimes called "Random call," is alluded to in both of these student quotes ("popcorn questions" is an engagement strategy where one student gets questioned, responds, and then questions another, which generally doesn't end until everyone has been "popcorned"). Whether that negative experience is more attributable to the "extremely rude" reaction of the instructor, or the nature of all students being expected to participate is not clear; both are likely contributing factors based on the responses.

In some ways, cold-calling inherently seems like it would be an inclusive practice, as one of the goals is to incorporate student voices across the classroom community. Indeed, data shows that when volunteers are asked to respond to questions, males are more likely to answer questions, and that implementing random call enhanced both the overall and voluntary participation of women in the class (Dallimore et al., 2019; Eddy et al., 2014; Waugh & Andrews, 2020). Further, in at least one study, random call also has been shown to increase voluntary engagement, attendance, and pre-class preparation over time (Broeckelman-Post et al., 2016; Waugh & Andrews, 2020). However, there are also studies which suggest that cold-calling increases student anxiety, may impact the students' ability to cognitively engage, and that some students may be more likely to face this anxiety based on their personal background (Cooper et al., 2018). To this point, modified versions of cold-calling that seek to maintain the benefits while also mitigating the inequities based on anxiety have been developed, such as "warm-calling," which provides students with both advance warning and the opportunity to opt out of sharing in front of the class (Metzger & Via, 2022).

In asynchronous online courses that rely heavily on written responses and discussions, it is often imperative that students respond to questions posed by the instructor. However, these courses also generally allow for more significant time between when the student first reads the question and when they need to respond, which theoretically reduces the performance anxiety that may be present during a live, in-person course. Still, depending on the course topic, there may be questions that students feel more or less comfortable answering for a variety of reasons. To this end, to enhance inclusivity and equity in Derek's own online teaching, he implements a course plan where there are multiple questions presented, and students are required to answer at least one of the questions, but not necessarily all. Further, the student responses are hidden from other students until a specified release time, at which point they can be viewed by all. This enhances equity and inclusion, by allowing students to answer the question of their choosing at their own pace and with their own process (prior to the specified release time), and not have to worry about other students "taking their answer" before they get the chance to respond.

The development and use of live-polling technologies in in-person courses has been a pathway that keeps the personal accountability of cold-calling, but actually allows for the incorporation of more student voices and what is likely a better picture of student understanding of a topic across the classroom population in real-time, as all students have the opportunity to respond to each question, even in large classes (Atkins, 2018). Moreover, polling is often done anonymously, which can take the burden off of students who are anxious about their responses. Further, live-polling can be successfully implemented in live online courses and in hybrid/hyflex courses, where some students are present in-person and some online (Phelps & Moro, 2022). Clickers were one of the first classroom response systems widely adopted, but advancing technology and the commonality of smartphones, tablets, and laptops in the student population has moved most of the live-polling done in classrooms to situations where students bring their own device to engage (Duncan, 2006; McGivern & Coxon, 2015; Sarvary & Gifford, 2017). There are a variety of basic and gamified live-polling tools freely available on the Internet, or available in fuller forms through paid subscriptions, as well as options built within various learning management systems. While being able to gather responses from an entire class at once clearly has benefits for inclusion and equity, one potential area where live-polling could be not inclusive and equitable is if there is differential access or ability to utilize the devices needed to submit responses. As such, it is critical that the instructor is aware of student access to the required devices.

One version of polling that seeks to avoid this potential pitfall is Plickers (Wood, 2017). Plickers is a polling process where students have unique printed cards that they hold up and rotate appropriately to designate answers, and the instructor is the only one who needs a device capable of detecting these responses. In addition to helping overcome the potential issues of access to technology across one's students, this platform has also been cited as being a useful tool for students with disabilities, by allowing them to answer in a private voice without calling attention to them if their response is incorrect (Mahoney & Hall, 2017). However, Plickers is limited to multiple-choice or true–false style questions, it can take some time for an instructor's device to visually detect each student response in a larger classroom, and modifications would need to be made for those with visual or motor skill impairment. Like Plickers, most live-polling systems allow the option of anonymous response collection, if desired, providing a potential benefit for neurodivergent and individuals with certain disabilities. Beyond these technology-based live-polling tools, there are also low- and no-tech options like using differently colored index cards to respond to multiple-choice questions. While some of the benefits of anonymity may be lost in these cases, it does help overcome barriers students and classrooms may have in terms of equitable access to the technology needed for online polling.

However, even these theoretically inclusive tools can also present barriers for some students. One particular student, who identified as having a visual disability, noted in their interview how live-polling and game-based learning activities that were timed and required visual cues were difficult, or even impossible, for her to participate with in real time. Nevertheless, within this context the student remarked on how her instructor was able to include her in a beneficial way by providing the polling questions in advance of class.

> *We were going to do … live active participation in some polls … and [my instructor] shared them with me ahead of time, so that I could put up my [responses] virtually, so I could have time to do it. And [while] in the moment where everyone got like a minute … I still got to share my opinion, but I didn't have the time crunch. It was at my own pace, which was really nice.*
>
> *—A student with a sensory disability who identifies as White and female*

This student also went on to acknowledge that when live-polls were used in classes, in addition to having time in advance to respond to the polls, keeping the visual aspects of the polls relatively simple was beneficial, rather than having too many graphics and visuals.

This all goes to show that incorporating student voice is important to students feeling that they are included in the daily activities of a course in an equitable way, and that while there are better ways to ask for and pose questions, responses, and opinions, that knowing the diversity of students in the class is a key.

Reflection Questions

- What are your personal feelings about cold-calling? Is it something you utilize in your classes, and what information do you have on how your students respond to it?
- Think about the potential barriers and brainstorm ways that you could incorporate the voices of students with the following:

    a Visual impairment
    b Hearing impairment
    c Motor impairment
    d Autism spectrum disorder
    e Other impairments or disabilities you have encountered in your student population

Appropriate Structuring and Management of Class Time

How the instructor navigates and uses the class time was another theme that was addressed by multiple students when speaking to experiences they had in a class's daily activities that were either successful or not successful at being inclusive.

Starting the Class Session

Some students spoke to how the manner in which the instructor began a class was important to their feeling included. In some instances, the way the course was begun was directly related to the class topic or the day's expectations:

> *[The instructor] would lay out expectations clearly for each class/rehearsal, and ensure each student had at least the minimum knowledge to succeed.*
> *—A part-time public university student who identifies as White, male, bisexual, and first-generation*

> *If there's [new] language you're teaching … and there are words that you just expect people to know … just assume no one knows. That way everyone's on an even footing and it takes away from any embarrassment that someone might feel later that helps with inclusion for people to want to keep participating.*
> *—A private university student who identifies as African American, female, neurodivergent, and 25–34 years old*

The ideas of clearly stating the learning goals for a class, as well as providing the requisite vocabulary for understanding the day's course topics, are concepts embedded within UDL principles (García-Campos et al., 2020; *UDL: The UDL Guidelines*, n.d.). This allows for students with differing background knowledge and experiences to have a more equitable opportunity to succeed in the learning that is intended to take place during the class session. James Lang provides four additionally useful means of starting a course in his 2016 article in the *Chronicle of Higher Education* including open with a question or two, asking what was learned last time, reactivating what was learned in previous courses or life experiences, and potentially writing some of the above down (Lang, 2016).

Other students spoke about mechanisms for beginning a class that were not directly related to the course subject matter, but set a tone for the day that was conducive to learning in an inclusive manner.

> *Have a meditation period prior to class. They helped me get into the mindset of wanting to learn and kept me engaged throughout.*
> *—A small, private liberal arts college student who identifies as Black, male, and demisexual*

I had a teacher that opened every class with a question. Like "What's your favorite movie?" [or] "What superpower would you have?" and this made the class feel light-hearted and fun.
—A public university student who identifies as White, female, and bisexual

Personally, Derek has used a strategy that was shared with him at an educational workshop where at the beginning of the semester the instructor collects information on the favorite songs or musical artists of each student in the class, and then compiles these into a musical playlist where one of the songs will be playing each day as students enter the class. Derek has received positive feedback from students on this approach, and has seen visible excitement when a student recognizes "their" song being played. This not only helps solidify each student's belonging to the class community, but also recognizes their individuality, and has a positive side effect of motivating students to arrive to class on time or even a few minutes early.

These comments speak directly to what was addressed in Chapter 3, creating a welcoming environment that fosters a sense of belonging for the students, by showing how this can be built consistently within every individual class session, and have a meaningful impact for the students on what happens in class that specific day.

Reflection Question

- Do you have a particular way in which you start your classes, before immediately jumping into the learning for the day? If not, what could you implement in the future?

Time for Learning Activities

Student learning is a core outcome of higher education, and presumably the goal of most class sessions is that learning will occur within that class time. However, as discussed previously, there are different mechanisms by which students may be doing that learning. One such aspect students in our study spoke to was related to the pace of lectures, and specifically related to the time allowed for taking notes.

[One example is my] Music History instructor who flew through the notes so quickly that about a third or more of the class wasn't able to write down what they needed to study, or the quality of their notes suffered dramatically.
—A part-time public university student who identifies as White, male, and first-generation

In my chemistry class the delivery of the material was very fast paced and often hard to keep up or ask for help.

—A private university student who identifies as White, female, and first-generation

In a course where lecturing is implemented to foster learning, allowing adequate time for both selecting appropriate information and actually writing that information are critical for student comprehension (Piolat et al., 2005). Further, studies show that note taking facilitates recall of factual material and the synthesis of new knowledge, leading to higher performance on exams, especially when those notes are reviewed after the class (DeZure et al., 2001; Kiewra et al., 1991). However, the pace at which an instructor moves through class topics has a direct impact on students' ability to take quality notes, as indicated in the quotes above and in the literature. Indeed, it has been reported that while most students typically write 17 to 20 words per minute, instructors present at approximately 110 words per minute (Boyle et al., 2015). Further, obstacles to effective note taking may be exacerbated for students with disabilities (Boyle et al., 2015; Maydosz & Raver, 2010).

There are a number of actions and supports that, depending on the particular class, may help alleviate some of the barriers to note taking that some students face. One of these is simply recognizing, and often slowing, the pace at which material is presented to students. This may be done by slowing the speed of speech or by incorporating intentional pauses where students can catch up or collaborate with a peer, which has been shown to improve student comprehension and retention (DeZure et al., 2001). Additionally, providing handouts of the material (including lecture slides if being used), outlines of the lecture as scaffolds for note taking, or even full instructor notes for the lecture have shown benefits in certain contexts. Technological tools, such as Livenotes or shared documents, can allow for students to cooperatively take notes in real time, which can both improve the quality of the notes taken and help alleviate the need for each student to record the entirety of the notes themselves (Kam et al., 2005). UDL guidelines would further suggest providing models or scaffolding tools to support students in development of their notetaking skills would be an inclusive approach to overcoming certain notetaking barriers (*UDL: The UDL Guidelines*, n.d.). Specifically, for those with disabilities, the use of the above strategies and tools like recording devices, note taking services/ scribes, interpreters, and even classroom setup can be beneficial in supporting note taking (Boyle et al., 2015; DeZure et al., 2001; Maydosz & Raver, 2010; Tincani, 2004).

One student from our survey specifically spoke to one of their instructor's varied approach to note taking as an inclusive experience for them:

> *[My] Biology teacher provided many ways to take notes.*
> *—A private university student who identifies as Hispanic, female, and first-generation*

Beyond note taking during lectures, time allotment is also an important aspect of inclusive teaching in active learning approaches, whether they be independent, paired, or in small groups. A student spoke to this when they stated they felt their instructors were not successfully inclusive in the following way:

> *In Spanish [the instructor will] give us 2 minutes to complete an activity.*
> *—A public university student who identifies as African American, female, and pansexual*

This was opposed to the positive experience a student noted whose Cell Biology instructor would take time to walk students through the worksheets they were asked to complete in class.

Specifically related to group work, a common practice used to overcome the challenge of limited time in the classroom is to have that group work occur outside of the class meeting times. While this can be a reasonable approach in certain instances, one of the students we interviewed spoke specifically to challenges presented by group work occurring outside of class.

> *I've also had experiences in STEM-based classes where we have done group work outside of class time, and I think that kind of structure as a part of the course is not necessarily inclusive. One because of student schedules. It's often hard for people to connect outside of class time in order to accomplish the tasks that they need to do, and also just kind of the nature of a lot of these classes, or that … not everyone is necessarily willing to commit the same amount of work to those projects, especially outside of class time. And I think that makes it really challenging for kind of students who want different things out of the class to work together, and then a lot of times the burden falls on a few students to kind of get the work done, or else it doesn't get done at all. I found that in two classes this semester … it's definitely frustrating, and I feel like even when talking to [the] professor they just kind of are like, "Well, that's group work. That's what we're doing. And you just need to figure it out."*
> *—A small, private liberal arts college student who identifies as White, female, and having an unspecified disability*

In this response, this student identified challenges in group work generally, differing student motivation and commitment, and also specifically related to it occurring outside of class time. They went on to note that, when the group work was more structured and guided by the instructor, this was beneficial, and that the ability of the instructor to check-in when the group work is occurring in-class is one particular reason why allowing time for group work to occur during class is ideal.

Reflection Question

- How do you navigate the challenges of limited time in the classroom, while still providing the necessary time for effective student learning?

Time for Critical Thinking and Sharing

Students also spoke to the need to allow sufficient time for critical thinking and discussion, when they mentioned classroom experiences they perceived as non-inclusive.

> *One of my [English] professors gives no time after [asking] "anybody have any questions?" for people to even raise their hand.*
> *—A public university student who identifies as White, female, and asexual*

> *During a biology undergraduate class, my biology professor would try to make us have in-class discussions but never gave us enough time for it (less than 5 min). So it felt counterproductive.*
> *—A private university student who identifies as African/Asian, female, and first-generation*

This is opposed to when an interviewed student mentioned:

> *[The] instructor then really did a good job of making sure we had discussion time. Not only was discussion allowed, but it was allocated a lot of time and it was a very purposeful process to make sure that everyone could speak up if they wanted to.*
> *—A public university student who identifies as White, non-binary gendered, and pansexual*

These quotes highlight the importance of both giving students time to think critically before needing to respond, and then allowing appropriate time for their response and discussion that follows. The concept of using "wait-time" to allow for student thinking prior to discussion was described in our previous book and has been recommended as an inclusive practice in numerous publications (Addy et al., 2021; Penner, 2018; Rowe, 1972; Tanner, 2013). Beyond this, specifically allocating time within a class session for meaningful critical thinking and discussion, rather than thinking of it as something to put in where it fits, can enhance the likelihood of it being a positive inclusive experience, as opposed to the opposite.

Time for Breaks

As noted in previous chapters, especially in class sessions that extend beyond 50 minutes, the importance of incorporating time for breaks to allow movement, or to take care of other personal needs, was highlighted as an inclusive experience in the following student quote:

> *Structuring the class with breaks allowed students to stretch their legs, use the bathroom, have a snack, and change activity to ensure that students' attention could come back to the class once the break was up.*
>
> *—A small, private liberal arts college student who identifies as White, agendered, and pansexual*

Supporting this contention, another student's response regarding a class experience that they found to not be inclusive:

> *Making [the students] sit still the whole time without regard to people who struggle to stay in one spot for long.*
>
> *—A public university student who identifies as White, female, and bisexual*

Ending the Class Session

> *We always had a task to complete at the end that was easy, yet beneficial to our learning topic.*
>
> *—A part-time public university student who identifies as White and female*

Much like how instructors begin a class session can be important to its inclusive nature, how they end a session is also critical. UDL guidelines would recommend providing time for self-assessment and reflection on the learning, as a mechanism of equity and to help students develop skills in self-regulation and executive functioning (*UDL: The UDL Guidelines*, n.d.). This can occur in a number of different manners, from daily minute papers where students are asked to write down the most important things they have learned during the class session, submitting their muddiest point, having a short task for students to complete, small group reviews, or having a brief guided discussion based on a relevant question for consideration (Angelo & Cross, 1993; Love, 2013; Tanner, 2013). While it can be challenging to preserve time at the end of a class session, practices like those mentioned above have been found to improve relationships and learning outcomes for students.

Reflection Question

- Do you have mechanisms for ending your class sessions? If not, how might you end them?

Timing in Asynchronous Online Courses

By their nature, in asynchronous online courses often there are not specified meeting times when the entire class gets together with their instructor. However, that does not mean that time management is not an important factor in these courses, only that it needs to be viewed a bit differently as students may engage with the material at their own pace. In situations where courses are constructive in nature, and have learning units confined to specific times and deadlines, each unit could theoretically be considered a class session. A number of the practices noted above can still be implemented. Strategies for successfully beginning and ending a unit, and for carefully considering the amount of time that students have to engage with learning materials, whether they be readings, videos, or otherwise, before being required to apply and respond, are all important.

A strategy that Derek has used to frame weekly learning units, is to record a short audio-visual welcome to the week, with a written transcript provided, which discusses what the class will be covering and how it relates to what was already learned. This allows students to understand the context of that week's learning goals and processes. Derek also provides an outline of a potential "plan for the week," which students can use to navigate the work that is expected to occur during that time frame, while acknowledging that each student has differing availability and schedules outside of the course, and that the plan can and should be modified to their needs. A challenge Derek previously faced in an online course that he taught was that some students would complete the work efficiently, while others would take large amounts of time completing the same work, or going further into the optional learning materials that Derek provided. To normalize this a bit, Derek now explicitly states what his expectations are for how long students should be spending on various learning activities, and encourages students to reach out to him if they find they are spending much more or less time, so that Derek can help them strategize and prioritize their learning, while still acknowledging that students might need differential amounts of time. Finally, while students interact with each other through discussion boards regularly within each week, Derek finds that one of the best ways to "close the loop" for a particular learning unit is for him, as the instructor, to provide substantial and meaningful feedback to each student on their work. This can be in the form of written feedback or, when possible and appropriate, even short, recorded audio-visual feedback, but regardless of format it is important that students can observe that their work is being acknowledged. Clearly, this is more practical in courses with smaller class sizes as opposed to large courses or massive open online courses (MOOCs), so in those classes recording a short learning unit wrap-up may be a beneficial approach before moving on to the next unit.

Reflection Question

- If you have taught an asynchronous course, how have you navigated student time allotment when you do not meet as a class for specified sessions?

There Is No One "Right" Way to Conduct a Class, But There Are "Better" Ways

Examining the responses of over 350 students to our national survey asking them to provide examples of when their instructors did something well or not well with regards to inclusive teaching related to daily class activities, it became clear that there was no one right way for an instructor to conduct their class inclusively as responses varied from student to student, and even at times seemed to contradict each other. However, on closer examination, the themes above became apparent, and that oftentimes it was how a particular approach or activity was implemented that mattered, even more so than what that particular approach or activity was. And, in a number of ways, this is supported by the literature that has been shared above and the authors' personal experiences. With this in mind, three additional core contexts can be applied to the above themes, which speak to the "better" ways an instructor can conduct their courses, including: understanding the instructor's role in the class and class community, considering the impact of instructor personality and identity, and the importance of equity-minded flexibility within day-to-day instruction.

Understanding the Instructor's Role

Historically, the instructor's position in the classroom has been at the head of a hierarchical power structure, where the instructor makes the rules, determines what material will be presented, how it will be presented, and how students will be assessed. And commonly, in day-to-day learning, this meant an instructor in front of the class lecturing to students. As described throughout this chapter, inclusive instruction often shares some of this power with the students in the class, and this requires a re-envisioning of the instructor role in how they conduct their class sessions. Indeed, in 1993 Alison King coined the phrase "from sage on the stage to guide on the side" to speak to this difference in instructor role, where the learning becomes student-centered and the instructor's role is more geared at facilitating students' interaction with the material and each other (King, 1993). This concept was shared in our student responses regarding what they found to be inclusive about how their courses were conducted, noting learning activities where the instructor wasn't the focus, but was willing to demonstrate, guide, or contribute as most appropriate.

> *Activities were often engaging and the professor was eager to jump into an activity or discussion with us.*
>
> *—A small, private liberal arts college student who identifies as White and male*

> *[The class was] mostly hands-on activities, but [the instructor] would always step-in if needed and demonstrate for the class beforehand.*
>
> *—A private university student who identifies as White and female*

Supporting this idea were the student comments that highlighted instructors who only utilized the "sage on the stage" role as non-inclusive practices; in one case, even when using a video documentary as a learning tool.

> *Some professors just lecture all class. I had one professor that put on a documentary, and then lectured over the documentary all class. It was too much and I couldn't focus on either.*
>
> *—A small, private liberal arts college student who identifies as White, female, and under the age of 18*

And extending this, a student specifically addressed how they believed the role of the instructor to be one of nurturing student engagement rather than simply lecturing, when they stated that the following was an experience that was not inclusive in an in-person, general education course:

> *[The instructor] did not vary activities, and when students sparked up a discussion (which is the point of these courses) did not nurture that conversation but kept enforcing his lecture.*
>
> *—A public university student who identifies as White, female, and first-generation*

Reflection Questions

- How do you view your role in the class, specifically related to in-class, day-to-day activities?
- How can you serve as a guide for your learners?

The Importance of Equity-Minded Flexibility

Complementing the concept of the instructor's role in the class as more of a facilitator of student engagement with the topic and skills being learned is the notion of the flexibility that the instructor should bring to the manner in which they conduct the class. The ability to adapt can and should be intentionally built into the design of the course, but also utilized in the moment of how the class is conducted. This flexibility is important both for ensuring equity in the course as well as nurturing student learning, as indicated in the previous quote where instead of the instructor being flexible enough to allow for student discussion, they defaulted back to their previous plan for lecturing. This can also be seen in additional quotes from students that referred to class experiences they found to be inclusive.

> *There was a lot of improvisation, as it was a jazz course, and [the instructor] did her utmost to ensure that all students felt comfortable playing alone in front of the group. If they weren't, she would often work with them outside of class time or simply not require them to play.*
>
> *—A part-time public university student who identifies as White, male, bisexual, and first-generation*

> *Classes are typically operated in an open forum type of situation. Each person is able to participate at their own comfort level.*
>
> *—A part-time public university student who identifies as White, male, and 45–54 years old*

> *One student pointed out that his religious holiday was not celebrated by the school. Our professor asked him if he would like the day off, and gave him extensions on deadlines.*
>
> *—A student who declined to provide demographic information*

In these quotes you can see an instructor demonstrating equity-minded flexibility, allowing students to participate as they are most comfortable, working with students to increase their confidence (outside of class if needed), and acknowledging the diverse backgrounds of their students and how that may impact their ability to be present in class and meet assignment deadlines. Other means of equity-minded flexibility converge with the use of varied approaches and the role of student choice in assessments addressed earlier in the chapter. One interviewed student, who identified as a female with an unspecified disability, spoke to this when noting how they felt included in a course where the instructor had created a particular assignment, but shifted that plan to allow for more student agency in choosing the format the assignment was completed in.

> *This was for fiction writing class ... the prompt was originally just [to write] some sort of personal essay that you wanted to create. And a lot of people did a photo essay. People had the opportunity to do a video essay ... speaking something more traditionally written, just kind of different opportunities for people to present the story that they were telling in whatever way was most comfortable for them, especially because these were specifically like non-fiction, personal anecdotes that people were sharing with the class, so that just made people a little bit more willing to share because they kind of got to choose what avenue they express that in.*
>
> *—A small, private liberal arts college student who identifies as White, female, and having an unspecified disability*

These student perspectives highlight that while it is certainly important for an instructor to have a plan for a course and particular class sessions, the ability to adapt as is most appropriate for the course and the student's learning in the course, was viewed by many as an inclusive practice that created equity.

Reflection Questions

- Think about a course that you teach or plan to teach. In what areas within specific class sessions, learning activities, or assessments could increased flexibility benefit your diverse student population?
- What specific challenges do you face as an instructor that can make flexibility in the class difficult? These could be related to course requirements, teaching experience, personal background, time in or out of the class, or other aspects.

The Influence of Instructor Personality and Identity

With all of the discussion on the diversity of our student populations, and the unique backgrounds and experiences that they bring to their courses, the diversity of the instructor and their unique personalities and identities are often not considered. At a broad level, instructor demographics can be considered. Based on a U.S. Department of Education study in 2021, of full-time faculty in degree-granting postsecondary institutions, there was a relatively even breakdown by gender, around 48 percent female and 52 percent male, though it is important to note that non-binary faculty were not reported. Further, nearly three-quarters of the full-time faculty were White (74 percent), with 12 percent Asian/Pacific Islander, 7 percent Black, and 6 percent Hispanic, with American Indian, Alaskan Native, and individuals of two or more races making up less than 1 percent (NCES, 2022). Less data is readily available related to the sexual orientation of faculty, but a 2022 report from the American Association of Medical Colleges noted that approximately 3.9 percent of faculty identified as LGB+ (AAMC, 2022). While these diversity numbers have been increasing, overall diversity in the faculty ranks still lags behind that of U.S. college students. Further, the level of instructor diversity varies across academic disciplines. Beyond these demographic categorizations, each instructor does bring their own personality, identity, and background to a course and its teaching, and this individuality can impact both how they teach and how their teaching is received.

While students in our survey did not specify how the demographics of their instructors impacted their feelings of inclusion in daily activities, there were a few responses that may indirectly address these topics. Two students specifically mentioned non-inclusive experiences where their instructors made assumptions or did not recognize the breadth of diversity in their students and course material, an issue that is potentially exacerbated by a faculty community that does not adequately represent the student population.

> *[The instructor] assumed a single student background (White, American, English as a mother tongue, etc.), which left out students whose experiences did not match up with this and made it hard for them to contribute equally because of "insider knowledge" which one would know only if they had a history of education that focused on U.S. history and politics, had a sizeable grasp of U.S. political jargon, and had an understanding of American news stories in the past 15 years.*
>
> *—A small, private liberal arts college student who identifies as White, agendered, and pansexual*

> *The professor would only acknowledge diversity in the African American community and not other ethnicities such as Hispanic, Native American, etc.*
>
> *—A small, private liberal arts college student who identifies as White and female*

This speaks to how instructors navigate their own demographic background in the context of their course, and the impacts that has on their students' experiences. A mechanism to avoid situations like these would include the faculty sharing their own demographic background that they bring to the class, their unconscious and implicit bias, and how these shape their perspectives and understanding related to the course topics and approach to teaching about it. Then, inviting student voices, and welcoming them to share the same if they so desire, which can promote a more diverse set of ideas, thoughts, and perspectives around the course material.

The inclusive benefit of instructors sharing other personal connections that they have to the material, beyond demographics, was also addressed in one of our student interviews.

The best professor would be one that has a strong personality ... and bring up small tidbits that they can relate the course that their own lives, so they feel [like] a little more human rather than an intimidating professor.

—A small, private liberal arts college student who identifies as Asian/ Central Asian/Eurasian/European/White, transgendered, bisexual, and neurodivergent

So while every instructor brings their own personality, identity, and demographic background to each class they teach, leveraging those aspects while also acknowledging and incorporating a diversity of perspectives through the selected course materials and student engagement can support an inclusive experience for their students.

In online courses, particularly asynchronous online courses, sometimes one of the biggest challenges that can present itself is for an instructor to connect with students who may be thousands of miles away and completing classwork at various times. Indeed, one student who spoke about their online learning experience addressed this when they said a negative aspect related to inclusion was that:

[The instructor was] not personable.

—A community college student who identifies as White, female, and first-generation

This student's perspective could be the result of either the instructor not seeming "personable" or the instructor not connecting with this student (and potentially others in the course). Aspects of being approachable, caring, and invested in the students and their learning, are qualities that apply both to online and face-to-face courses. However, as noted above, if the issue has more to do with connection between the instructor and their students, then there are some challenges that are specific to the online format. Indeed, studies have shown that how connected a student feels to their instructor in an online course is positively related to their success in those courses and online programs (Jones et al., 2022; Joyner et al., 2014; Young & Bruce, 2011; Zajac & Lane, 2021). A common theme in a number of these studies that examine student–instructor connectedness in an online learning setting was the need for the instructor to be present. More specifically, factors that were most associated with student connectedness with their instructors were: contact with the instructor, that the instructor was responsive, and that they trusted their instructor to handle inappropriate interactions (Young & Bruce, 2011). Some specific strategies that have been shown to support this connectedness includes a video-based introduction, substantive feedback to student work, and using writing as a means of support (Diekelmann & Mendias, 2005; Martin et al., 2018). In addition to these strategies, ways that Derek has sought to build connectedness between himself and his students in online asynchronous courses includes having a discussion thread devoted to personal introductions, which talk about personal interests and favorite hobbies, which both he and his students participate in, and can build on throughout the term. Additionally, offering the opportunity for one-on-one virtual meetings that last five to ten minutes, Derek has found to help "bridge the virtual gap." These meetings are certainly more manageable in courses with small class sizes, so in larger classes some of the other approaches noted may be more practical.

Reflection Questions

- What are aspects of your personality or identity (visible or invisible) that impact your teaching? What challenges might those present? Alternatively, how can you leverage those characteristics within your courses?
- If you teach online, what strategies have you used successfully to connect with your students? Or, if you have found that connection difficult, what can you try in the future?

Conclusion

In this chapter, we listened to student voices to identify what specific student experiences in the daily activities of how a course is conducted have impacted their perception of inclusion, and four major themes emerged: utilizing varied approaches can be beneficial, incorporating student voices is critical, time management matters, and that there is no one "right" way to conduct a class, but there are "better" ways to do so. These themes intersect, overlap, and complement each other in a number of places, and strategies for how to effectively implement them were provided both in face-to-face and online courses. Moreover, the themes found when analyzing student responses about the day-to-day activities in their courses also connected to those that were identified in Chapters 2 and 3, addressing course design and creating a welcoming environment.

In Part Two of this book, the focus will shift, building on what was learned from student perspectives on effective inclusive teaching practices here in Part One, to how instructors can interrogate their teaching practice, through self-reflection, observational feedback, and assessment and scholarship of teaching and learning projects.

References

AAMC. (2022). *Perceptions of Diversity, Equity, and Inclusion of LGB+ Faculty at U. S. Medical Schools.* https://www.aamc.org/media/62091/download.

Addy, T. M., Dube, D., Mitchell, K. A., & SoRelle, M. (2021). *What inclusive instructors do: Principles and practices for excellence in college teaching*. Sterling, VA: Stylus Publishing.

Agrawal, N., Rathi, S., Gupta, N., Aggarwal, A., Garg, A., & Gupta, J. (2021). The use of anonymous pop-quizzes as an innovative teaching-learning tool to reinforce learning among undergraduate dental students. *SRM Journal of Research in Dental Sciences*, 12(2), 74–74.

Allen, K. L., & Katz, R. V. (2011). Comparative use of podcasts vs. lecture transcripts as learning aids for dental students. *Journal of Dental Education*, 75(6), 817–822. doi:10.1002/j.0022-0337.2011.75.6.tb05110.x.

Alsalamah, A. (2020). Using captioning services with deaf and hard of hearing students in higher education: A systematic review. *American Annals of the Deaf*, 165 (1), 114–127. doi:10.1353/aad.2020.0012.

Angelo, T. A., & Cross, P. (1993). *Classroom assessment techniques: A handbook for college teachers*, 2nd ed. New York: Wiley. https://www.wiley.com/en-us/Classroom+Assessment+Techniques%3A+A+Handbook+for+College+Teachers%2C+2nd+Edition-p-9781555425005.

Atkins, T. (2018). *Amplifying Diverse Voices: Strategies for Promoting Inclusion in the Law School Classroom* (SSRN Scholarly Paper No. 3469793). https://papers.ssrn.com/abstract=3469793.

Bender, T. (2012). *Discussion-based online teaching to enhance student learning: Theory, practice and assessment*. Sterling, VA: Stylus Publishing.

Bligh, D. A. (1998). *What's the use of lectures?*Bristol, UK: Intellect Books.

Boardman, A. M., & Maynard, D. (2023). Beyond "great job"—providing peer feedback in college classrooms. *College Teaching*. doi:10.1080/87567555.2023.2238955.

Bouchey, B., Castek, J., & Thygeson, J. (2021). Multimodal learning. In J. Ryoo & K. Winkelmann (Eds.), *Innovative learning environments in STEM higher education: Opportunities, challenges, and looking forward* (pp. 35–54). New York: Springer. doi:10.1007/978-3-030-58948-6_3.

Bovill, C. (2020). Co-creation in learning and teaching: The case for a whole-class approach in higher education. *Higher Education*, 79(6), 1023–1037. doi:10.1007/s10734-019-00453-w.

Boyle, J. R., Forchelli, G. A., & Cariss, K. (2015). Note-taking interventions to assist students with disabilities in content area classes. *Preventing School Failure: Alternative Education for Children and Youth*, 59(3), 186–195. doi:10.1080/1045988X.2014.903463.

Bradbury, N. A. (2016). Attention span during lectures: 8 seconds, 10 minutes, or more? *Advances in Physiology Education*, 40(4), 509–513. doi:10.1152/advan.00109.2016.

Broeckelman-Post, M., Johnson, A., & Reid Schwebach, J. (2016). Calling on students using notecards: Engagement and countering communication anxiety in large lecture. *Journal of College Science Teaching*, 45(5), 27–33. doi:10.2505/4/jcst16_045_05_27.

Brookfield, S. D., & Preskill, S. (1999). *Discussion as a way of teaching. tools and techniques for democratic classrooms*. Hoboken, NJ: Jossey-Bass.

Carter, C., & Gentry, J. A. (2000). Use of pop quizzes as an innovative strategy to promote critical thinking in nursing students. *Nurse Educator*, 25(4), 155.

Christensen, C. R., & Others, A. (1991). *Education for judgment: The artistry of discussion leadership*. Boston, MA: Harvard Business School Press.
Cicirello, V. A. (2009). On the role and effectiveness of pop quizzes in CS1. *ACM SIGCSE Bulletin*, 41(1), 286–290. doi:10.1145/1539024.1508971.
Clouder, L., Karakus, M., Cinotti, A., Ferreyra, M. V., Fierros, G. A., & Rojo, P. (2020). Neurodiversity in higher education: A narrative synthesis. *Higher Education*, 80(4), 757–778. doi:10.1007/s10734-020-00513-6.
Cooper, K. M., Downing, V. R., & Brownell, S. E. (2018). The influence of active learning practices on student anxiety in large-enrollment college science classrooms. *International Journal of Stem Education*, 5(1), 23. doi:10.1186/s40594-018-0123-6.
Dallimore, E., Hertenstein, J., & Platt, M. (2019). Leveling the playing field: How cold-calling affects class discussion gender equity. *Journal of Education and Learning*, 8(2), Article 2. doi:10.5539/jel.v8n2p14.
Davidson, N., Major, C., & Michaelsen, L. (2014). Small-group learning in higher education—cooperative, collaborative, problem-based, and team-based learning: An introduction by the guest editors. *Journal on Excellence in College Teaching*, 25(3–4), 1–6.
DeZure, D., Kaplan, M., & Deerman, M. A. (2001). Research on student notetaking: implications for faculty and graduate student instructors. https://www.researchgate.net/publication/247399328_RESEARCH_ON_STUDENT_NOTETAKING_IMPLICATIONS_FOR_FACULTY_AND_GRADUATE_STUDENT_INSTRUCTORS
Diekelmann, N., & Mendias, E. P. (2005). Being a supportive presence in online courses: Knowing and connecting with students through writing. *Journal of Nursing Education*, 44(8), 344–346. doi:10.3928/01484834-20050801-02.
Dommett, E. J., Dinu, L. M., Van Tilburg, W., Keightley, S., & Gardner, B. (2022). Effects of captions, transcripts and reminders on learning and perceptions of lecture capture. *International Journal of Educational Technology in Higher Education*, 19(1), 20. doi:10.1186/s41239-022-00327-9.
Duncan, D. (2006). Clickers: A new teaching aid with exceptional promise. *Astronomy Education Review*, 5(1), 70–88. doi:10.3847/AER2006005.
Eddy, S. L., Brownell, S. E., & Wenderoth, M. P. (2014). Gender gaps in achievement and participation in multiple introductory biology classrooms. *CBE Life Sciences Education*, 13(3), 478–492. doi:10.1187/cbe.13-10-0204.
Effective Lectures. (n.d.). *Academy for Teaching and Learning | Baylor University.* Retrieved May 30, 2023, from https://www.baylor.edu/atl/index.php?id=965135.
Freeman, S., Eddy, S. L., McDonough, M., Smith, M. K., Okoroafor, N., Jordt, H., & Wenderoth, M. P. (2014). Active learning increases student performance in science, engineering, and mathematics. *Proceedings of the National Academy of Sciences*, 111(23), 8410–8415. doi:10.1073/pnas.1319030111.
García-Campos, M.-D., Canabal, C., & Alba-Pastor, C. (2020). Executive functions in universal design for learning: Moving towards inclusive education. *International Journal of Inclusive Education*, 24(6), 660–674. doi:10.1080/13603116.2018.1474955.
Garrett, C. E. (2020). Three key principles for improving discussion-based learning in college classrooms. *Journal on Empowering Teacher Excellence*, 4(1), Article 8. doi:10.15142/VNKZ-P273.

Glazer, N. (2014). Formative plus summative assessment in large undergraduate courses: Why both? *International Journal of Teaching and Learning in Higher Education*, 26(2), 276–286.

Herman, J. H., & Nilson, L. B. (2018). *Creating engaging discussions: Strategies for "avoiding crickets" in any size classroom and online*. Sterling, VA: Stylus Publishing.

Ismail, S. M., Rahul, D. R., Patra, I., & Rezvani, E. (2022). Formative vs. summative assessment: Impacts on academic motivation, attitude toward learning, test anxiety, and self-regulation skill. *Language Testing in Asia*, 12(1), 40. doi:10.1186/s40468-022-00191-4.

Jones, K., Polyakova-Norwood, V., Raynor, P., & Tavakoli, A. (2022). Student perceptions of faculty caring in online nursing education: A mixed-methods study. *Nurse Education Today*, 112, 105328. doi:10.1016/j.nedt.2022.105328.

Joyner, S. A., Fuller, M. B., Holzweiss, P. C., Henderson, S., & Young, R. (2014). The importance of student-instructor connections in graduate level online courses. *Journal of Online Learning and Teaching*, 10(3), 436–445.

Kam, M., Wang, J., Iles, A., Tse, E., Chiu, J., Glaser, D., Tarshish, O., & Canny, J. (2005). Livenotes: A system for cooperative and augmented note-taking in lectures. *Proceedings of the SIGCHI Conference on Human Factors in Computing Systems*, 531–540. doi:10.1145/1054972.1055046.

Kamuche, F. U. (2007). The effects of unannounced quizzes on student performance: Further evidence. *College Teaching Methods & Styles Journal*, 3(2), 21–26.

Kent, M., Ellis, K., Latter, N., & Peaty, G. (2018). The case for captioned lectures in Australian higher education. *TechTrends*, 62(2), 158–165. doi:10.1007/s11528-017-0225-x.

Khanna, M. M. (2015). Ungraded pop quizzes: Test-enhanced learning without all the anxiety. *Teaching of Psychology*, 42(2), 174–178. doi:10.1177/0098628315573144.

Kiewra, K. A., DuBois, N. F., Christian, D., McShane, A., Meyerhoffer, M., & Roskelley, D. (1991). Note-taking functions and techniques. *Journal of Educational Psychology*, 83, 240–245. https://doi.org/10.1037/0022-0663.83.2.240.

King, A. (1993). From Sage on the Stage to Guide on the Side. *College Teaching*, 41 (1), 30–35. doi:10.1080/87567555.1993.9926781.

Knight, J. K., & Wood, W. B. (2005). Teaching more by lecturing less. *Cell Biology Education*, 4(4), 298–310. doi:10.1187/05-06-0082.

Lang, J. (2016). Small changes in teaching: The first 5 minutes of class. *The Chronicle of Higher Education*. https://www.chronicle.com/article/small-changes-in-teaching-the-first-5-minutes-of-class/.

Loughlin, C., & Lindberg-Sand, Å. (2023). The use of lectures: Effective pedagogy or seeds scattered on the wind? *Higher Education: The International Journal of Higher Education Research*, 85(2), 283–299. doi:10.1007/s10734-022-00833-9.

Love, B. (2013). Finishing strong: End-of-class review to improve relationships, measurement, and learning outcomes. *College Teaching*, 61(4), 151–152. doi:10.1080/87567555.2013.773417.

Mahoney, J., & Hall, C. (2017). Using technology to differentiate and accommodate students with disabilities. *E-Learning and Digital Media*, 14(5), 291–303. doi:10.1177/2042753017751517.

Martin, F., Wang, C., & Sadaf, A. (2018). Student perception of helpfulness of facilitation strategies that enhance instructor presence, connectedness, engagement and learning in online courses. *The Internet and Higher Education*, 37, 52–65. doi:10.1016/j.iheduc.2018.01.003.

Maydosz, A., & Raver, S. (2010). Note taking and university students with learning difficulties: What supports are needed? *Journal of Diversity in Higher Education*, 3, 177–186. doi:10.1037/a0020297.

Mayer, R. E. (2014). Cognitive theory of multimedia learning. In R. E. Mayer (Ed.), *The Cambridge handbook of multimedia learning* (2nd ed., pp. 43–71). Cambridge: Cambridge University Press. doi:10.1017/CBO9781139547369.005.

McGivern, P., & Coxon, M. (2015). Student polling software: Where cognitive psychology meets educational practice? *Frontiers in Psychology*, 6, 55. doi:10.3389/fpsyg.2015.00055.

Metzger, K. J., & Via, Z. (2022). Warming up the cold callencouraging classroom inclusion by considering warm- & cold-calling techniques. *The American Biology Teacher*, 84(6), 342–346. doi:10.1525/abt.2022.84.6.342.

Morris, R., Perry, T., & Wardle, L. (2021). Formative assessment and feedback for learning in higher education: A systematic review. *Review of Education*, 9(3), e3292. doi:10.1002/rev3.3292.

Mulder, R. A., Pearce, J. M., & Baik, C. (2014). Peer review in higher education: Student perceptions before and after participation. *Active Learning in Higher Education*, 15(2), 157–171. doi:10.1177/1469787414527391.

NCES. (2022). *Characteristics of Postsecondary Faculty.* https://nces.ed.gov/programs/coe/indicator/csc/postsecondary-faculty

Nicol, D., Thomson, A., & Breslin, C. (2014). Rethinking feedback practices in higher education: A peer review perspective. *Assessment & Evaluation in Higher Education*, 39(1), 102–122. doi:10.1080/02602938.2013.795518.

Paulus, M., Kunkel, J., Schmidt, S. C. E., Bachert, P., Wäsche, H., Neumann, R., & Woll, A. (2021). Standing breaks in lectures improve university students' self-perceived physical, mental, and cognitive condition. *International Journal of Environmental Research and Public Health*, 18(8), 4204. doi:10.3390/ijerph18084204.

Penner, M. R. (2018). Building an inclusive classroom. *Journal of Undergraduate Neuroscience Education*, 16(3), A268–A272.

Phelps, C., & Moro, C. (2022). Using live interactive polling to enable hands-on learning for both face-to-face and online students within hybrid-delivered courses. *Journal of University Teaching and Learning Practice*, 19(3). doi:10.53761/1.19.3.08.

Piolat, A., Olive, T., & Kellogg, R. T. (2005). Cognitive effort during note taking. *Applied Cognitive Psychology*, 19(3), 291–312. doi:10.1002/acp.1086.

Ranchal, R., Taber-Doughty, T., Guo, Y., Bain, K., Martin, H., Paul Robinson, J., & Duerstock, B. S. (2013). Using speech recognition for real-time captioning and lecture transcription in the classroom. *IEEE Transactions on Learning Technologies*, 6(4), 299–311. doi:10.1109/TLT.2013.21.

Regmi, K. (2012). A review of teaching methods—lecturing and facilitation in higher education (HE): A summary of the published evidence. *The Journal of Effective Teaching*, 12(3). https://files.eric.ed.gov/fulltext/EJ1092144.pdf

Ritzhaupt, A. D., Pastore, R., & Davis, R. (2015). Effects of captions and time-compressed video on learner performance and satisfaction. *Computers in Human Behavior*, 45, 222–227. doi:10.1016/j.chb.2014.12.020.

Roettger, C., Roettger, L. O., Walugembe, F., & Makerere (2007). Teaching: More than just lecturing. *Journal of University Teaching and Learning Practice*, 4(2), 65–80. doi:10.53761/1.4.2.6.

Rose, D. H., & Meyer, A. (2002). *Teaching every student in the digital age: Universal design for learning*. Alexandria, VA: Association for Supervision and Curriculum Development.

Rowe, M. B. (1972). *Wait-Time and Rewards as Instructional Variables: Their Influence on Language, Logic, and Fate Control*. https://eric.ed.gov/?id=ED061103.

Sankey, M., Birch, D., & Gardiner, M. (2010). Engaging students through multimodal learning environments: The journey continues. *Proceedings ASCILITE 2010: 27th Annual Conference of the Australasian Society for Computers in Learning in Tertiary Education: Curriculum, Technology and Transformation for an Unknown Future*. http://ascilite.org.au/conferences/sydney10/Ascilite%20conference%20proceedings%202010/Sankey-full.pdf.

Sarvary, M. A., & Gifford, K. M. (2017). The benefits of a real-time web-based response system for enhancing engaged learning in classrooms and public science events. *Journal of Undergraduate Neuroscience Education*, 15(2), E13–E16.

Serrano-Aguilera, J. J., Tocino, A., Fortes, S., Martín, C., Mercadé-Melé, P., Moreno-Sáez, R., Muñoz, A., Palomo-Hierro, S., & Torres, A. (2021). Using peer review for student performance enhancement: Experiences in a multidisciplinary higher education setting. *Education Sciences*, 11(2), Article 2. doi:10.3390/educsci11020071.

Smith, G. G., Ferguson, D., & Caris, M. (2003). The web versus the classroom: Instructor experiences in discussion-based and mathematics-based disciplines. *Journal of Educational Computing Research*, 29(1), 29–59. doi:10.2190/PEA0-T6N4-PU8D-CFUF.

Tanner, K. D. (2013). Structure matters: Twenty-one teaching strategies to promote student engagement and cultivate classroom equity. *CBE—Life Sciences Education*, 12(3), 322–331. doi:10.1187/cbe.13-06-0115.

Timmer, M. C. J., Steendijk, P., Arend, S. M., & Versteeg, M. (2020). Making a lecture stick: The effect of spaced instruction on knowledge retention in medical education. *Medical Science Educator*, 30(3), 1211–1219. doi:10.1007/s40670-020-00995-0.

Tincani, M. (2004). Improving outcomes for college students with disabilities: Ten strategies for instructors. *College Teaching*, 52(4), 128–133. doi:10.3200/CTCH.52.4.128-133.

Tisdell, C., & Loch, B. (2017). How useful are closed captions for learning mathematics via online video? *International Journal of Mathematical Education in Science and Technology*, 48(2), 229–243. doi:10.1080/0020739X.2016.1238518.

Tronchoni, H., Izquierdo, C., & Anguera, M. T. (2022). A systematic review on lecturing in contemporary university teaching. *Frontiers in Psychology*, 13, 971617. doi:10.3389/fpsyg.2022.971617.

UDL: The UDL Guidelines. (n.d.). Retrieved May 30, 2023, from https://udlguidelines.cast.org/.

Waugh, A. H., & Andrews, T. C. (2020). Diving into the details: Constructing a framework of random call components. *CBE Life Sciences Education*, 19(2), ar14. doi:10.1187/cbe.19-07-0130.

Willyard, C. (2010) The benefits of pop quizzes. *Science—AAAS*. https://www.science.org/content/article/benefits-pop-quizzes.

Wilson, K., & Korn, J. H. (2007). Attention during lectures: Beyond ten minutes. *Teaching of Psychology*, 34(2), 85–89. doi:10.1080/00986280701291291.

Wood, T. A. (2017). *Faculty and student perceptions of Plickers*. 2017ASEE Zone II Conference.

Ying, J. (2020). The importance of the discussion method in the undergraduate business classroom. *Humanistic Management Journal*, 5(2), 251–278. doi:10.1007/s41463-020-00099-2.

Young, S., & Bruce, M. A. (2011). Classroom community and student engagement in online courses. *Journal of Online Learning and Teaching*, 7(2).

Yüksel, H. S., & Gündüz, N. (2017). Formative and summative assessment in higher education: Opinions and practices of instructors. *Online Submission*, 3(8), 336–356. https://eric.ed.gov/?id=ED576679.

Zajac, L. K., & Lane, A. J. (2021). Student perceptions of faculty presence and caring in accelerated online courses. *Quarterly Review of Distance Education*, 21(2), 67–78.

PART II

Assessing Our Practices

5

STARTING TO REFLECT ON YOUR PRACTICE

In Part Two of this book, we take what was heard from listening to learner feedback on inclusive, and non-inclusive teaching practices they have experienced as students in higher education, and activate those lessons learned as we discuss how we as instructors can develop as reflective practitioners. In this chapter, the focus is on mechanisms of self-reflection and incorporating feedback from students within the courses. We highlight a variety of reflective practices that have been successful for instructors, provide tools for acquiring student feedback around topics of equity and inclusion, and offer suggestions for how to make reflection and acquired feedback actionable. Some of the specific resources described might become unavailable after the production of this book, so therefore several are listed as potential starting points, and these lists are not exhaustive. We encourage instructors to seek out additional general and disciplinary resources.

The Importance of Reflective Practice

> "Inclusive teaching is a perpetual work in progress informed by research, dialogue, and reflection. It is necessarily a process of negotiation between teacher and students, since no single set of practices is possible for every teacher to enact, or responsive to every learner."
>
> —*Full Professor, Baccalaureate College, Education*

The above quote comes from a national survey of instructors in higher education on the topic of inclusive teaching, used to inform our previous book, *What Inclusive Instructors Do*. It echoes some of the key themes that came from our more recent student survey, such as the importance of

DOI: 10.4324/9781003442929-7

student voice and how there is not only one correct way to teach inclusively. Moreover, it emphasizes the concept that inclusive and equitable teaching is not a destination, but a journey of continued development, and one that requires self-reflection and the use of the information, experiences, and tools available to us as instructors.

As Stephen D. Brookfield notes in the book, *Becoming a Critically Reflective Teacher*, our actions as instructors are built on assumptions that we hold on the best ways to help students learn, and depending on the situation those assumptions may be accurate, inaccurate, or anywhere in between (Brookfield, 2017). Reflecting on our teaching is essentially the process of checking the accuracy and validity of those assumptions and how they are manifesting for our students. Reflective practice allows for the development of new knowledge, skills, and dispositions which can be employed in our future teaching to improve its efficacy (Slade et al., 2019). The knowledge and skills acquired create a toolkit, which the instructor can utilize in their future teaching, and allow instructors to adjust and respond to challenges and issues in a justified manner (Brookfield, 2017). Reflective practice can further lead to employing pedagogies that demonstrate an understanding of student cultures, and has the potential to be significantly impactful in situations of teacher–student difference, allowing us as instructors to better support the learning of a diverse student body (Carrington & Selva, 2010; Shandomo, 2010).

Reflection Questions

- What do you believe are the main specific benefits of reflecting on one's teaching?
- Do you consider yourself an effective reflective practitioner of teaching? If not, what barriers make reflection difficult for you?

Attitudes and Approaches of Reflective Practitioners

Reflective practice has been embedded in K-12 teacher education for a number of years, however most instructors within higher education are more likely to have been trained in their specific discipline of expertise rather than in education, and thus there is a need to discuss means by which instructors who have not been formally trained in reflective teaching practices can nonetheless become effective reflective practitioners (Brandt, 2008; Carrington & Selva, 2010; Mortari, 2012; Shandomo, 2010; Slade et al., 2019).

In 1938, John Dewey spoke to attitudes that form the basis of effective reflective practice, including open-mindedness, responsibility, and wholeheartedness (Dewey, 1938). Open-mindedness represents being open to other points of view, a willingness to consider new evidence, and admitting the possibility of error. Responsibility acknowledges that our choices as instructors impact our students in foreseen and unforeseen ways. And wholeheartedness asks for a commitment to learning and a belief that growth is possible (Reflective Practice, 2022). These attitudes are complemented by a series of attributes of reflective practitioners as individuals who: engage in ongoing inquiry, reflect on and learn from experience, solicit feedback, remain open to alternative perspectives, assume responsibility for their own learning, take action to align with new knowledge and understandings, observe themselves in the process of thinking, are committed to continuous improvement in practice, strive to align behavior with values and beliefs, and seek to discover what is true (Larrivee & Cooper, 2006).

With these core attitudes and attributes of instructors seeking to grow as reflective practitioners, there are various modes through which reflection can occur, and the most effective reflective practitioners will utilize them all. Reflection-in-action occurs when instructors take note of thinking and actions as they are occurring and make immediate adjustments as the events unfold. Reflection-on-action is retrospective, and looks back on an experience or event that occurred in the past. Reflection-for-action is application minded, with the goal of analysis leading to change, and can include both reflection-in-action and reflection-on-action. And reflection-within is self-reflection that inquires about personal purposes, intentions, and feelings (Reflective Practice, 2022). In each of these modes of reflection, various lenses can be applied to achieve the broadest perspective and yield the most positive growth. These lenses include the autobiographical (self) lens, the student lens, the colleague lens, and the theoretical lens which incorporates literature and research (Brookfield, 2017).

In this chapter, we provide a number of means by which to apply each of these lenses within the various modes of reflection, with a particular focus on reflection -on and -for action. Then, the following chapters explore the concepts of the colleague lens, through acquiring observational feedback, and the theoretical lens, by involving oneself in the scholarship of teaching, in more specific depth.

Reflection Questions

- In regards to reflective teaching, do you feel that you have the three attitudes for effective reflective practice (open-mindedness, responsibility, and wholeheartedness)? If not, which are absent and why?
- Which attribute of reflective practitioners is your strongest? Which is one that could use more development?
- Which lens of reflective teaching, if any, have you most employed? Which lens have you employed the least?

Methods and Resources for Reflection

Journaling

The practice of teacher journaling, or keeping a teaching diary, is one that has been around for many years (Dreyer, 2015; McDonough, 1994; Stevens & Cooper, 2009). The goals of this practice are to provide an opportunity to create a record of the events occurring in the course and an opportunity for current and post-reflection on those events. Indeed, journaling has been found to specifically help teachers confronting challenging contexts and situations (Lowe et al., 2013).

There are a number of variables through which an instructor can personalize their journaling process, and make it most effective for them. One of these is the form the journal is created in. Some prefer a physical notebook or journal, while others prefer a digital version. One of the benefits of the physical journal is that entries can be made essentially anytime and anywhere, so long as the instructor has a journal and a writing utensil. Benefits of the digital version is that it may be more accessible, if saved in a manner that makes it accessible on different devices and different locations, and journal entries may be more easily searchable as one "looks back in time" for key words, ideas, or events. Digital journals can be kept by simply utilizing word processing programs, web-based services, and mobile applications. Of note, a number of the web-based services also have mobile app versions, and vice versa.

Another variable is the timing and regularity of the journal entries. Perhaps the most effective approach comes when instructors create regular entries, either daily, after each class session, or weekly. This creates a regular, habit-forming opportunity for instructors to think about each specific block of time in a meaningful way, rather than relying on specific events triggering the feeling that a journal entry would be beneficial. It also prevents too much time from elapsing and reducing the accuracy of the entry. It is important that the instructor intentionally makes time for this journaling, though it does not need to be particularly long. Committing 5–10 minutes directly after each class session, or 20–30 minutes at the end of each week, are common practices that work well for some instructors Derek has found that devoting the last 15 minutes of each workday to updating his own teaching journal has provided a nice balance of time after his classes for retrospection and recall of the events he would like to record and examine.

Also important is the content included within the journal entries. The journal may be a narrative account of the class; a record of incidents, problems, and insights from the lessons; or a source of information to be reviewed and shared with others. One simple strategy for a teaching journal could include the questions: What went well today? What could I have done differently? How will I modify my instruction in the future? (Reflective Teaching, 2016). Others have used a structure based on the Harvard Visible Thinking Routine, organizing the entries around the "I see, I think, I wonder" format (Lowe et al., 2013). Still another incorporates four questions: What did my students learn today? What helped them learn? What got in the way? What specific evidence can I quote to back up my claims? (Richards & Farrell, 2005). Determining your own particular goal for your teaching journal can help frame what questions it should address, and what content it should include.

To create a teaching journal that is focused on equity and inclusion, instructors can utilize the feedback from students on what they find to be most inclusive and equitable, to incorporate some specific questions that could be addressed in each journal entry. These could include:

- What teaching approaches were utilized? Were there multiple means of representation and engagement allowed for? Did students have a choice in how they engaged with the material?
- Were student ideas, opinions, and perspectives welcomed and included in our learning? If so, whose voices did we hear, and what were their additions?
- Were student questions encouraged? If so, who asked questions? How did they ask them? What was their content?
- Was sufficient time allowed for learning activities, critical thinking, and sharing? Why do I think this?
- Were there any violations of our course expectations? If so, how were they handled and is additional follow-up needed?
- How did I assess student learning in an equitable or inclusive manner? How does this fit with other assessments throughout the course?
- Did I notice any barriers to learning for any students facing barriers to their learning in class? If so, how were they addressed or can they be addressed in the future?

Another important parameter to consider when creating a teaching journal is who the journal is for. Is it simply a record for yourself, or is it intended to be shared more broadly? If the intention is the latter, then the blog format may be an appropriate form for the journal to take. Blogs are websites consisting of journal-style entries, commonly without substantial oversight or professional editing. This allows others to learn from your experiences; however, it does change the type of content that can and should be included. For example, specific student names or identifying characteristics should not be included in an outward facing blog. Also, if the goal is identifying incorrect assumptions and improving ineffective methods of one's personal teaching, it may not be desirable to have this openly accessible to a broader audience. As such, we encourage instructors to think about and approach personal teaching journals and shared teaching journals, like blogs, differently from one another, and recommend starting with the personal journaling first.

Using Blogs, Podcasts, Webinars, Websites, and Social Media

While journaling is commonly an introspective practice, where an instructor looks inwardly at their own teaching and courses, instructors around the globe share their experiences, tips, and tools through a variety of accessible media which can be valuable resources for reflective practice by providing context and scope beyond one's own teaching.

As mentioned above, blogs are one means by which the experiences and opinions around teaching are shared. Sometimes blogs can have a single owner who makes all the entries, and other times they are collections from various contributors, known as multi-author blogs, and may be professionally curated and edited. While there are teaching blogs that exist on a wide berth of topics, there are also a number that specifically speak to concepts of inclusion and equity. Examples include the University of Michigan Center for Research on Learning & Teaching's "Blogs on Inclusive Teaching" (*Blogs on Inclusive Teaching | CRLT*, n.d.) and the Rochester Institute of Technology's Sara Schley and Carol Marchetti-helmed "Included" blog (INCLUDED Blog, 2021).

Podcasts are another resource available for instructors looking to reflect on their own practice by incorporating the experiences, ideas, and perspectives of others. Podcasts are generally audio-based media, generally with a specific theme across episodes, and a particular focus or foci within individual episodes. Again, like blogs, there are too many education-related podcasts to note here, and new ones being created regularly, but there are some that commonly focus on topics related to inclusion and equity which bear mention. "Dead Ideas in Teaching and Learning" hosted by the Columbia University Center for Teaching and Learning Executive Director Catherine Ross (Ross, n.d.), "Teaching in Higher Ed" hosted by Bonni Stachowiak (Stachowiak, n.d.), the "Inclusive Education Project" podcast hosted by Amanda Selogie and Vickie Brett (Selogie & Brett, n.d.), the "Think UDL" podcast hosted by Lillian Nave (Nave, n.d.), and "Tea for Teaching" with John Kane and Rebecca Mushtare (Kane & Mushtare, n.d.) are just a few examples.

Webinars on inclusive teaching are also commonly available online, hosted by institutions of higher education, book publishers, and others vested in diversity, equity, and inclusion. The Association of College and University Educators (ACUE) is a service that has full courses for higher education teaching professional development, but also posts select webinars specifically related to inclusive teaching that can be accessed free of charge (*ACUE*

Webinar Series, n.d.). For teachers looking for insight on how to make online courses inclusive, Quality Matters is a program similar to ACUE but with a focus on online pedagogy and also offers selected free webinars (*Free Webinars | Quality Matters*, n.d.).

Inside Higher Ed, a well-respected resource with over 2 million monthly readers, provides news articles, editorial and opinion articles, blogs, and podcasts related to higher education all in one location (*Inside Higher Ed | Higher Education News, Career Advice, Events and Jobs*, n.d.). These very commonly address issues of diversity, equity, and inclusion, and indeed there is a "Diversity" tab that allows visitors to sort through its contents related to race & ethnicity, sex & gender, socioeconomics, religion, disability, and age. *The Chronicle of Higher Education* is another Internet resource that hosts news articles, advice commentaries, and virtual events related to teaching and higher education, many of which speak to diversity, equity, and inclusion (*The Chronicle of Higher Education | Higher Ed News, Opinion & Advice*, n.d.).

Social media platforms are also means of sharing experiences and constructing dialogue around topics in higher education, including the topics of inclusion and equity. These provide avenues not only for an instructor to hear and see what colleagues and experts are experiencing around the globe in real time, but also a means of networking and building relationships that can allow for more informed reflection on their own practice. This may come in the form of following the social media presence of some of the foremost thought leaders on inclusive education, or institutions, or advocacy groups. Information and conversations on inclusive teaching in higher education can be found across Instagram, Facebook, X (formerly Twitter), and other platforms, and by their very nature can comment on, discourse, and respond to current events of importance in near real time. As noted when the action of blogging was discussed, careful consideration should be given to any information shared through social media platforms about our teaching experiences, ensuring that we are protecting and respecting the privacy of our students, colleagues, and others.

The Inclusive Teaching Visualization Project

The Inclusive Teaching Visualization Project is a resource which was designed to support reflection specifically around inclusive teaching in higher education (*Inclusive Teaching Visualization*, n.d.). It consists of a collection of short video vignettes in which instructors are implementing inclusive teaching practices in a mock college class. These vignettes include examples within a social science lecture, a first-year seminar, and a STEM laboratory. While watching these videos, viewers are asked to identify the inclusive approaches being used and their strengths, reflect on how they could be implemented within their own courses, perhaps in a modified format, and to brainstorm what other inclusive approaches could be used in the setting of the video. By combining the processes of viewing inclusive practices in action, and pairing that with the reflection questions, this resource provides a novel way to support the development of our inclusive teaching that can complement what other resources provide.

Utilizing Teaching Inventories

Teaching inventories are standardized instruments, generally consisting of multiple-choice questions or prompts that can be used to reflect on one's teaching. A number of validated inventories have been created, geared at various aspects of teaching and the teaching process, and they create a framework for critical reflection on that specific aspect. The *Teaching Perspectives Inventory* is aimed at helping instructors identify the actions, intentions, and beliefs that make up their perspectives on teaching (Pratt, 1998; Pratt et al., 2001). After completing the 45-item inventory, a profile is created which can then be interpreted and reflected on, and used as a tool for understanding one's own philosophies and biases related to teaching. The *Teaching Goals Inventory* is focused on helping an instructor determine what they value about teaching and learning, specifically related to what they want to accomplish within individual courses (Angelo & Cross, 1993; *The Teaching Goals Inventory (TGI) | Office of Teaching, Learning & Technology*, n.d.; Ulosevich, 1994). By completing and reflecting on the results of this instrument, instructors are better suited to revise instructional goals, identify and create appropriate assessment tools, and discuss teaching and learning goals with colleagues. The *Teaching Practices Inventory* was originally designed to characterize teaching practices an instructor utilizes in undergraduate science and mathematics lecture courses, though it has been adapted for more broad application, including the natural and social sciences (Wieman, 2015; Wieman & Gilbert, 2014). Reflecting on the results of this inventory can aid in gauging the extent that evidence-based teaching practices are being employed in one's classes and, when shared, within and across departments and institutions.

Specifically related to inclusive and equitable teaching, the University of Michigan Center for Research on Learning and Teaching developed the *Inventory of Inclusive Teaching Strategies* to help instructors reflect on their pedagogical practices and provide specific strategies for building inclusive classes (*Inventory of Inclusive Teaching Strategies—Inclusive Teaching*, n.d.). This inventory is founded on five research-based principles, which include: critical engagement of difference, academic belonging, transparency, structured interactions, and flexibility. Upon completing the inventory, the instructor can more clearly reflect on what strategies they are already utilizing, ones they would like to implement or investigate further, and ones that may not work for them and their class. Others include the Inclusive Teaching Higher Education Rubric and the Social Justice Syllabus Design Tool (Taylor et al., 2019; Hu & Deramo, 2021).

These various instruments can be completed at any point in the arc of one's teaching career, and also at any point within the development, implementation, or after completion of a particular class, but some may be most useful at specific times depending on the goals of the instructor taking them.

Discussions with Colleagues and Education Developers

The value of the experiences and perspectives that one's colleagues can provide cannot be understated. The other instructors within one's own department have context that is available to perhaps no one else regarding the student population, the program's curricular goals, and the institutional structure. Leveraging this contextual understanding within informal conversations around one's teaching can be very beneficial in making meaningful adjustments that are also practical for one's setting. Beyond informal conversations, departments holding workshops or setting aside specific time for these conversations can be useful for the faculty and for emphasizing the value placed on inclusive and equitable teaching. Broadening the pool of colleagues to members of the division, school, or institutional level may be necessary in some instances but, even when it is not, can also bring in new perspectives from outside of one's discipline that otherwise may not have been discussed. Many institutions of higher education have centers devoted to teaching and learning, staffed with education developers and experts whose role it is to support instructors in their teaching. Meeting and having discussions with these individuals specifically around means of inclusive teaching can be especially helpful, as they very likely have networks that extend beyond one's home institution and can help an instructor reflect on their own practice and provide information on evidence-based practices being used more broadly. Further, when interest warrants, these centers can be useful in creating instructor learning communities and holding other professional development events around these topics. In Chapter 6, we explore in significant detail how having colleagues, education developers, and others observe teaching can be a useful part of reflective practice.

Beyond one's own institution, connecting with other instructors can occur through listservs, commonly run by disciplinary associations like the American Society of Microbiology (ASM) MICROEDU listserv, social media as described previously in this chapter, and academic conferences focused on teaching. All of these resources can be valuable in acquiring ideas, information, and perspectives which impact your reflecting on your teaching.

Investigating the Literature

Finally, there is an ever-increasing breadth of published information on inclusive and equitable teaching in higher education. This includes evidence-based practices in the form of peer-reviewed journal articles. Journals specific to topics of inclusion and equity include the *International Journal of Inclusive Education, Inclusive Practices*, and others which touch on teaching at various levels, including higher education. Topics addressing inclusion and equity can also often be found within non-discipline specific journals specific to college teaching such as *Review of Educational Research, Educational Researcher, Teaching in Higher Education, To Improve the Academy, College Teaching*, the *International Journal of Teaching and Learning in Higher Education, Higher Education, Research in Higher Education*, and the *Journal of the Scholarship of Teaching and Learning*, among others. And then there are numerous disciplinary-specific teaching and learning journals where articles addressing inclusion may be found. Moreover, academic books like our previous title, *What Inclusive Instructors Do* (Addy et al., 2021b), *Inclusive Teaching* by Kelly A. Hogan and Viji Sathy (Hogan & Sathy, 2022), *Inclusive College Classrooms* by Lauren S. Cardon and Anne-Marie Womack (Womack & Cardon, 2022), *Promoting Inclusive Classroom Dynamics in Higher Education* by Kathryn C. Oleson (Oleson, 2020), and others cited throughout this book speak to means of promoting equity and inclusion in the college classroom and can be useful tools for reflecting on your own teaching. Chapter 7 will go into more depth for instructors who are seeking to engage in assessment projects and the scholarship of teaching and learning with their own projects, providing strategies and examples of ways these can be approached effectively.

Reflection Questions

- What is one means or resource for reflection from the options above, if any, that you have used previously? How effective was it for you? What alterations could be made to make it even more effective?
- What is one means or resource for reflection from the options above, if any, that you have not used or have only minimally used, and would like to use more? How specifically will you do so?

The Importance of Student Feedback

As the driving force of Part One of this book was the voices of students around their inclusive and non-inclusive college experiences, we clearly believe that in many ways the most important resource for understanding what is working in our own teaching related to inclusion and equity is what we can learn by directly asking our students. Much like the various content and skill assessments used in a course aid instructors in understanding what the students have learned and what knowledge and skill gaps may still exist, acquiring feedback from students related to inclusion and equity can help us better understand why some of those gaps exist and why there may be differences in terms of success in the course across the classroom community. And moreover, they can also often provide insight on how to improve in this realm. Indeed, research has shown that student feedback can be a valuable stimulus for teacher reflection and a tool for improvement (Mandouit, 2018). Moreover, collecting feedback specifically related to inclusion can directly inform effective practices for inclusive pedagogy (Faulkner et al., 2021). Further, the students in our own survey noted how they felt their course was made more inclusive and equitable when their instructor incorporated student feedback, as indicated when one student said their instructor did well because:

> *[The instructor] allowed all feedback.*
>
> *—A private university student who identifies as White, male, and 25–34 years old*

And another said their instructor did not do well because:

> *[The instructor] didn't care for student feedback.*
>
> *—A public university student who identifies as White, female, and bisexual*

Reflection Questions

- What do you believe to be the main specific benefits of acquiring student feedback?
- When you acquire student feedback, do you specifically ask for responses related to inclusion and equity? If not, why not and do you think it would be beneficial to include in the future?

Mechanisms for Acquiring Student Feedback

There are a variety of different mechanisms by which an instructor can acquire student feedback. Most commonly, end-of-term course evaluations are completed by students to provide information related to their experience in the course, and insight into the instructor's teaching of the course (Gravestock & Gregor-Greenleaf, 2008). These student evaluations are commonly used as a means of assessing the instructor for retention, promotion, and tenure, though they have the added benefit of being a tool for instructor reflection as well. However, in most situations, the instructors have little if any control over the questions that are a part of the survey, and what types of information students are asked to provide. Indeed, a study of the end-of-term course evaluations from 310 higher education institutions found that only 15.5 percent of the institutions included even one question related to diversity, equity, and inclusion over the 15-year period between 2006 and 2021, and only 0.13 percent of all questions related to these topics (Jackson, 2022). Further, students do not always see the value in these end-of-term course evaluations, so in cases where their completion is not mandated, response rates can be lower than ideal. Moreover, there is considerable evidence that there are significant issues of bias related to an instructor's race, ethnicity, and gender in these end-of-course student evaluations, bringing their reliability and validity into question (Aragón et al, 2023; Chávez & Mitchell, 2020; Esarey & Valdes, 2020; Fan et al., 2019). As such, the remainder of this section will focus on means of acquiring student feedback that the instructor does have more direct control over, and can gear toward aspects of inclusion and equity. These are intended to provide formative feedback for the instructor, rather than evaluative feedback for the instructor's supervisor and employers.

With each of the mechanisms of collecting student feedback discussed below, when that feedback is collected must be considered. The most common options include early-term, mid-term, end-of-term, and continuous. Each of these has specific utility that can help in determining what is most appropriate. While there is clearly benefit in end-of-term student feedback, as the students have had the opportunity to experience the entire arc of the course, only utilizing end-of-term feedback options does not provide tangible benefits to the students in the course giving the feedback (Keane & Labhrainn, 2005). Pre- or early-term feedback can be useful for getting to know the particular community of students within that class, which can be informative for aspects of course design, however the students will not have first-hand experience within the course to provide feedback on. Mid-term feedback is often thought of as the "sweet spot," as students have theoretically experienced enough of the course to have informed opinions, but there is still time for the instructor to build on the course's strengths and implement changes for improvement based on the feedback (Lewis, 2001; McGowan, 2011; Waitz, 2019). Likely the best approach to acquiring student feedback includes multiple touch points throughout the term's beginning, middle, and end, or allows for fully continuous feedback over the course of the term (Goldfarb & Morrison, 2014). However, there is almost certainly a threshold in which students could become overwhelmed by the amount of feedback they are being asked to provide, and it could begin to take away from time devoted to learning the content of the course itself. Additionally, certain means of feedback collection lend themselves more effectively to certain times of implementation. As such, thoughtfully considering what mechanisms of feedback collection are being used, when, and how often, is critical to maximizing their positive impact for the student and instructor alike.

Surveys, Forms, and Questionnaires

One of the most common means of acquiring student feedback is through the use of surveys, forms, or questionnaires, and research supports their use as a means for measuring effective teaching (Mandouit, 2018; Richardson, 2005). However, there are a number of considerations when utilizing surveys as a means of collecting student feedback, including modality, setting, length, anonymity, completion requirements, and validity.

Surveys may be completed on paper or digitally. For digital implementation, various tools are available that can host digital student surveys. Further, learning management systems commonly used in higher education generally have built-in tool sets that allow for the creation and implementation of surveys or questionnaires. There are also some platforms that utilize SMS text messaging for survey distribution and response, with some preliminary studies suggesting their effectiveness, though there are still some concerns that remain around privacy aspects (Peterson, 2019; Thompson et al., 2020). Paper surveys tend to benefit from increased response rate when compared with digital surveys (Nulty, 2008). However, digital surveys have the advantages of having various parameters that can be set as desired, at times offering useful automatically generated analysis or reporting, and can be particularly helpful in online courses that don't meet face to face. Further, some digital survey platforms have accessibility features that make them more manageable for a diverse set of student respondents. These features can include screen magnifiers, text-to-speech features, speech-to-text response features, and accessible color contrast.

Regarding the setting in which the survey is implemented, the highest response rates will normally occur with a survey that is conducted during class time for face-to-face and online synchronous courses, as opposed to one that asks students to complete it outside of class (Marquette Univ., n.d.). In terms of length, while there is no specific rule for the appropriate length of a survey, a good guideline is to keep the survey as short as possible to acquire the desired information. This will improve the chances of students completing the survey in its entirety. Further, a study from 2017 found that when instructors simply show students they care about course evaluations, response rates increase (Chapman et al., 2017).

The instructor should also consider whether the respondents should be anonymous or identifiable. The benefits of a survey in which respondents are identifiable is that instructors then have the ability to take specific feedback and respond directly to the student, and if multiple surveys are conducted it is easier to track a particular individual's responses. Alternatively, anonymous surveys are commonly said to benefit from higher response rates and honesty, as respondents may feel more comfortable providing sensitive or private information (Murdoch et al., 2014; Ong & Weiss, 2000). However, there are situations where even anonymous surveys still can lead to identifiable responses, in cases where there are identifiable personal characteristics being reported. One way to navigate this, when anonymity is desired, is to ensure that responses are automatically aggregated prior to review, so that responses from an individual are not linked. When considering whether a survey should be mandatory or voluntary, while requiring completion of a survey in some manner may increase the total number of responses, this can be challenging to do in the cases of anonymous surveys, and may decrease the quality of the data received. Generally, it would be advisable to utilize anonymous and voluntary student feedback surveys, especially when related to topics of inclusive and equitable teaching. This will provide the students who want to respond with the opportunity to do so in a safe manner. And even with this anonymous context, instructors can also invite students to directly connect with them if there is information within their responses that they would like the instructor to know who it came from.

Whenever possible, survey instruments that have been determined to be valid and reliable with evidence should be used. This process entails the survey having a theoretical model of its goals, intentional formatting, clarity in its questions, and pilot testing to examine the reliability (statistical analysis such as Cronbach's alpha) and internal consistency (Cobern & Adams, 2020). This process essentially confirms that the instrument is measuring what it is intended to, and that it can do it consistently across the intended respondent population (Elangovan & Sundaravel, 2021). However, validated instruments do not always exist. That does not mean that student surveys that are not validated cannot provide useful information to help inform an instructor's reflection on their teaching, but rather that special care must be taken when analyzing what the questions are asking, what the responses are saying, and what the major conclusions are.

Some institutions have attempted to ascertain information related to equity and inclusion about students'college experiences more broadly. In 2018 Penn State University conducted its Pre-health program for Underrepresented Leaders in STEM Education (PULSE) survey, and in 2021 Stanford University conducted its Inclusion, Diversity, Equity, and Access in a Learning Environment (IDEAL) survey, both focusing on aspects of student inclusion and belonging, and these institutional efforts and those like them will be discussed more in Chapter 8. Additionally, certain centers for teaching and learning provide some guidance or examples on questions that could be included in student feedback surveys by instructors to begin to address diversity, equity, and inclusion (BUILD, n.d.; Student Evaluation of Teaching Questions Related to DEI—DU VPFA, 2022).

To support the efforts of instructors seeking to acquire feedback from learners within their classes specifically related to equity and inclusion, we have created "How's Class Going?,"a student feedback form (Appendix II).

While this form has not yet been validated, it was created using good survey construction processes and considered the quality of effective questions (Jenn, 2006). It includes 24 Likert-scaled questions and 6 open-ended questions. This question set was created to cover a wide breadth of topics related to inclusive and equitable teaching, specifically informed by the themes that emerged from our national survey of students on the topic, and organized as the questions relate to course design, creating a welcoming environment, and conducting the course. As noted in the earlier chapters themselves, it is important to understand that these categories are not mutually exclusive, but rather complement each other and overlap in numerous important ways, and so to do some of the questions. The "How's Class Going?" form can be utilized either in its entirety or individual questions most relevant to an instructor's particular course or goals could be curated from the list. The intention is that the survey would be conducted anonymously, and on a voluntary basis, with data reported in aggregate if possible. Importantly, the form is intended for use during the semester rather than at the end of the term, so that the instructor can put the feedback to use in making course modifications if needed. We suggest implementing the "How's Class Going?" form around the quarter-way mark through the term of the course, though it could be implemented at mid-semester or even multiple times throughout the term to gauge progress.

There may be benefits in pairing the "How's Class Going?" form with the "Who's in Class?" form available and described in our previous book, *What Inclusive Instructors Do* (Addy et al., 2021b) and article from 2021 (Addy et al., 2021a). The "Who's in Class?" form is a survey implemented prior to or at the very beginning of the semester, to help the instructor understand features of their specific class community that may impact the student experience and their ability to succeed in the class. In addition to providing potentially useful and actionable information about the student population, it also serves as an opportunity to meaningfully address the importance that equity and inclusion have to the instructor and within the course. In Derek's teaching, he has learned about a number of connections students have to the course that he would not have otherwise known (e.g., personal work experiences, family members in the field, etc.), and has been able to tailor the class to leverage those assets and interests. Further, Derek was able to learn about the invisible disabilities of some of his students, who, however, did not choose to receive institutional accommodations for them. These included having diabetes and needing to have their phone to check their glucose levels, having Attention Deficit Hyperactive Disorder (ADHD) and occasionally needing to move around the room, among others.

Knowing this information about the class early to allow appropriate modifications, and then implementing the "How's Class Going?" form later in the semester, can reinforce the importance of inclusivity and personal value in a tangible way, and provide a mechanism for the faculty to ensure the needs of the students are being met. Of note, it is recommended that when asking students to provide feedback using these forms, or any other means, the instructor takes time to talk with the students about why these questions are being asked and how the information learned from the student responses will be used.

Reflection Questions

- Do you conduct student feedback surveys in or after your courses, other than your institution's end-of-term course evaluations? If so, are any questions specifically related to diversity, equity, and inclusion?
- Examine the "How's Class Going?" form in Appendix II. Would implementing this tool in your courses be beneficial? If so, consider the following:

    a Would you want to utilize the form in its entirety, or just use selected questions?

    b If you would only use selected questions:

    - Which specifically will you use?
    - Will you ask these in their own survey, or include them as part of a larger survey?

    c Are there other questions not included on the "How's Class Going?" form related to equity and inclusion that you would like to have your students respond to? If so, what are they?

Student Comment Boxes and Exit Tickets

Another means by which student feedback about aspects of inclusion and equity can be acquired throughout the term is through the use of a student comment box. A student comment box is a means for continuous feedback, as it is available for students to access at any point during a course. If the instructor is specifically interested in feedback on inclusion and equity in the course, then they should either emphasize these topics when explaining the purpose of the comment box to the students, or even give it a name that makes that intention obvious (i.e., "The Inclusivity Dropbox"). A comment box can take a physical form, where there is a literal box with a slot in the top that students can put comments and suggestions into before, during, or after class sessions. Students should be informed that they can either submit their comments anonymously or add their name, as they feel most comfortable. To allow for anonymity, it is important that there is time when students can access the box without the instructor being present. This could occur either by having the box outside of the classroom and out of view of the instructor before or after class, or by the instructor leaving the classroom for a few minutes to allow students the time to submit. Further, when a physical box is used, it is important that the box be opaque in nature, to ensure the privacy of the feedback. When class is not in session, these boxes could also be available at the instructor's office.

Student comment boxes can also be digital in nature, which, if the proper settings are selected, can ensure the anonymity of the responses (if the student desires for it to remain anonymous, which may not always be the case). Another benefit is their continuous availability both in terms of timing and location. Students do not need to be in-class or on-campus to submit a comment, nor do they need to do it during specific times of the day that are convenient for the instructor. That makes digital comment boxes particularly beneficial for hybrid and fully online courses. These digital comment boxes can come in many forms, whether it is one of the number of web-based tools that provide this sort of service or an openly available comment forum using one the survey platforms noted earlier in the chapter. If student names or other identifying information could be provided, then it would be important to make sure appropriate privacy settings were applied.

Another form of near-continuous feedback is the use of exit tickets. Exit tickets are in some ways similar to the minute papers described in Chapter 4, as they are prompts given to students at the end of a class period, week, or learning unit, which are then submitted by the students back to the instructor in order to "exit" the session (Angelo & Cross, 1993; Danley et al., 2016; Marzano, 2012). While exit tickets are often used to assess understanding of content, they can just as easily be used for students to provide feedback on the inclusivity of the course itself, depending on the prompts provided by the instructor. In a class that meets multiple times per week, certain days might be devoted to content-related prompts and others are to feedback-related prompts. In terms of the feedback-related prompts, one possibility would be utilizing the questions from the "How's Class Going?" form (Appendix II), one or two per ticket throughout the term. Those related to course design would likely want to be utilized early in the course, while those about the welcoming environment and how the course is conducted could be included throughout the term as appropriate.

Reflection Questions

- What benefits and challenges do you see for you and your courses for students having the ability to continuously provide feedback throughout a course, via mechanisms like a physical or digital comment box?
- Do you utilize exit tickets in your teaching?

a If so, did they focus more on course content or course experience? Do you think it would be practical and beneficial to allow for both types of feedback?
b If not, do you think exit tickets could be utilized in any of your courses, specifically to address aspects of inclusion and equity? How regularly would you have students complete these exit tickets; every day, every week, every unit? What specific prompts would you want to include?

One-on-One Conferences

Office hours are a common mechanism by which students can get one-on-one time with their instructor, typically to help students understand aspects of course content. These can be held in-person, online using virtual meeting software, or in both formats, making them possible to implement in both face-to-face and online courses. However, not all students may understand how to take advantage of, or feel comfortable using office hours. This can be particularly true for those who do not have "insider" knowledge on navigating college academics, such as first-generation students. Further, office hour meetings do not need to be exclusive to understanding course content alone, but can also be used to support the development of an inclusive and equitable course. To this end, the concept of essential office hours, brief but required one-on-one meetings with the instructor, was discussed in *What Inclusive Instructors Do* as a tool for building and maintaining a welcoming environment. Holding one-on-one conferences with students during office hours (or even class time when students are working on independent projects) can be an effective way to build rapport with students and gather feedback from them (Starcher, 2011). Some have noted the utility of holding the first of these one-on-one meetings early in the term, specifically during the first two weeks, but they can also be useful at mid- and end-term depending on the goals of the particular meetings (Day, 2018; Kapoor, n.d.). An important note is that while these one-on-one meetings can provide useful feedback, they are inherently not anonymous, which can potentially cause some students to not share certain aspects openly, especially as in many classroom situations the students perceive the instructor as having the power in the relationship, including control of their grade in the course. To minimize this, using strategies to openly minimize the power differential in the class can be important, as well as incorporating other avenues by which students can provide anonymous feedback.

Clearly, meeting with every student one-on-one can be a challenge, particularly in courses with large class sizes, so these meetings tend to be brief (commonly, 5 to 15 minutes), but framing a portion of these meetings around specific topics an instructor would like feedback on can help promote their efficiency and effectiveness. Further, additional strategies for acquiring face-to-face feedback from students in classes where one-on-one conferences may not be possible due to time constraints are addressed below.

Small Group Feedback

To reduce the amount of time for one-on-one meetings, instructors could change the format of the one-on-one meeting to include two to four students at a time. However, there might be challenges associated with how the students are grouped, and the issue of non-anonymity still remains.

To this end, Clark and Redmond developed the process of Small Group Instruction Diagnosis (SGID), which is a method that has been utilized and adapted across higher education (Clark & Redmond, 1982; Seattle Univ., n. d.; Stanford Univ., n.d.; Vanderbilt Univ., n.d.). SGID is traditionally used at the mid-term, as an approach to gain feedback for instructional improvement, but it can and has been used earlier or later in the term when appropriate. For SGID, an individual external to the course, commonly a trained facilitator or consultant from the institution's center for teaching and learning, will meet with the instructor to understand the course and feedback goals, and then be the one who conducts the feedback session with the students. In this session, the students break into groups of around five, and discuss specific prompts for approximately ten minutes each. Three common prompts are: What do you like about the course? What do you think needs improvement? What suggestions do you have for bringing about those improvements? After these discussions, the class reconvenes as a whole, the groups report out on their discussions, and the information is recorded so it can later be provided to the instructor. After the instructor and facilitator meet to discuss the feedback, the instructor reviews the takeaways with the class including any intended changes to the course stemming from the feedback. While students' comments are not anonymous in the SGID process, working in small groups initially can decrease student anxiety about sharing their perspectives, and from that point on the feedback is aggregated by the facilitator and shared with the instructor.

Student Representatives

Another means of gathering student feedback that can be especially effective and time efficient in large class sizes is the use of student representatives (Addy, n.d.; Carey, 2013). In this practice, one or more students from the class act as a representative for the class to discuss issues and ideas. These representatives can either be selected by the instructor, a student who is reliable and respected by their classmates, or ideally chosen by the students, a process which more strongly considers and incorporates the students as partners (Matthews & Dollinger, 2023). The representative will communicate with their classmates throughout the term, to collect their feedback. This could occur in a number of ways, from providing designated class time where the instructor is not present, to the representative holding out-of-class focus groups, informal conversations, using email or social media, or conducting their own short questionnaire (Choi, 2020). Then, the representatives should have regular meetings with the instructor to relay and discuss this information. One published approach utilized a ratio of one student representative per eight students in the course, and the group of representatives and the instructor formed what was referred to as "the course council" as they met monthly (Heise & Himes, 2010). However, depending on the class size, it may be appropriate for a student to serve as a representative for a significantly higher number of students. Benefits to this model of gathering feedback are that it values the students' agency in course design and implementation, maintains anonymity for the students, and allows for face-to-face discussions rather than just the textual feedback of a survey. A disadvantage to this model is that, just like any scenario with representatives or elected officials, the feedback is going through the personal lens of the representative, and it is always possible that a particular view is not fully understood or relayed, or that certain issues are missed entirely, especially if they are only impacting a minority of the students in the course. For these reasons, it is suggested that if a student representative model for gathering feedback is utilized, it is supplemented with the opportunity for individual students to provide feedback as well, perhaps through a comment box or short survey.

Reflection Questions

- What would be the maximum class size for which you feel you could meet with every student, even just once a semester for five to ten minutes, to discuss their experiences and assess aspects of inclusion and equity?
- When in the term do you believe would be the most appropriate time for one-on-one conferences with students in your courses? Do you feel for your class it would be necessary to meet more than once with each student?
- If you teach larger classes, which of the approaches of collecting student feedback do you find more useful for your classes between the small group or student representatives methods? Alternatively, do you feel that using surveys would be more practical and provide similar benefits?

Actionizing Your Reflection and Feedback

All of the means discussed for us as instructors to become more reflective practitioners, through self-reflection, the use of resources like social media, published literature, our colleagues, and the feedback of our students, are only meaningful if actionized in a productive manner. For end-of-term reflection and feedback, this generally means taking what is learned and applying both to future teaching of that particular course, but also more broadly to other courses you may teach. However, for the reflection and feedback that occur within a course, it is important to create and implement a plan for modifications, additions, or subtractions from the course in real time. Unfortunately, as each course is distinct in content and community, there is no one action that can be shared here to address particular challenges, but it is important to let the reflection and feedback process guide what would be most appropriate. Recording the themes and ideas generated through reflection and feedback in writing can be an important part of building the bigger picture of aspects of the course that could benefit from change. The next step would be brainstorming or utilizing the previously discussed resources to create specific modifications that could address those aspects. If multiple options are available, sharing these options with the class, either as a whole, via student representatives, or with the individuals who would be most impacted, can be a valuable way to ensure that the changes being made will actually address the challenges faced. Regardless of what degree students from the class are involved in actually determining the change that is made, it is important for the instructor to be transparent with their students, and close the loop, especially when alterations directly stem from student feedback.

In Derek's courses, if a student survey is implemented, or other feedback is collected, he makes sure to take the time thereafter to let students know that he did review their responses and hear their voices, share what his interpretations of the important takeaways were, and note how that feedback will impact the course moving forward. He also welcomes any students who feel that he did not hear or address aspects of their specific feedback, to connect with him so that they can discuss more directly. By taking what only needs to be a small amount of time in class to devote to this, students see the impact of their perspectives and the importance of inclusion and equity within the course.

Conclusion

In this chapter, we have explored the means by which every instructor can develop as a reflective practitioner, highlighting how we instructors need to be life-long learners just as we encourage our students to become. Each class community is different and, as such, what works well for one course may not work quite as well for the same course in the future. There is no one best method for reflection, nor one perfect method for acquiring student feedback, but to build a truly inclusive and equitable course it is vital that student feedback be collected, considered, and acted upon. Instructors can consider the options discussed within this chapter, and their personal approach to teaching, learning, and professional development, ideally experimenting with different means and potentially combining a variety of inclusive reflection "ingredients" into the recipe that best fits their palate and will most benefit their students. While the process of developing as a reflective practitioner has been presented in this chapter as a means for improving one's teaching to the benefit of our students, this work can also be directly incorporated into, and be beneficial for, the process of promotion and tenure within the academic ranks as well. In the next chapter, the power of utilizing student, peer, and educational developer observation of one's teaching, and a protocol for doing so effectively, will be discussed, which can similarly provide both formative and evaluative benefits.

References

ACUE Webinar Series: Inclusive Online Teaching. (n.d.). *ACUE*. Retrieved June 9, 2023, from https://acue.org/inclusive-online-teaching-webinars/.

Addy, H. (n.d.). *Class representatives: A Formative Feedback Strategy for Teaching Development*. https://taylorinstitute.ucalgary.ca/sites/default/files/teams/1/Class%20representative%20Heather%20Addy%20Sep%2011%202017_Part1.pdf.

Addy, T. M., Mitchell, K. A., & Dube, D. (2021a). A tool to advance inclusive teaching efforts: The "Who's in Class?" form. *Journal of Microbiology & Biology Education*, 22(3), e183–121. doi:10.1128/jmbe.00183-21.

Addy, T. M., Dube, D., Mitchell, K. A., & SoRelle, M. (2021b). *What inclusive instructors do: Principles and practices for excellence in college teaching*. Sterling, VA: Stylus Publishing.

Angelo, T. A., & Cross, P. (1993). *Classroom assessment techniques: A handbook for college teachers*, 2nd ed. New York: Wiley. https://www.wiley.com/en-us/Classroom+Assessment+Techniques%3A+A+Handbook+for+College+Teachers%2C+2nd+Edition-p-9781555425005.

Aragón, O. R., Pietri, E. S., & Powell, B. A. (2023). Gender bias in teaching evaluations: The causal role of department gender composition. *Proceedings of the National Academy of Sciences of the United States of America*, 120(4), e2118466120. doi:10.1073/pnas.2118466120.

Blogs on Inclusive Teaching | CRLT. (n.d.). Retrieved June 9, 2023, from https://crlt.umich.edu/inclusive-teaching.

Brandt, C. (2008). Integrating feedback and reflection in teacher preparation. *ELT Journal*, 62(1), 37–46. doi:10.1093/elt/ccm076.

Brookfield, S. D. (2017). *Becoming a critically reflective teacher*. New York: John Wiley & Sons.

BUILD. (n.d.). Evaluation of teaching items in course evaluations. *BUILD.* Retrieved June 12, 2023, from https://www.boisestate.edu/build/inclusive-excellence-resources/inclusive-resources-evaluation-of-teaching-items-in-course-evaluations/.

Carey, P. (2013). Representation and student engagement in higher education: A reflection on the views and experiences of course representatives. *Journal of Further and Higher Education*, 37(1), 71–88. doi:10.1080/0309877X.2011.644775.

Carrington, S., & Selva, G. (2010). Critical social theory and transformative learning: Evidence in pre-service teachers' service-learning reflection logs. *Higher Education Research and Development*, 29(1), Article 1.

Chapman, D. D., Joines, J. A. (2017). Strategies for increasing response rates for online end-of-course evaluations. *International Journal of Teaching and Learning in Higher Education*, 29(1), 47–60.

Chávez, K., & Mitchell, K. M. W. (2020). Exploring bias in student evaluations: gender, race, and ethnicity. *Political Science & Politics*, 53(2), 270–274. doi:10.1017/S1049096519001744.

Choi, J. (2020, August 10). How can a student rep gather feedback? *Unitu.* https://unitu.co.uk/student-rep-journey-gather-student-feedback/.

Clark, D. J., & Redmond, M. V. (1982). *Small Group Instructional Diagnosis: Final Report.* https://eric.ed.gov/?id=ED217954.

Cobern, W. W. & Adams, B. AJ. (2020). Establishing survey validity: A practical guide. *International Journal of Assessment Tools in Education*, 7(3), 404–419. doi:10.21449/ijate.781366.

Danley, A., McCoy, A., & Weed, R. (2016). Exit tickets open the door to university learning. *InSight: A Journal of Scholarly Teaching*, 11, 48–58. doi:10.46504/11201603da.

Day, B. (2018). Exploration of the effectiveness of one-on-one meetings with students. *THE NOVICE PROFESSOR.* http://www.thenoviceprofessor.com/1/post/2018/10/exploration-of-the-effectiveness-of-one-on-one-meetings-with-students.html.

Dewey, J. (1938). *Logic: The theory of inquiry.* New York: Henry Holt and Company. https://ia801500.us.archive.org/13/items/JohnDeweyLogicTheTheoryOfInquiry/%5BJohn_Dewey%5D_Logic_-_The_Theory_of_Inquiry.pdf.

Dreyer, L. M. (2015). Reflective journaling: A tool for teacher professional development. *Africa Education Review*, 12(2), 331–344. doi:10.1080/18146627.2015.1108011.

Elangovan, N., & Sundaravel, E. (2021). Method of preparing a document for survey instrument validation by experts. *MethodsX*, 8, 101326. doi:10.1016/j.mex.2021.101326.

Esarey, J., & Valdes, N. (2020). Unbiased, reliable, and valid student evaluations can still be unfair. *Assessment & Evaluation in Higher Education*, 45(8), 1106–1120. doi:10.1080/02602938.2020.1724875.

Fan, Y., Shepherd, L. J., Slavich, E., Waters, D., Stone, M., Abel, R., & Johnston, E. L. (2019). Gender and cultural bias in student evaluations: Why representation matters. *PLOS ONE*, 14(2), e0209749. doi:10.1371/journal.pone.0209749.

Faulkner, S. L., Watson, W. K., Pollino, M. A., & Shetterly, J. R. (2021). "Treat me like a person, rather than another number": University student perceptions of inclusive classroom practices. *Communication Education*, 70(1), 92–111. doi:10.1080/03634523.2020.1812680.

Free Webinars | Quality Matters. (n.d.). Retrieved June 9, 2023, from https://www.qualitymatters.org/professional-development/free-webinars.

Goldfarb, S., & Morrison, G. (2014). Continuous curricular feedback: A formative evaluation approach to curricular improvement. *Academic Medicine*, 89(2), 264. doi:10.1097/ACM.0000000000000103.

Gravestock, P., & Gregor-Greenleaf, E. (2008). *Student Course Evaluations: Research, Models and Trends.* Higher Education Quality Council of Ontario, Toronto.

Heise, B., & Himes, D. (2010). The course council: An example of student-centered learning. *Journal of Nursing Education*, 49(6), 343–345. doi:10.3928/01484834-20100115-04.

Hogan, K. A., & Sathy, V. (2022). *Inclusive Teaching: Strategies for Promoting Equity in the College Classroom.* http://wvupressonline.com/inclusive-teaching.

Hu, D., & Deramo, M. (2021). Is Your Teaching Inclusive? In R. Kumar & B. Refaei (Eds.), *Equity and inclusion in higher education: Strategies for teaching* (pp. 200–208). Cincinnati, OH: University of Cincinnati Press.

INCLUDED Blog. (2021, May 20). *Inclusive Higher Ed Pedagogy.* https://www.inclusivefaculty.com/included-blog.

Inclusive Teaching Visualization. (n.d.). *Inclusive Teaching Visualization.* Retrieved June 9, 2023, from https://inclusiveteachingvisualization.com/.

Inside Higher Ed | Higher Education News, Career Advice, Events and Jobs. (n.d.). Retrieved June 9, 2023, from https://www.insidehighered.com/.

Inventory of Inclusive Teaching Strategies—Inclusive Teaching. (n.d.). Retrieved June 9, 2023, from https://sites.lsa.umich.edu/inclusive-teaching/inventory-of-inclusive-teaching-strategies/.

Jackson, S. (2022). Course evaluations: Are diversity, equity, inclusion, and belonging experience questions asked, and who is the driving force? *Anthology.* https://www.anthology.com/blog/course-evaluations-are-diversity-equity-inclusion-and-belonging-experience-questions-asked-and.

Jenn N. C. (2006). Designing a questionnaire. *Malaysian Family Physician: The Official Journal of the Academy of Family Physicians of Malaysia*, 1(1), 32–35.

Kane, J., & Mushtare, R. (n.d.). *Tea for Teaching—A Podcast on Teaching and Learning.* Retrieved June 9, 2023, from https://teaforteaching.com/.

Kapoor, A. (n.d.). How to conduct one-on-one meetings with students. Retrieved June 13, 2023, from https://teachingresources.stanford.edu/resources/how-to-conduct-one-on-one-meetings-with-students/.

Keane, E., & Labhrainn, I. M. (2005). Obtaining student feedback on teaching & course quality. https://www.universityofgalway.ie/media/celt/files/coursedesign/ReviewofTeachingEvaluationMethods.pdf.

Larrivee, B., & Cooper, J. M. (2006). *An educator's guide to teacher reflection.* Boston, MA: Houghton Mifflin.

Lewis, K. G. (2001). Using midsemester student feedback and responding to it. *New Directions for Teaching and Learning*, 2001(87), 33. doi:10.1002/tl.26.

Lowe, G. M., Prout, P., & Murcia, K. (2013). I see, I think I wonder: An evaluation of journaling as a critical reflective practice tool for aiding teachers in challenging or confronting contexts. *Australian Journal of Teacher Education*, 38(6), 1–16. doi:10.3316/ielapa.686932935010667.

Mandouit, L. (2018). Using student feedback to improve teaching. *Educational Action Research*, 26(5), 755–769. doi:10.1080/09650792.2018.1426470.

Marquette University. *Strategies to Increase Course Evaluation Response Rates*. https://www.marquette.edu/institutional-research-analysis/moces/response-rates.php.

Marzano, R. (2012). Art and science of teaching/The many uses of exit slips. *ASCD*, 70(2). https://www.ascd.org/el/articles/the-many-uses-of-exit-slips.

Matthews, K. E., & Dollinger, M. (2023). Student voice in higher education: The importance of distinguishing student representation and student partnership. *Higher Education*, 85(3), 555–570. doi:10.1007/s10734-022-00851-7.

McDonough, J. (1994). A teacher looks at teachers' diaries. *ELT Journal*, 48(1), 57–65. doi:10.1093/elt/48.1.57.

McGowan, W. R. O. (2011). 12 student and faculty perceptions of effects of mid-course evaluation. *To Improve the Academy: A Journal of Educational Development*, 29. doi:10.3998/tia.17063888.0029.016.

Mortari, L. (2012). Learning thoughtful reflection in teacher education. *Teachers and Teaching*, 18(5), 525–545. doi:10.1080/13540602.2012.709729.

Murdoch, M., Simon, A. B., Polusny, M. A., Bangerter, A. K., Grill, J. P., Noorbaloochi, S., & Partin, M. R. (2014). Impact of different privacy conditions and incentives on survey response rate, participant representativeness, and disclosure of sensitive information: A randomized controlled trial. *BMC Medical Research Methodology*, 14, 90. doi:10.1186/1471-2288-14-90.

Nave, L. (n.d.). *Think UDL*. Retrieved June 9, 2023, from https://thinkudl.org/.

Nulty, D. D. (2008). The adequacy of response rates to online and paper surveys: What can be done? *Assessment & Evaluation in Higher Education*, 33(3), 301–314. doi:10.1080/02602930701293231.

Oleson, K. C. (2020). *Promoting inclusive classroom dynamics in higher education*. Sterling, VA: Stylus Publishing. https://styluspub.presswarehouse.com/browse/book/9781620368992/Promoting-Inclusive-Classroom-Dynamics-in-Higher-Education.

Ong, A. D., & Weiss, D. J. (2000). The impact of anonymity on responses to sensitive questions. *Journal of Applied Social Psychology*, 30(8), 1691–1708. doi:10.1111/j.1559-1816.2000.tb02462.x.

Peterson, E. L. (2019). *Student Survey Response: Use Of SMS in Higher Education to Encourage Survey Participation* [Thesis, University of Wisconsin—Stout]. https://minds.wisconsin.edu/handle/1793/79635.

Pratt, D. D. (1998). *Teaching Perspectives Inventory*. http://www.teachingperspectives.com/tpi/.

Pratt, D. D., Collins, J. B., & Selinger, S. J. (2001). *Development and Use of the Teaching Perspectives Inventory (TPI)*. In annual meeting of the American Educational Research Association, Seattle, Washington.

Reflective Practice. (2022, December 8). *NSW Department of Education*. https://education.nsw.gov.au/teaching-and-learning/professional-learning/teacher-quality-and-accreditation/strong-start-great-teachers/developing-focus/reflective-practice.html.

Reflective Teaching. (2016, November 1). *Poorvu Center for Teaching and Learning*. https://poorvucenter.yale.edu/ReflectiveTeaching.

Richards, J. C., & Farrell, T. S. C. (Eds.). (2005). Keeping a teaching journal. In *Professional development for language teachers: Strategies for teacher learning* (pp. 68–84). Cambridge: Cambridge University Press. doi:10.1017/CBO9780511667237.007.

Richardson, J. T. E. (2005). Instruments for obtaining student feedback: A review of the literature. *Assessment & Evaluation in Higher Education*, 30(4), 387–415. doi:10.1080/02602930500099193.

Ross, C. (n.d.). *Dead Ideas in Teaching and Learning* [podcast]. Columbia Center for Teaching and Learning.

Seattle Univ. (n.d.). *Small Group Instructional Diagnosis | Learning and Teaching | Services | Center for Faculty Development.* Seattle University. Retrieved June 13, 2023, from https://www.seattleu.edu/faculty-development/services/learning-and-teaching/small-group-instructional-diagnosis/.

Selogie, A., & Brett, V. (n.d.). *Inclusive Education Project (IEP) Podcast on Apple Podcasts.* Retrieved June 9, 2023, from https://podcasts.apple.com/us/podcast/inclusive-education-project-iep-podcast/id1307157016.

Shandomo, H. M. (2010). The role of critical reflection in teacher education. *School-University Partnerships*, 4(1), 101–113.

Slade, M. L., Burnham, T., Catalana, S. M., & Waters, T. (2019). The impact of reflective practice on teacher candidates' learning. *International Journal for the Scholarship of Teaching and Learning*, 13(2). doi:10.20429/ijsotl.2019.130215.

Stachowiak, B. (n.d.). *Teaching In Higher Ed Podcast.* Retrieved June 9, 2023, from https://teachinginhighered.com/episodes/.

Stanford Univ. (n.d.). *Small Group Feedback Session | Evaluation & Research.* Retrieved June 13, 2023, from https://evals.stanford.edu/mid-term-feedback/small-group-feedback-class.

Starcher, K. (2011). Intentionally building rapport with students. *College Teaching*, 59(4), 162. doi:10.1080/87567555.2010.516782.

Stevens, D. D., & Cooper, J. E. (2009). *Journal keeping: How to use reflective writing for effective learning, teaching, professional insight, and positive change.* Sterling, VA: Stylus Publishing.

Student Evaluation of Teaching Questions Related to DEI—DU VPFA. (2022, October 4). https://duvpfa.du.edu/2022/10/student-evaluation-of-teaching-questions-related-to-dei/.

Taylor, S. D. (2019) The social justice syllabus design tool: A first step in doing social justice pedagogy. *JCSCORE*, 5(2). doi:10.15763/issn.2642-2387.2019.5.2.132-166.

The Chronicle of Higher Education | Higher Ed News, Opinion & Advice. (n.d.). *The Chronicle of Higher Education.* Retrieved June 9, 2023, from https://www.chronicle.com/.

The Teaching Goals Inventory (TGI) | Office of Teaching, Learning & Technology. (n.d.). Retrieved June 9, 2023, from https://teach.its.uiowa.edu/handbook-teaching-excellence-7th-edition/who-are-you/teaching-goals-inventory-tgi.

Thompson, S., Hebert, S., Brunelli, R., Creech, C., Drake, A., Fagbodun, S., Garcia-Ojeda, M., Hall, C., Harshman, J., Lamb, T., Robnett, R., Shuster, M., Cotner, S., & Ballen, C. (2020). A call for data-driven networks to address equity in the context of undergraduate biology. *CBE Life Sciences Education*, 19. doi:10.1187/cbe.20-05-0085.

Ulosevich, S. N. (1994). *Using the Teaching Goals Inventory (TGI) to improve teaching effectiveness.* Second Annual College of Continuing Education Faculty Symposium on Teaching EffectivenessApril 1994. https://commons.erau.edu/cgi/viewcontent.cgi?article=1024&context=bollinger-rosado

Vanderbilt Univ. (n.d.). *Mid-semester feedback through small group analysis.* Vanderbilt University. Retrieved June 13, 2023, from https://cft.vanderbilt.edu/services/individual/small-group-analysis/.

Waitz, I. (2019). *A Case for Mid-Semester Feedback.* https://web.mit.edu/fnl/volume/321/waitz.html.

Wieman, C. (2015). A better way to evaluate undergraduate teaching. *Change: The Magazine of Higher Learning*, 47(1), 6–15. doi:10.1080/00091383.2015.996077.

Wieman, C., & Gilbert, S. (2014). The teaching practices inventory: A new tool for characterizing college and university teaching in mathematics and science. *CBE—Life Sciences Education*, 13(3), 552–569. doi:10.1187/cbe.14-02-0023.

Womack, A. M., & Cardon, L. S. (2022). *Inclusive college classrooms: Teaching methods for diverse learners.* London and New York: Routledge. doi:10.4324/9781003121633.

6

USING OBSERVATIONAL FEEDBACK

The goals of Chapters 2 through 4 were to provide insider views of how the students we surveyed and interviewed perceived the inclusive teaching approaches of their instructors. Perhaps some practices were familiar to you, and others seemed promising. In reading about these approaches you may have increased your awareness of what hinders an inclusive classroom from the viewpoints of the learners we surveyed. Chapter 5 was focused on how you can take students' perspectives into account as you reflect on your own teaching. Perhaps some of the actions described are things you already do as a reflective practitioner or one who partners with instructors as they deliberate on their teaching efforts. The current chapter focuses on the observation of inclusive teaching practices providing a variety of tools and instruments that can support instructors across disciplines in advancing their inclusive teaching and learning efforts. One of the key instruments described that can be used as a tool to examine praxis is the Protocol for Advancing Inclusive Teaching Efforts (PAITE) and how it has been, and is being, used to make classrooms more inclusive (Addy et al., 2022). Given that the development of the PAITE is published in a separate article, this book focuses on connecting the usage of the protocol to inclusive teaching practice.

There are a number of reasons why having one's teaching observed is of value (Fletcher, 2018). Even with good intent, the approaches an instructor thinks they use in the classroom might not be consistent with what they actually implement and what their learners experience. Various studies in the literature have shown this can occur with active learning, as described in Chapter 4, which are a diverse array of inclusive teaching approaches that engage students in their learning and have been shown to reduce equity gaps (Ebert-May et al., 2011; Freeman et al., 2014; Fung & Chow, 2002; Kane

DOI: 10.4324/9781003442929-8

et al., 2002; Murray & Macdonald, 1997). For example, an instructor might believe that they engage their students with high amounts of active learning, but when it comes to most classes they might lecture the majority of the time. Sometimes they might not actually be aware of this discrepancy in practice. To better understand what practices one does indeed utilize, the perspectives of outside observers can be very useful. Additionally, various tools focused on observational feedback can be helpful to get a sense of one's practices. Sometimes in higher education the classroom is a closed off space but it ought not be.

In general, low-stakes observational feedback can help instructors maximize their usage of various inclusive teaching approaches, as well as reveal opportunities for further implementation. While experiencing nervousness is typical for any observation, formative feedback on inclusive teaching decreases the pressure on an instructor in that the goal is not to use the information for hiring, tenure, or promotion. Instead, the feedback is used for continuous improvement, and if high-stakes observations are subsequently conducted, the instructor has the opportunity to further solidify their practices beforehand. Having teaching experience is generally important in improving practice, but granting someone the gift of teaching learners and expecting them to automatically know how to be inclusive for their learners is problematic and this is often the case in higher education. If we examine other professions, such as becoming a medical doctor or a lawyer, observation and feedback are critical to their growth. Medical students work with an attending physician that will provide them with feedback. Within K-12 education, pre-service teachers are observed and given feedback to support their teaching practices.

We hope we have emphasized sufficiently that taking a multi-pronged approach to informing practice, gathering students' perspectives, engaging in self-reflection, as well as obtaining observational feedback can provide a window into an inclusive instructor's classroom. Observations are critical across the career of an instructor. Whether they are new to teaching or have been teaching for many years, all instructors have the potential to learn something new about their teaching through observation.

Fellow instructors, educational developers in centers for teaching and learning, or student partners can conduct these observations. The lenses through which each views teaching and learning can differ and they can collectively provide a larger picture that can support inclusive teaching and learning more holistically. Instructors who teach similar courses and conduct observations are poised to comment both within a disciplinary context as well as on approaches they have found useful in their own teaching with the same student population. They too can learn from the observations and reflect on their own teaching. Such discussions have the potential to inspire departmental conversations around teaching. Instructors newer to teaching who do not teach the same courses might be able to provide input based on outside experiences and potentially be more open to novel ways of teaching. Experienced instructors might be able to share some of their wisdom.

Student partners who are trained to give feedback on teaching can provide an understanding of how learners might be experiencing the class. For example, they may see or reveal things happening in the classroom that an instructor might not see from their perspective. These students might engage in training through a center for teaching and learning. Educational developers with a broad range of expertise and knowledge on teaching across disciplines and observing a variety of courses can also have valuable insights. They might be poised to refer those being observed to literature or resources based on evidence-based practices. They might have experience using specialized observation instruments such as those that will be subsequently described, that enable instructors to obtain feedback on their teaching.

More information about how to navigate "who" conducts the observation is included in subsequent paragraphs. All observations should be held confidential, unless the observer otherwise specifies, and conducted by trusted individuals who are genuinely interested in supporting the teaching efforts of instructors. Further, having observers perform multiple observations over time is ideal given that each one only provides a snapshot view. Aiming for two to three observations of a single course during a term is a good starting point, with more observations allowing for a better understanding of the instructor's teaching approaches.

One item we absolutely cannot neglect to address is the role of emotion in observation of teaching. Sometimes it might feel anxiety-producing to have another person view a course even when it is not for evaluative purposes. Many instructors experience such nervousness, it's natural. Tracie, who has conducted a number of confidential classroom observations, can attest that the benefits often far outweigh the costs for instructors. In her experiences, she has seen how valuable instructors have perceived the feedback and used it to change their practices. Sometimes instructors have been unaware of how certain instructional behaviors impacted the learning environment and they tried something different with much success. When instructors open their classrooms, they may be more willing to see the perspectives of another to truly change their practices. This teaching maturity sits in a special space and can invite a wonderful partnership.

Reflection Questions

- How do you feel about your teaching being observed?
- If you feel some discomfort, what might help you feel more comfortable?

How Can I Obtain Observational Feedback?

Resources for the observation of inclusive teaching vary with institutions. For example, some institutions might have established centers for teaching and learning or peer observation of teaching programs for instructors while others may not. Below are several ways to make observations work at the institution regardless of resource level.

Lower Resource

At minimum, if outside observation is not possible, an instructor can record their own class sessions and later watch them to reflect on their teaching. Some on-site classrooms might be equipped with cameras and, if not, even a cell phone camera might be able to capture aspects of classroom teaching. For synchronous online courses, an instructor can create a recording using their video conferencing software. They can save the chat to assess equitable participation amongst members of the class. In an asynchronous online course, student responses to discussion and other forums can provide an understanding of their engagement patterns.

The Decibel Analysis for Research in Teaching (DART) is a tool that instructors can use to analyze how much talking with multiple voices occurred in a class. This may signify how much lecturing compared with student talking is occurring, a proxy for measuring active learning (Owens et al., 2017). The instructor can upload the audio file of their class session to obtain this analysis.

Additionally, an instructor could use various observation protocols on their classroom recordings, such as the PAITE, which will be described subsequently in full detail in this chapter (*Inclusive Teaching Visualization*, n.d.) or the Classroom Observation Protocol for Undergraduate STEM (COPUS) (Smith et al., 2013), which provides an understanding of various active learning approaches in which the instructor and students engage. The advantage of using a recording is that instructors can always revisit and visually see how exactly they were teaching the course. They might be surprised at how well something went and it might be different from their recollection. Instructors can also record themselves multiple times over the course of the semester to analyze the changes they have made. Such reflections can be helpful to add to a teaching portfolio. The limitations to using recordings are that they are dependent on the audio and video quality. They may not be able to capture non-verbal communication if the camera is only focused on the instructor. If sound quality is not good, it limits what can be assessed. Generally, if the quality is sufficient, an instructor has the potential to learn a lot from the recording.

If an instructor has trusted colleagues teaching similar courses, there may be opportunities to engage in observations of one another through teaching circles (Marshall, 2008). For example, they can reciprocally observe each other's courses. In the event that a department has joint goals around inclusion, observation of teaching can encourage dialogue around what practices can support inclusion within various courses. Asking a colleague outside of the department's observed courses might also be preferred in some instances if it is preferred to hear additional voices, to potentially have a more low-stakes engagement, or if departmental colleagues are unavailable.

Higher Resource

Institutions with centers for teaching and learning might have additional opportunities for requesting formative observations of teaching. Educational developers who have expertise in teaching and learning and experience observing courses across disciplines might be able to conduct observations. Some institutions might have student pedagogical partners who also conduct observations of teaching that can provide feedback from the perspective of a learner. Further, centers for teaching and learning might facilitate programming such as Teaching Squares or Triangles that pair faculty with one another to observe each other's classes and reflect on teaching (Haave, 2014). Or, centers that conduct assessment might run formal, formative peer observation of teaching programs.

There are a variety of possibilities for observation of inclusive teaching, and what matters most is knowing what is possible and makes sense within the institutional context.

Reflection Questions

- What are the resources available to you for reflection on your teaching?
- How can you obtain observational feedback on your inclusive teaching efforts? Who might you ask?

Observation Procedures and Tools

For any observation that is to be conducted, scheduling both pre- and post-observation debriefings are recommended practices (Chism, 2007). The pre-observation debriefing provides an opportunity to discuss the course, plans for the class session, inclusivity goals and what the instructor would like the observer to look out for. The post-observation debriefing is held ideally within a week or less of the observation to share feedback within a timeframe where both the observer and the observed can recall what happened during the course. There are a variety of ways to conduct observations of teaching to support inclusion efforts. Below are a few examples.

General Observation of Inclusive Teaching

An instructor might have interest in general feedback from the observer. Having specific goals to work toward can be useful for this stage, but also an observer can give overall feedback, perhaps comparable to a diagnostic type of assessment. In this scenario the observer may or may not use a formal protocol or observation instrument but take notes according to what they observe is highly recommended. To focus their observational efforts, the observer might take notes on the general classroom climate, inclusive teaching approaches and strategies utilized by the instructor, accessibility, or other related items. Observers may also provide feedback on syllabi as well as assignments.

In such scenarios observers may think more holistically about the course, with simultaneous benefits and limitations that they are viewing it through their own lens and experiences. They will also need some basic competency in identifying possible inclusive teaching instructional behaviors. In this vein, having multiple observers with more perspectives can allow for more comprehensive feedback, yet is not always feasible to accomplish in practice.

The Protocol for Advancing Inclusive Teaching Efforts (PAITE)

An instructor can also request usage of an observational instrument to obtain feedback on their teaching if those trained at the institution have the capacity or if they themselves learn and use the tool on a recording of their teaching efforts. The PAITE can be a helpful launching point for an instructor to learn more about various inclusive teaching approaches they utilize or have the opportunity to utilize (Addy et al., 2023). The PAITE highlights 15 inclusive teaching approaches used by instructors in a data-driven manner. The codes used for the PAITE (the instructor's teaching behaviors) are consistent with what students shared through their perspectives, as highlighted in the earlier chapters of this book. Some sample codes include calling students by their names, giving students choice, providing affirmation, reinforcing community guidelines, creating an active learning environment that engages learners, and using approaches that encourage equitable participation.

When using the PAITE, observers record what the instructor is doing every two minutes and create a data visualization of their practices in a data-driven manner using pie charts, graphs, and/or tables. The observer also comments upon the accessibility practices used by an instructor as well as the level of structure enacted during the class session (see Figures 6.1 and 6.2). For example, if an instructor displays closed captioning when playing media, such would be noted by the observer. If an instructor has a lesson plan that includes a variety of structured activities, this would also be recorded.

FIGURE 6.1 Pie chart PAITE data visualization.

FIGURE 6.2 Bar chart PAITE data visualization.

Observers (e.g., student partner, faculty colleague, educational developer) can learn to use the PAITE by using the training guide and the various training vignettes provided through the Inclusive Teaching Visualization Project (*Inclusive Teaching Visualization*, n.d.). From Tracie's experience, the most effective usages of PAITE findings from instructors have been when instructors set goals for inclusion, participate in an observation and feedback session, iterate, and engage in subsequent observations and feedback sessions. Such a process provides the instructor the opportunity to witness and document the changes that they made in their teaching.

There are a variety of usages of PAITE within institutional contexts. Originally the PAITE was used in an intensive academy focused on inclusive teaching by student pedagogical partners as well as within a new faculty learning community. Others have described their intent or usage of the PAITE within instructor teaching circles, with instructors participating in grants focused on inclusive excellence, during general observations of teaching run by centers for teaching and learning, and peer observation teaching programs. The protocol is generally discipline-agnostic and versatile. For the PAITE, as in many other observation protocols, observers should have the capacity to understand the language in which the course is taught. For example, if an instructor is teaching an upper-level language course that is spoken in that language, the observer should have sufficient fluency to be able to follow when the instructor and students are speaking. Otherwise, it would be difficult to apply certain codes on the PAITE (e.g., affirmation, community standards, prior knowledge assessment, and others).

The PAITE was not designed to capture every inclusive teaching approach, as that is a lofty goal given the diversity of such methods. There are other approaches as well as course design elements that are not included on the PAITE. Instead, the protocol was designed to focus on several inclusive teaching practices that can be reliably observed. Observers can still, and are encouraged to, comment upon inclusive teaching approaches that are not included on the PAITE. The PAITE, however, is a launching point that allows for a general baseline of the implementation of several key inclusive teaching approaches.

Reflection Questions

- Which inclusive teaching practices do you implement, if any?
- How might visualizing your inclusive teaching approaches using the PAITE help you to enhance your practice?

Decoding PAITE Codes

Below are several instructional examples where usage of the PAITE can further goals for equity and inclusion.

Visualizing an Ethic of Care through Actions Establishing a Positive Classroom Climate

The commonly used phrases by students who participated in our study included words such as "comfortable" and "valuable," as highlighted in the two quotes below.

> *My algebra professor was very adamant about getting to know us and making everyone feel comfortable and included.*
>
> *—A public university student who identifies as Puerto Rican, female, heterosexual, and first-generation*

> *[I] feel like the teachers here at [college name] care about me as a person and listen to me when i can get dificult [sic] and stress out.*
>
> *—A small, private, liberal arts student who identifies as White and non-binary*

Many of these students described how when their instructors created a classroom environment that made them feel relaxed and perhaps at ease, and this made them feel welcome. Interestingly, they did not appear to be describing being comfortable about the process of learning, but rather the atmosphere of the class itself. The PAITE identifies several instructional behaviors that help an instructor create an ethic of care and a positive classroom climate. The behaviors include establishing community standards, relationship building, using affirmation, adopting growth mindset language, using students' names, addressing exclusionary acts, and avoiding forced spokespersonship.

Reinforcing Community Standards

When entering any new space, whether within a virtual or onsite classroom setting, there can be a sense of uncertainty with the norms and expectations of the community. When instructors establish respectful guidelines for the classroom environment which they might also co-create students, such can set a tone for inclusion, and help create a positive climate. The PAITE code "COM" is marked each time an instructor reinforces such guidelines as a gentle reminder as well as in times where they may have been violated. Knowing these accepted norms, students can feel more relaxed in the environment and have an increased readiness to learn.

Building Relationships

Evident in the two quotes provided above are the instructors' abilities to get to know students and build relationships. To do so requires intentionality, and sometimes interactions might occur outside of the classroom such as during student hours (office hours), co-curricular events, or other gatherings. A variety of these relationship-building activities can also occur in the classroom if an instructor conducts a wellness check-in, provides opportunities for students to get to know one another, and more. The code "REL" captures this act, and observers can further note what types of activities were carried out to build such relationships.

Using Students' Names

Sometimes a small action can make a big impact toward inclusion. Many of the students in our study confirmed that when their instructor knew their name they felt that the course was more inclusive. Sometimes instructors might not be aware of how many times they call students by their names in a course. The PAITE code "NAME" allows the frequency of how often an instructor uses a name to be measured. Such usage of names can make the environment feel more welcoming to students. We found in our general survey that 69 percent of students perceived that most, or all, of their instructors knew their names by the end of a course. There are a variety of strategies that instructors can use to learn students' names. At some institutions, a photo is provided of all students in the class on the learning management system. An instructor might use that to practice memorizing the names of students in class. Handing back assignments also reinforces names.

Instructors might also use name tents, which can help in all classes including larger-sized classes. Students can write phonetic spellings of their names on name tents as well as their pronouns. Writing names on the front and back of name tents can support other students learning such names sitting behind the students. These approaches are based on the content found in Chapter 3. Using the PAITE, an instructor can be aware of how often they use students' names. If there are no, or few instances, there might be opportunities for growth.

Addressing Exclusionary Acts and Avoiding Forced Spokespersonship

In this book we describe both what our student respondents consider an inclusive classroom environment and what they do not. Two behaviors that are known to not be inclusive are when instructors do not acknowledge or address those challenging moments in the classroom when comments are made that are exclusionary in some way (PAITE code "EXCL"), as well as when students are asked to speak on behalf of their social identity (PAITE code: "IDEN") (Boysen, 2012). Based on experience, these two codes have perhaps been the least used on the PAITE but can be very impactful in cultivating an inclusive classroom.

Using Growth Mindset and Affirmation Language

Additional actions, based in socio-psychological work, include using growth mindset language and the language of affirmation. Fixed mindsets can limit individuals from achieving their full potential (Dweck, 2006, 276). In higher education, this can prevent students from achieving what they are capable of in a course. Such beliefs that intelligence is fixed are limiting, and other work has shown that when instructors have fixed mindsets they too can negatively impact the mindsets of students (Yeager et al., 2022). Some work has found that STEM instructors with fixed mindsets can induce stereotype threat in their learners, and that their female-identifying students can be even more negatively impacted with regards to performance (Canning et al., 2021). Instructors interested in examining the language they use that promotes a growth mindset can find the PAITE helpful in their understanding of the words they use in their courses. In addition to including such language on course syllabi such as "with practice you can improve" or "some course material may be difficult at times but if you work through it you can develop a deeper understanding," instructors who also reinforce such principles in their classes can promote a growth-focused environment that fosters learning.

The code "GROW" on the PAITE directly addresses growth mindset language. Instructors who set goals around growth mindset can work with observers to understand how they are using such verbiage in their courses. Observers can not only tally the number of instances in each class, they can also take note of the types of statements made by the instructors and the responses of the students.

Some instructors with growth mindset goals might simultaneously be interested in using more affirmation in their courses, another code on the PAITE, "AFFIRM." Affirmation statements focus on the positive aspects of what students contribute to the course environment. To some students this messaging can be incredibly impactful in increasing their self-efficacy. Similar to growth mindset language, observers take note of any affirmation language used by the instructor.

Affirmation language and actions in our student study also seemed entwined with creating a welcoming space. For example, a neurodivergent student indicated a critical component of such environments: "[I]t feel['s] like there's a lack of judgment." In this example, even if students went off topic they were not reprimanded. In effect, they were still affirmed in that course even if the instructor did later need to redirect attention to the course content at hand.

Such affirmations are also described in the documentary film *Autism Goes to College* (*Autism Goes To College Resource Center*, n.d.). In this film, one of the students with autism spectrum disorder (ASD) would at times get up and walk to the front of the class while their instructor was teaching. Rather than being publicly reprimanded, the professor patiently affirmed the student with understanding. In doing so, the instructor was affirming the student with ASD in that classroom environment. Affirmation therefore can manifest in a variety of ways in a class.

Applying Teaching Frameworks that Build Inclusive Classrooms

A variety of frameworks, such as UDL (About Universal Design for Learning, n.d.) and Culturally Responsive Teaching (Gay, 2002), focus on practices that are responsive to the diversity of students within a course setting.

Integrating Diverse Media and Examples

Several students, including those who were neurodivergent or had physical or learning disabilities in our study, described the importance of the instructor using diverse visuals and media in the course to support their learning. The PAITE code "MED" is selected when the instructor uses videos, props, demos, models, or other materials to supplement their teaching. As noted in Chapter 4, seeing course concepts represented in multiple ways can support the learning of all students. An example might be of an instructor showing an anatomical model, a simulation, or a case vignette.

In addition to using a variety of media during a class, the incorporation of diversity with regards to perspectives, people, and ideas as related to course content can create a more inclusive experience for students. Such can allow students to learn viewpoints, or about people and cultures beyond their own, as well as see examples that are more similar to their social identities. When instructors use such diverse examples in the class, the observer selects the code "DIVEX" and takes note of the specific usages.

Real-world Scenarios

When an instructor applies course content outside of the classroom, such examples can support students' learning by understanding it within other contexts (PAITE code "REAL"). Some examples might include discussions of case studies, recent news articles, or applications of the material to students' daily lives.

Student Choice

Giving students decision-making capabilities (PAITE code "CHOICE") within class activities can give them agency and allow them to have more control over their learning.

Applying the Science of Learning

Prior Knowledge and Comprehension Check

There are some general principles that are just as evident in the science of how people learn. One is understanding what students already know, or are able to do, and building on their knowledge and skills. Instructors who check for students' prior understanding (PAITE code "PRIOR") can better scaffold learning in a course environment. Some sample strategies include classroom brainstorms about a particular concept, topic, or principles, or a poll that checks prior knowledge. The observer can take note of what was asked of the students as well as how the information was used to support learning.

Additionally, questions might test for general comprehension of information recently learned (PAITE code "COMP") with the goals of ensuring that students are following along and processing the course information.

Active Learning and Equitable Participation

Instructors who want to incorporate more active learning (PAITE code "ACTIVE") in their courses might focus on how often they utilize such approaches in their courses. In addition to coding such approaches using the

PAITE, observers can also take note of which practices are utilized and potential future opportunities for implementation. Instructors teaching courses that are lecture-based can consider how they can further integrate more active learning activities. Here is where we note some cautions for instructors and observers to be aware of with active learning activities to ensure they are inclusive of students who are neurodivergent and with learning disabilities (Pfeifer et al., 2023). For example, while group work can have positive aspects such as helping students form relationships, and promote metacognition, there can be challenges if the assignment instructions are unclear or their peers do not want to work with each other. Neurodivergent students and students with learning disabilities recommended that their instructors be aware of how their teaching practices implicate student success in their course, acknowledge differences between students, explain their reasoning, give a roadmap to accommodations, as well as incorporate more videos and interactive notes.

Courses that include active learning might benefit from secondary observations that use tools such as the COPUS, which provides perspectives on both what the students and the instructors are doing during class (Smith et al., 2013). Many of the students in our study, including several who identified as neurodivergent or with learning disabilities, indicated that they felt group work and other active learning activities made them feel more included in their courses. Simultaneously, we also note that students on the autism spectrum might find group work challenging, and that neurodivergent and all students can benefit from carefully scaffolded group experiences. These are all conversation points for debriefing sessions between the instructor and the observer.

A separate but related code to active learning is equitable participation ("EQPART"). This approach has a broader scope than active learning. Where this differs is that the instructor has created an environment in which the majority of students are able to contribute. For example, setting up a poll that all students can respond to, a free writing activity in which all students engage, or a reflection on their course experience. An instructor can integrate active learning activities to also encourage equitable participation in a class session.

Hypothetical Case Applications of PAITE

Case 1: General Feedback

An English instructor is interested in obtaining a general overview of various inclusive teaching approaches they implement in their classes. They agree to have the observer use the PAITE, and they find that they are using a number of the strategies to some degree but want to enhance the language that they use in the course to make it more affirmative and focused on growth mindset as students improve in their writing. They consider their upcoming class sessions and the topics for discussion, and the types of work the students will undertake, and consider some ways that they can use more affirmative and growth mindset language. An increase is evident in a subsequent PAITE analysis.

Case 2: Increasing Active Learning

A STEM instructor is interested in enhancing the active learning strategies used in their large enrollment introductory lecture course. An initial PAITE observation reveals that the instructor implements active learning for a very small duration of the class time. During the debriefing session the instructor and observer brainstorm more ways that the instructor can incorporate active learning. They choose to incorporate more active problem-solving and written reflection during the class sessions. Upon second observation with the PAITE, the frequency of how often the instructor uses active learning in the course increases. Subsequently, the instructor informally and anonymously surveys the students to obtain their feedback on the use of active problem-solving and written reflection. The majority of students appreciate the change and a theme emerges for the instructor to provide some more worked examples prior to the student problem-solving sessions, which the instructor acts upon. This case illustrates how an instructor can use formative observational feedback as well as formative student voice to enhance their implementation of inclusive teaching approaches.

Case 3: More Relationship Building

An Art instructor teaches fairly small classes where students engage in individual long-term art projects. They are interested in building positive relationships with their students and using class time as a space for informal conversation and interaction. Their initial PAITE observation reveals few relationship-building activities in the course, and during the debriefing they brainstorm other possibilities with the observer such as icebreakers or low stakes conversations that can occur while students are working. The second and third observations reveal these happening to a large degree. The instructor notices that more comments in their course evaluations are even more positive around the classroom climate compared with previous semesters.

PAITE as a Tool for Advancing Inclusive Teaching

When instructors undergo a PAITE observation, they can increase their awareness of their inclusive teaching practices and be more reflective practitioners, building on approaches described in Chapter 5. Specifically, instructors can reflect on which inclusive teaching approaches they are currently using, if any, and how they are being implemented in their courses. They can explore and experiment with new approaches and assess the impact on their students. The PAITE truly is a launching point for reflection and observation on inclusive teaching for those new to teaching as well as those with more experience.

Reflection Questions

- Considering the instructional behaviors included on the PAITE, which would you be most interested in focusing on for a classroom observation?
- What type of outcomes would you hope to see?

Building Upon the PAITE: Other Observational Tools

PAITE is a tool used to examine a variety of general inclusive teaching approaches. Instructors who want a deeper analysis of some of the codes may benefit from some of the other observation instruments that are currently available, or consider adapting them to their contexts, as described in the following sections. We provide two analogies that illustrate how instructors can use PAITE findings as a launching point, and then engage in follow-up observations with other tools. One is considering the data received analogous to preliminary clues that are provided about the teaching environment. PAITE findings can give instructors an initial understanding about which approaches they are using but they might want to know about additional impacts of the tool. Instructors might consider future analyses that allow them to answer such questions. Another analogy is from the discipline of statistics. One might perform tests of significance on data. If there is significance, depending on the test, the next step might be to conduct a post-hoc analysis to better understand where the significance lies. The PAITE provides useful information about the types of inclusive teaching approaches instructors utilize, and it might be necessary to have subsequent analyses that answer deeper questions about what is observed. Two areas where instructors might consider taking a deeper approach after using the PAITE, where there are existing observational tools, include the general active learning approaches they utilize and how they foster equitable participation.

Active Learning

Given that the PAITE focuses globally on any active learning approach utilized, instructors whose goals are to implement more of such methods in their courses might be interested in more specific observational feedback on their instructional strategies. The COPUS, validated in STEM classrooms, can give a picture of what approaches the instructor is using in the classroom as well as the actions of the students (Smith et al., 2013). As noted previously, the COPUS might be used as a follow-up to the PAITE, and in Tracie's center for teaching and learning programming this has provided useful information for many instructors regarding their practices. Additionally, an instructor might be interested in proxy measures of active learning such as to what degree there are multiple voices being heard in the classroom (i.e., more students speaking) and not just the instructor. This can be captured by submitting an audio recording of the class session to analyze through the DART, as previously described, which provides varying frequencies of instruction (Owens et al., 2017).

Equitable Participation

If an instructor would like to find out more information about which students are participating in their class, and their types of contributions, the Equity QUantified In Participation (EQUIP) tool may be appropriate (EQUIP App, n.d.). EQUIP is a web-based tool that can provide an analysis of how students participate in a course. The observers will track which students are participating and the types of contributions they make.

Perhaps, for example, male-identifying students are answering the most questions in a course with roughly 50 percent female- and 50 percent male-identifying students. The instructor might want to consider other strategies for encouraging equitable participation, such as those previously described in earlier chapters (e.g., polling, warm calling, free writing, and others).

EQUIP allows versatile usage within any discipline, and researchers reported using it in undergraduate mathematics courses and finding that female-identifying students were more likely to contribute to small group discussions but less so in whole-class discussions, and how the actions of the instructor might hinder their participation if calling only on male-identifying students or the first students to raise their hands (Ernest et al., 2019). Because mathematics is a male-dominated field, such scenarios can perpetuate inequities and it can be very empowering for instructors, who become aware that this is happening in their courses, to take action.

Another study revealed some powerful reflections that instructors and students made on inclusive teaching efforts after EQUIP was used to analyze their course or they experienced their instructor using it in their course (TPB Publication, 2023).

An instructor shared:

> Through this process I learned strategies that enabled me to reverse the exclusionary conditions of the classroom and work towards creating an inclusive classroom environment. Ultimately, inclusive classrooms are like a

> symphony, and this study provided the pedagogical tools and mentoring necessary to effectively facilitate the harmonizing of student voices.
>
> *(p. 116)*

Two students shared (p.117):

> Latinx students are often not included in learning environments because "the culture doesn't value education" or because of the language barrier or for whatever other reason. This software sheds a light on explicit or implicit bias that may show the exclusion of Latinx students and can help make their inclusion more intentional.
>
> As an Asian woman, we are generally quieter/less comfortable speaking in front of the group than our white and/or male counterparts so being cognizant of this and not cold calling would have been something I appreciated as a student.

There are a variety of other observational protocols that have been used in courses that might augment the observational feedback an instructor receives from PAITE or to focus on their teaching, many of which have been developed in STEM disciplines (Anwar & Menekse, 2021; Asgari et al., 2021; Lund et al., 2015).

Sample Reflective Analysis

In the spirit of backward design, instructors can decide what their goals are with regards to inclusive teaching and next determine if existing tools might help them achieve them. Below is a sample reflective analysis.

I am interested in:

- General inclusive teaching approaches I am implementing in my courses and how I can build upon them (PAITE observation)
- To what extent I am facilitating an environment that encourages equitable participation (PAITE observation)
    - Which students are responding in this environment and how (EQUIP follow-up observation)
- To what extent that I am creating an active learning environment (PAITE observation)
    - How my students are responding in this environment (COPUS follow-up observation)
    - How much of my classroom involves my voice versus students engaged in dialogue (DART follow-up observation)

Choosing Observation Types

There are arguments that narrative, holistic observation in a form of naturalistic inquiry is preferable to breaking down inclusive teaching practices into more bite-sized chunks (McCreary, 2023). In some ways, this parallels when to use qualitative and when to use quantitative research methods, with mixed methods research integrating both. Instructors' approaches to observation generally should be driven by what questions they most want to answer about their teaching practices. Providing instructors with a choice of approaches can better tailor to their goals.

From Tracie's experience, some instructors want to know, "Overall, what are you observing in my classroom?" In this case a narrative of overall teaching and learning actions is generally appropriate, with the understanding that such observation and feedback relies heavily on the lens of the observer(s).

Some instructors, however, want to know, "Which specific inclusive teaching approaches do I use and to what degree?" or "Over time am I increasing the usage of the approaches as aligned with my goals for inclusion?"

Some instructors might be interested in both having a general classroom observation as well as one that classifies specific approaches. Both are valid ways to support instructors in their implementation of inclusive teaching approaches. Given that time, resources, and expertise for observations are often limited at most institutions, instructor choice of what they find the most useful to enhance their practice provides flexibility. Instructors might not recognize the various options available to them. Here we provide a menu of choices from low to high resource to accommodate for the many different contexts in which instructors work and the questions they are most interested in answering through observational feedback.

Advice for Asynchronous Online Courses

While some of the tools described may have some utility in synchronous online courses, they may not be validated, or have significant limitations, for usages in asynchronous online courses. A critical analysis unit for inclusivity in asynchronous courses is in their design. The flexibility they provide in their design can support inclusivity, allowing students to complete course assignments within fewer time-bound restrictions than a synchronous course. Having an intuitive layout, welcoming videos and language, responsiveness and instructor presence, ensuring digital accessibility of materials (e.g., colors, alt text, closed captioning), creating opportunities for equitable participation (e.g., reflections, forums with guidelines for respectful dialogue), can create a more inclusive environment.

Advice for Observers

Observers can provide valuable feedback to instructors on their inclusive teaching efforts. A recommendation is for the observer (e.g., student partner, faculty colleague, or educational developer) to ask the instructor whether they are wanting a general overview of inclusive teaching approaches they are utilizing or whether they have specific goals, and what they are. Together, decide what the best ways for providing feedback on those goals might be; either a general observation, or an observation with PAITE or another tool. Observers will need to ensure that they are trained on any relevant tools and have sought the appropriate training resources. In general, discuss the importance of multiple observations to monitor growth over time and ideally schedule subsequent observations early. These observations are generally announced by the instructor with observers being a parenthetical fly on the wall in the classroom to focus on the observation and provide feedback.

Reflect on your own biases and mindsets before conducting observations and be open-minded. Observers should make sure that they focus on what they observe rather than any preconceived notions about an instructor or a course. Observations are best conducted when observers are open to the possibilities of the classroom and what teaching and learning can look like.

Advice for Educational Developers

In general, being trained and able to use a diverse array of tools for classroom observations can be very useful. Educational developers can announce to faculty members that they are available to conduct formative classroom observations which can provide useful feedback on teaching. In addition, educational developers can encourage instructors to set inclusive teaching goals and be critical partners in this process. They also have the ability to create communities or facilitate initiatives that allow faculty members to observe one another's practices as well as provide brave spaces for faculty members to obtain feedback on their practices. Conducting observations can also be an opportunistic time to learn and, if the faculty member agrees, to promote their efforts through faculty panels, newsletters, social media, or other highlights to showcase their dedication to inclusive teaching and how they have been going about such.

Conclusion

Observation can be a powerful method for obtaining feedback on inclusive teaching practices. Instructors can consider their inclusivity goals as well as the approaches they utilize and seek out individuals who can attend their classes or view their asynchronous course platforms to provide such feedback. Various tools are also available for the purposes of obtaining feedback on inclusive teaching practices such as PAITE, EQUIP, and COPUS, among others.

References

About Universal Design for Learning. (n.d.). *CAST.* Retrieved May 20, 2023, from https://www.cast.org/impact/universal-design-for-learning-udl.

Addy, T., Younas, H., Cetin, P., Cham, F., Rizk, M., Nwankpa, C., & Borzone, M. (2022). The development of the Protocol for Advancing Inclusive Teaching Efforts (PAITE). *Journal of Educational Research and Practice*, 12. doi:10.5590/JERAP.2022.12.0.05.

Anwar, S., & Menekse, M. (2021). A systematic review of observation protocols used in postsecondary STEM classrooms. *Review of Education*, 9(1), 81–120. doi:10.1002/rev3.3235.

Asgari, M., Miles, A. M., Lisboa, M. S., & Sarvary, M. A. (2021). COPUS, PORTAAL, or DART? Classroom observation tool comparison from the instructor user's perspective. *Frontiers in Education*, 6. https://www.frontiersin.org/articles/10.3389/feduc.2021.740344.

Autism Goes To College Resource Center. Hey U Here We Come! (n.d.). Retrieved May 20, 2023, from https://www.autismgoestocollege.org/.

Boysen, G. A. (2012). Teaching and student perceptions of microaggressions in college classrooms. *College Teaching*, 60(3), 122–129.

Canning, E. A., Ozier, E., Williams, H. E., AlRasheed, R., & Murphy, M. C. (2021). Professors who signal a fixed mindset about ability undermine women's performance in STEM. *Social Psychological and Personality Science*, 13(5), 927–937. doi:10.1177/19485506211030398.

Chism, N. (2007). *Peer review of teaching: A sourcebook.* Bolton, MA: Anker.

Dweck, C. S. (2006). *Mindset: The new psychology of success.* New York: Random House.

Ebert-May, D., Derting, T. L., Hodder, J., Momsen, J. L., Long, T. M., & Jardeleza, S. E. (2011). What we say is not what we do: Effective evaluation of faculty professional development programs. *BioScience*, 61(7), 550–558. doi:10.1525/bio.2011.61.7.9.

EQUIP App. (n.d.). Retrieved June 13, 2023, from https://www.equip.ninja/.

Ernest, J. B., Reinholz, D. L., & Shah, N. (2019). Hidden competence: Women's mathematical participation in public and private classroom spaces. *Educational Studies in Mathematics*, 102(2), 153–172. doi:10.1007/s10649-019-09910-w.

Fletcher, J. A. (2018). Peer observation of teaching: A practical tool in higher education. *The Journal of Faculty Development*, 32(1), 51–64.

Freeman, S., Eddy, S. L., McDonough, M., Smith, M. K., Okoroafor, N., Jordt, H., & Wenderoth, M. P. (2014). Active learning increases student performance in science, engineering, and mathematics. *Proceedings of the National Academy of Sciences*, 111(23), 8410–8415. doi:10.1073/pnas.1319030111.

Fung, L., & Chow, L. P. Y. (2002). Congruence of student teachers' pedagogical images and actual classroom practices. *Educational Research*, 44(3), 313–321. doi:10.1080/0013188022000031605.

Gay, G. (2002). Preparing for culturally responsive teaching. *Journal of Teacher Education*, 53(2), 106–116. doi:10.1177/0022487102053002003.

Haave, N. (2014). Teaching squares: A teaching development tool, *The Teaching Professor*, 28(10), 1.
Inclusive Teaching Visualization. (n.d.). Retrieved May 19, 2023, from https://inclusiveteachingvisualization.com/.
Kane, R., Sandretto, S., & Heath, C. (2002). Telling half the story: A critical review of research on the teaching beliefs and practices of university academics. *Review of Educational Research*, 72(2), 177–228. doi:10.3102/00346543072002177.
Lund, T. J., Pilarz, M., Velasco, J. B., Chakraverty, D., Rosploch, K., Undersander, M., & Stains, M. (2015). The best of both worlds: Building on the COPUS and RTOP observation protocols to easily and reliably measure various levels of reformed instructional practice. *CBE Life Sciences Education*, 14(2), article 18. doi:10.1187/cbe.14-10-0168.
Marshall, M. J. (2008). Teaching circles: Supporting shared work and professional development. *Pedagogy*, 8(3): 413–431.
McCreary, M. (2023). Quality doesn't matter: Educational development as a young science. *New Directions for Teaching and Learning*, 2023(173), 75–85. doi:10.1002/tl.20536.
Murray, K., & Macdonald, R. (1997). The disjunction between lecturers' conceptions of teaching and their claimed educational practice. *Higher Education*, 33(3), 331–349. doi:10.1023/A:1002931104852.
Owens, M. T., Seidel, S. B., Wong, M., Bejines, T. E., Lietz, S., Perez, J. R., Sit, S., Subedar, Z.-S., Acker, G. N., Akana, S. F., Balukjian, B., Benton, H. P., Blair, J. R., Boaz, S. M., Boyer, K. E., Bram, J. B., Burrus, L. W., Byrd, D. T., Caporale, N., … Tanner, K. D. (2017). Classroom sound can be used to classify teaching practices in college science courses. *Proceedings of the National Academy of Sciences*, 114(12), 3085–3090. doi:10.1073/pnas.1618693114.
Pfeifer, M. A., Cordero, J. J., & Stanton, J. D. (2023). What I wish my instructor knew: How active learning influences the classroom experiences and self-advocacy of STEM majors with ADHD and specific learning disabilities. *CBE—Life Sciences Education*, 22(1), article 2. doi:10.1187/cbe.21-12-0329.
Smith, M. K., Jones, F. H. M., Gilbert, S. L., & Wieman, C. E. (2013). The classroom observation protocol for undergraduate STEM (COPUS): A new instrument to characterize university STEM classroom practices. *CBE—Life Sciences Education*, 12(4), 618–627. doi:10.1187/cbe.13-08-0154.
TPB Publication. (2023, April 17). *ACES Online*. https://acesonline.net/tpb-publication/.
Yeager, D. S., Carroll, J. M., Buontempo, J., Cimpian, A., Woody, S., Crosnoe, R., Muller, C., Murray, J., Mhatre, P., Kersting, N., Hulleman, C., Kudym, M., Murphy, M., Duckworth, A. L., Walton, G. M., & Dweck, C. S. (2022). Teacher mindsets help explain where a growth-mindset intervention does and doesn't work. *Psychological Science*, 33(1), 18–32. doi:10.1177/09567976211028984.

7

MEASURING AND SHARING OUTCOMES

Let's take a moment and just be explicit about the path we are following in this book. Initially we describe practices that students consider to be inclusive. We next spend time considering how an instructor can reflect on their implementation efforts through various means as well as observational feedback. In this chapter we consider the next level of engagement, more formally measuring the outcomes related to inclusive teaching, both those that focus on the instructor's growth as well as student outcomes. We essentially address, how do we know that the inclusive teaching approaches are having their intended effects? We discuss which outcomes can be measured through an assessment project as well as the next level of performing a systematic research investigation for measuring outcomes at the instructor level. Our suggestions go beyond traditional grades and measures that might be overlooked but are quite valuable.

Outcomes are important to measure not only for continuous improvement, but they also provide evidence supporting inclusive teaching practices that can also be provided on a teaching portfolio or even shared when an instructor's inclusive teaching approaches are questioned.

Assessment Framework

Sometimes instructors might benefit from using a framework that guides them through the assessment process. In *Equity & Inclusion in Higher Education: Strategies for Teaching* (Kumar & Refaei, 2021) we provide steps that instructors can follow. This framework is openly available, and includes the following components:

DOI: 10.4324/9781003442929-9

- Identify any existing disciplinary challenges
- Clarify pedagogical goals
- Choose an appropriate scope for the project
- List expected outcomes
- Specify data sources and formulate an assessment plan
- Gather preliminary data/information
- Implement project and collect data
- Analyze data, draw conclusions, and consider next steps

For example, an instructor might be particularly interested in facilitating equitable participation in a particular course. They alter the lens through which they view participation and see it as skill building (Gillis, 2019) rather than how many times a student speaks up in class or raises their hand, which can be imperfect metrics for quiet students, students who take more time to process information, and generally for students who have not had opportunities to grow in their participation skills. They encourage students to set goals and choose how they will participate in class, and administer small assignments where students reflect on their progress toward their goals. Their data sources consist of such reflections, which include comparative analyses of how they engaged in this class as well as others in addition to how well they have achieved their goals by the end of the semester. The instructor finds that students have been able to set small goals and accomplish them for participation. Employing this new framework appeared to result in equitable participation by all students.

Sometimes assessing outcomes can feel anxiety-inducing. For example, an instructor might feel they are to blame for the results that they see. Here we describe a different viewpoint. There are systemic challenges that learners can face, and data can help us make more actionable changes. However, we know that many of these go broader than what a single instructor might be capable of doing in their course, but even within the classroom community changes can be made.

Instructor Outcomes

In higher education we may focus on student outcomes for good reason, as the hope is that students will be transformed through their learning experiences. However, it is important that an instructor considers simultaneously and critically their own outcomes with regards to inclusion so that they can assess their own growth, no matter where they are, to continue growing as an inclusive instructor.

Sample outcomes include awareness of diversity (e.g., cultural awareness), frequency of implementation of inclusive teaching approaches, and the degree of variation in the approaches utilized. Whether an instructor is new to teaching or has been teaching for 30 years, they should be always growing.

Cultural Diversity Awareness

One substantial instructor barrier highlighted in our previous work is awareness of diverse students' inclusivity needs in addition to inclusivity practices themselves (Addy et al., 2021b). For example, instructor growth in cultural competence and humility can be an asset to working with students from various cultures, opening up possibilities for instructors to learn more about their students with a humble mindset and the challenges that they might face, as they facilitate transformative learning experiences. By cultural competence, we refer to being able to work across cultural differences, and by cultural humility acknowledging and respecting those from cultures different from one's own.

A recent study focused on cultural competence of mentors also has potentially transferable implications for teaching in the classroom as well as mentoring students inclusively beyond courses. When instructors underwent professional development in cultural diversity they engaged in more effective mentoring relationships (Byars-Winston et al., 2023). The researchers ran a randomized controlled trial of mentors and undergraduate mentees and found that the mentors who underwent professional development indicated that they were more confident and better able to address diversity scenarios, and their mentees also rated them higher in this ability.

Such cultural diversity awareness for an instructor teaching students in course experiences similarly has the potential to have beneficial effects on students. Thus, one sample instructor outcome is growth in awareness of cultural diversity, while another is being more confident to address scenarios where there is difference. Centers for teaching and learning, as well as multicultural centers, might run initiatives to help increase such awareness.

There exist assessments that can measure growth in cultural competence such as the Intercultural Development Inventory (IDI), a theory-based tool (IDI, n.d.). Tracie had the opportunity to take the IDI as part of a leadership development opportunity. The assessment provides an overview of where someone sits on a continuum from monocultural to intercultural mindsets, where they are able to bridge across differences. The report provides actionable feedback, guiding individuals toward further growth in intercultural development. The assessment also allows for collective understanding of where a group falls, as well as the individual. These types of assessments are tools that instructors can use in their own growth as they work with their students across differences. An instructor's self-reflection of their growth can be useful through journaling or discussion.

Reflection Questions

- In the last year (or other time frame), what, if any, growth have you noticed, regarding the awareness of your own cultural identity and your students' cultural differences or circumstances?
- What are some opportunities that you have on your own campus to grow in your own cultural competence or humility?

Increased Implementation of Inclusive Teaching Approaches

A second major outcome for instructors, depending on their goals and current practices, is more frequent implementation of inclusive teaching approaches. For example, instructors might want to learn more ways to incorporate active learning or other approaches into their courses. The extent to which they do such can be measured through data-driven instruments such as the Protocol for Advancing Inclusive Teaching Efforts described in the previous chapter if the instructional strategy is included on the protocol. In this scenario, the observer can provide the number of occurrences within the time frame of the course and the instructor can monitor whether they see increases in the number of subsequent observations. Additionally, observers could also be asked to quantify other approaches. Simultaneously, noting how the approaches were utilized is important for such observations.

There is no gold standard for the number of times that any particular approach should be used. Implementation is always context specific to a particular course, with a particular instructor, and their learners.

Varied Inclusive Teaching Approaches

Another instructor outcome is the variety of inclusive teaching approaches utilized. By engaging in observation and reflection on their inclusive teaching efforts, instructors can get a sense of the diversity of approaches they implement to foster an equitable learning environment.

Reflection Questions

- Reflect on any inclusive teaching practices that you implement in your courses. What types of approaches do you implement? What is the frequency with which you use such approaches? How broad a scope of approaches do you utilize?
- What might be the next steps for you with regards to the frequency with which you use various approaches and the variation of those approaches?
- What, if any, additional instructor-level outcomes would be meaningful to you?

Student Outcomes

Ultimately, a major goal is that the approaches utilized in the classroom improve the student learning experience. There are a variety of potential student outcomes with a sample noted below, both academic and psychosocial.

Equitable Achievement

As a proxy for achievement, students' grades are accountability measures that are embedded within the framework of many institutions. The problems with grades continue to be described (Kohn & Blum, 2020) as a less than optimal measure of student learning. However, given that grades remain part of the experience of most instructors, as an imperfect measure, examining change in grades in a course, in addition to disaggregated grades by student demographics (e.g., but not limited to race/ethnicity, gender, sexual identity, major, class year, international status, first-generation status), can provide some sense of how students are achieving in a course. Coupled with other outcome measurements, this might provide a helpful story for an instructor to reflect upon their courses and the pedagogical approaches utilized.

For a variety of reasons, inequities could be apparent unrelated to the pedagogical approaches and course design, such as systemic barriers. Yet, there is a body of evidence demonstrating that equity gaps can be reduced using particular inclusive teaching approaches (e.g., Dewsbury et al., 2022). As a standalone measure, the comparison of outcomes does not always tell the full story. Students can have different stories that might contribute to their achievement in a course. Being able to subsequently gain insight into other aspects of students' backgrounds and experiences using additional measures, as noted below, is also important.

Learning Growth

Arguably, even more important than the final measure of a grade is the progress students make in their learning from the beginning to the end of the course. For example, students may enter a course with different levels of preparedness because of inequitable systems, and yet, learn a considerable amount by the end of the course. How even more impactful is the inclusive learning experience if entering students make substantial gains in their learning and it provides a sort of mobility that allows students from less privileged backgrounds to significantly grow?

Within any institution of higher education, students can face obstacles and barriers to their achievement when situations arise in their personal lives whether they be family, financial, health-related, social, or others that can directly affect their ability to successfully complete a course. The final grade that they receive does not shed light on those circumstances with regards to where they started and where they ended. Learning is more than a grade; we can view it as a process and a journey. Assessments such as portfolios and student reflections can provide more insight into the difference between where a student started and where they ended up by the end of the course with regards to their knowledge, skills, and attitudes, and can be even more powerful and insightful markers than a final grade. Ideally an instructor would find that all students are making individual progress in substantial ways. If inequities exist, an instructor can further reflect on how to tailor their teaching approaches to support students who are not experiencing such gains.

Persistence

Completing coursework is the hope of students entering colleges and universities. Having a sense of belonging correlates with student persistence in college (Gopalan & Brady, 2020). A variety of factors can contribute to this and some described have been increased help-seeking and social engagement (Won et al., 2021). A course withdrawal is not necessarily the failure of an instructor—there are many reasons why students might not complete a course that are beyond the instructor's control; sometimes students might need to take time away. Inclusive environments, however, can help students to persist and complete courses. Therefore, an instructor can assess who is completing their courses and who is not.

While presenting on the PAITE, Tracie recalls an audience attendee who worked at a Historically Black College or University indicating that traditional measurements of achievement and grades would not capture the full story of their students. Students might rebound after navigating difficulty and persist in their academic journeys. When creating inclusive environments it's important to remember that overcoming obstacles is also an outcome that can be documented. An instructor might consider not only whether students complete their course as a metric, but also qualify whether such persistence was in the midst of personal hardship or circumstances (if known).

Sense of Belonging

In our first book, *What Inclusive Instructors Do*, we cited a number of studies that describe the significance of students' sense of belonging being critical in higher education (Addy et al., 2021b). Within a course setting, a sense of belonging, and students feeling that they matter and that their perspectives are valued, is critical for fostering an environment where diverse students can grow. Over time, a variety of tools have been deployed to assess students' sense of belonging with colleges, programs, or courses. These include both survey instruments as well as interviews and focus groups for general and targeted groups to better understand student attitudes (Knekta et al., 2020; Yorke, 2016). Such questions can be asked to obtain more insights about the course climate and how it contributes to students' sense of belonging.

Empowerment

While the outcomes thus far have been heavily focused on academic completion and achievement, another potential impact of an inclusive learning experience is students feeling empowered in their learning, increasing their self-efficacy, as well as well-being. The inclusive classroom should be a place of empowerment and self-discovery, allowing students to achieve their maximum potential, exposing them to new ways of thinking, experiences, and people. This empowerment can also encourage more equitable engagement by learners. For assessing this outcome, and analyzing who is contributing to the classroom environment through more equitable engagement, as well as the type of participation, the Equity QUantified In Participation (EQUIP) protocol that we discussed previously in Chapter 6 is a tool that can help classify student engagement (EQUIP App, n.d.), by who is participating and the type of questions that they are answering. Instructors might find that, through implementing different inclusive teaching strategies, they empower more voices to participate in the course, and this might not always be through oral responses. It might also be through creating backchannels where students can contribute to discussions through digital technologies, as noted in other chapters.

Enhanced Connections

A number of students in our study described how they viewed collaborative activities as approaches that can build a more inclusive learning environment. Perhaps not often discussed, courses can be opportunistic times for students to build connections not just with their instructors but with one another. When an instructor sets up opportunities for students to meet, they can form new relationships. One measure of how connections can be built in a course is asking students how many people they know in the class at the beginning of the course and then intentionally setting up opportunities for active learning and small group discussion, both formal and informal, to allow students to interact with one another. At the end of the course, instructors can ask students to reflect on how many new connections they have made through the class and any perceived benefits. While not all student–student connections might blossom, some might be a gateway to peer mentorship as well as academic and social support.

More Accessible Learning

An inclusive classroom can allow diverse students with disabilities, neurodivergent students, students from lower-socioeconomic classes, and first-generation students to have access to an education that allows them to grow and achieve. When instructors create accessible learning environments, they facilitate conditions that allow all students to have access. Sometimes it can be difficult to measure whether or not the pedagogical approaches utilized are opening doors for learners unless asked to students. Such might involve probing students whether various approaches utilized impacted their learning. For example, an instructor might display captions on all videos in class, which can be helpful for all learners including those with hearing impairments.

Relationship Between Instructor and Student Outcomes

To more effectively create an inclusive classroom an instructor should be aware of, and acknowledge, the diversity of learners in their class and use a variety of inclusive teaching approaches throughout class sessions. Such can help create the conditions to allow for various outcomes to be achieved: equitable achievement; enhanced academic progress; sense of belonging; persistence; empowerment and well-being; enhanced social networks; and accessible learning. The instructor and student outcomes can also impact one another. For example, if the instructor utilizes approaches and finds that their students' achievement is somewhat more equitable, they might consider additional approaches they can implement to enhance their students' learning experience.

By selecting a few key outcomes, instructors have already started their journeys to build more inclusive learning environments. A next step is to consider how to "measure" each of these outcomes in meaningful ways and consider how to report it in teaching documentation. An assessment project is an informal measure, typically not a systematic investigation that is disseminated more broadly, and typically only for the instructor's usage.

Reflection Question

- Which student outcomes most resonate with you and your courses?

Sample Assessment Projects

Below are hypothetical examples of projects that an instructor might perform to measure the outcomes of their inclusive teaching efforts.

Example 1: Facilitating Connections

An instructor teaches primarily first-year students in a majors course. In addition to teaching their course material, they aim to foster a welcoming environment for their students as they navigate college and ensure that they connect with peers and develop their social networks within and beyond the course. The instructor embeds a variety of community-building activities that enable students to get to know one another during the course as well as the greater campus community. The instructor is curious as to whether their efforts are making a difference on their students and how. At the beginning of the course, the instructor gives students a survey that asks them to indicate how many other students they have previously interacted with in the course as well as others on campus. At the end of the course the students are surveyed again with regards to how many more connections they have formed through the course and any impacts these have had on their college experience. They find that the students increased the number of connections they formed and were able to obtain peer mentorship and advice, as well as other support through these course activities. They also find that students who were first-generation and international students noted that they particularly benefited from these community connections.

Example 2: A Focus on Growth

An instructor finds themselves dissatisfied with the traditional grading systems they have been using. In their experience, the grading seemed inequitable and disadvantaged students, and also did not completely align with their teaching philosophy of focusing on student growth. They adopt an alternative grading approach for their course, which allows students to demonstrate progress in their learning and skill development in a structured manner. The instructor is curious to know whether their new approaches are leading to their intended outcomes. They incorporate end-of-course reflection assignments where students describe what they know at the beginning of the semester related to course content and how much they learned by the end of the semester. The instructor also separately notes their own observations of student growth. The instructor enjoys reading the essays and, based on these self-reflections and their own observations, finds that some students grew immensely over the course. However, instructors might face teaching scenarios where there are tensions between a focus on growth and on final outcomes that the students achieve. For example, some programs are more stringent or have specialized examinations that students must pass to advance in the profession. In these cases, while student growth in knowledge and skills remains important, ultimately students must develop a basic level of competency to continue in the career.

Example 3: Learning Students' Names

Teaching a large lecture course of over 300 students felt like a large challenge to an instructor to get to know their learners. They wanted to make sure they could still call students by their names and engage with them in dialogue. They decided to implement name tents in the course and took time to call on students by their names. They conducted a few informal check-ins and found that the students commented more upon appreciating the instructor using their name and feeling like more than a number in the course.

Example 4: Student Persistence in a Course

In previous years students had various troubles finishing a required course taught by an instructor. The withdrawal rate was concerning. The instructor has a conversation with their department chair about ways to improve the course that still allow students to achieve their learning goals. The instructor decides to do a more in-depth assessment of why students have not historically been persisting in this course. They have approval to hire an assistant who performs confidential interviews with students who did not finish the course to ask them what made it difficult for them. The findings pointed to a particular major assignment in the course that seemingly served as a gatekeeper for students with less academic preparation. Many of the students who withdrew found that their own personal circumstances prevented them from completing this assignment and because it was worth such a high percentage of their grade this was a barrier for them. As a result, the instructor made several changes by modifying the assignment using the Transparency in Learning and Teaching framework (TILT), which focuses on creating assignments that have a clearly defined purpose, tasks, and criteria for assessment (TILT Higher Ed, n.d.). The instructor broke the assignment down into smaller assignments rather than a single assignment with a high percentage of grades. They also implemented more opportunities for students to ask questions about the assignment.

Advice for Educational Developers

You can be an integral partner to instructors who are looking to measure the outcomes of their efforts by providing valuable guidance and stepping through how to carry out such assessment projects.

Share the assessment framework described earlier with the instructors with whom you partner and use it to scaffold them as they build out designs for their assessment projects. If you know of other instructors who have performed such work, consider also connecting them with one another for peer mentorship and guidance. In this way, you as an educational developer can serve the important role of a broker (Addy & Frederick, 2023). You can also hold specific drop-in hours or initiatives for these purposes. For some institutions, educational developers can play key roles in supporting departments in their assessment for accreditation purposes.

As an example, perhaps an instructor of a first-year writing intensive course suspects that there is inequitable achievement in their course. They observe how students enter the course with a wide range of writing skills with about a third of the class lacking substantial early opportunities to develop as writers. The instructor decides to implement a fail-forward approach at the beginning of the semester, weighting early writing assignments less and providing more formative low-stakes opportunities for students to practice their writing early in the course. You step through the assessment framework with them as described below:

- Disciplinary challenge—incoming students vary in their writing skills, which can result in inequities as they seek to gain a foothold on college writing
- Pedagogical goals—to provide students with more opportunities to develop their writing using approaches gives all students an opportunity to improve
- Choose an appropriate scope for the project—this project is implemented in one course
- List expected outcomes—all students will develop stronger writing skills
- Specify data sources and formulate an assessment plan—the instructor plans to use an adapted Written Communication AAC&U rubric to assesses students' writing skills on assignments from the beginning of the semester, and at the end, and compare in a course before the intervention as well as in one after; they disaggregate the data by student demographics
- Gather preliminary data/information—the instructor gathered available student demographic information
- Implement project and collect data—they implemented their project
- Analyze data, draw conclusions, and consider next steps—they find that after the intervention students' writing is stronger

If you need more experience with outcomes assessment, consider what training or resources might support your work. The Assessment Institute in Indianapolis is an annual conference with a Faculty Development track. Associated with the Institute are a publication and a podcast on relevant topics in assessment. The Association of American Colleges and Universities also hosts conferences on assessment and has a variety of resources.

Reflection Questions

- Consider a course and choose one or two outcomes for inclusive teaching. How might you measure them?
- What might help you better assess outcomes of your teaching efforts?

Conducting a Study

Those interested in delving deeper into a systematic investigation that can be presented and published to inform the field about equity work might consider writing scholarly articles on their efforts. If data will be shared, this typically involves completing training on conducting research with human participants. Such studies involve participants providing informed consent prior to engaging in a research project. Typically, classroom studies are approved with exemption status. However, it's also possible for instructors to write about their teaching in a more narrative style, such as a reflective essay that does not involve a formal research study. Additionally, some instructors might consider writing op-ed articles to share their work on inclusive teaching. Such writing can be a starting point for further work.

Why would an instructor want to publish their own study? There are a variety of reasons. Such scholarship allows an instructor to disseminate their work more broadly and make a more public contribution to teaching and learning. Other instructors might find their work inspiring and use it to inform their own practices. Within some institutions, performing scholarly research on teaching and learning can be used for promotion and tenure review processes to document teaching excellence. An increasing number of disciplinary journals publish articles focused on teaching and learning.

With regards to inclusive learning environments in higher education, there are several areas of potential which would benefit from more research. If your work falls within these topic areas, consider if you want to share it with others.

- Alternative grading approaches
- Specific inclusive teaching approaches and their measurable impacts
- Teaching neurodivergent learners and students with learning disabilities in higher education
- Teaching inclusively as an instructor of color at historically White institutions
- Teaching inclusively as an international faculty member at U.S. institutions
- Teaching as a faculty member with a disability
- Equity and emerging technologies, such as generative artificial intelligence in higher education
- Student mental health and impacts on learning

Research in teaching and learning follows particular methodologies that can be learned. There are a variety of books that can help instructors get started, such as *Engaging in the Scholarship of Teaching and Learning: A Guide to the Process, and How to Develop a Project from Start to Finish* (Bishop-Clark & Dietz-Uhler, 2012). Additionally, centers for teaching and learning staff or colleagues who have conducted such research, may be able to provide helpful guidance. Look into whether your main disciplinary societies have sections focused on teaching and learning. These might provide opportunities to present your work.

To support the scholarship of teaching and learning (SoTL), students can be co-researchers on SoTL projects (Waller & Prosser, 2023). If involved in a research study that will be disseminated, just like the researcher, they will need to complete Human Subjects Training. Typically, such information is housed on the Institutional Review Board's website at a college or university. Tracie has had experiences working with faculty who work with undergraduate research assistants on SoTL projects. This can considerably support their work and efforts, and potentially be valued by certain institutions' promotion and tenure processes.

Instructors need not share their work in only research article format. There are a number of journals that invite writing of other types, such as more journalistic-style essays, lessons learned articles, classroom lessons, as well as op-ed articles. Sharing reflections or opinions on inclusive teaching practices more broadly can help initiate dialogues around higher education teaching and learning. There is typically a shorter onramp to writing such pieces compared with when data from a systematic investigation is being shared that has undergone required Institutional Review Board processes.

Advice for Educational Developers

The Professional and Organizational Development Network in Higher Education (POD Network) special interest group on the Scholarship of Teaching and Learning and the International Society for the Scholarship of Teaching and Learning (ISOTTL) can be helpful resources for educational developers who conduct scholarly research or partner with instructors on such work.

To support instructors in their SoTL work, develop communities of practice that allow instructors to get support as well as mentor others in their research. In addition, provide funding for SoTL work. In Tracie's experience, some of the biggest challenges that instructors face when performing SoTL is knowing how to design a study and how to juggle their teaching scholarship with their other responsibilities. Sometimes short op-ed or reflective pieces might be the most feasible for some instructors.

Additionally, MegaSoTL projects are promising ways for instructors to combine efforts in their scholarship (Mojarad & Cruz, 2022). These projects examine specific research questions and involve collaborations between several researchers. Educational developers can provide an infrastructure for carrying out such research and allow for the measurement of outcomes beyond a single course.

Advice for Instructors from Groups Historically Excluded

Research and perspectives published on and by instructors from groups historically excluded who are teaching in higher education are much needed in the field. The dominant voices in much of the teaching and learning literature are often those from majority demographic backgrounds but the experiences of faculty of color, international faculty, neurodivergent faculty and faculty with disabilities, LGBTQIA+ faculty, and instructors of additional social identities are lacking. We truly need to hear more diverse voices. Consider whether there are contributions that you can share more broadly to have a wider audience than within a single institution. As an example, the book chapters in *Picture a Professor: Interrupting Biases about Faculty and Increasing Student Learning* (Neuhaus, 2022) provide advice through the experiences of instructors from diverse backgrounds including instructors identifying as blind, faculty of color, queer, and transgender (e.g., Mayes-Tang, 2022).

Additional Sample Articles

The projects below represent examples already published in the literature to give instructors a sense of what they can do.

Op-ed article: Pittman and Tobin published the op-ed article "Academe Has a Lot to Learn About How Inclusive Teaching Affects Instructors," which makes a call to the field to further investigate the impacts of instructor identity on implementation of inclusive teaching approaches (Tobin & Pittman, 2022). This type of article can help encourage further research and dialogue that looks at outcomes where there are gaps in the literature; in this case, the impacts of inclusive teaching on instructors from identities historically excluded.

Research article in online teaching: This example is an intersection of classroom climate and social presence with assessment and growth of students. In a study of the feedback channel provided in an online course environment for a written assignment, researchers compared how much students improved and their perceptions of the type of feedback they received, whether text, audio, or video (Espasa et al., 2022). They found that the type of feedback received made no significant difference to student performance, however students perceived that the video feedback was more effective and enabled them to feel more connected to the instructor.

Lesson-style article: Sometimes an instructor might publish a lesson or framework that others could model. Tan and Venkatesh (2023) shared the framework they developed to create more inclusive scientific journal club sessions. In their article they highlight how they use backward design to create more inclusive journal club meetings.

Investigation of the first-year experience: Researchers were interested in how social support played a role in the academic experiences of first-year students (Wilcox et al., 2005). Through their qualitative analysis of 34 interviews with first-year students, they found that finding friends that were compatible was essential for learners to feel a part of the institution. Making friends with people in their classes, as well as with peer mentors and others, was also important, and provided different types of support distinct from compatible friendships.

Conclusion

By measuring the outcomes of their inclusive teaching efforts, instructors can leverage change within their classrooms that can have large impacts. Determining which outcomes to assess and taking steps to gather the information needed are critical. Having a mindset of continual improvement is essential to the growth of any instructor. Assessment can be a vehicle for change.

References

Addy, T. M., & Frederick, J. (2023). Educational developers as conveners, brokers, and expansionists: How networks enhance our work. *The Journal of Faculty Development*, 37(1), 35–40.

Addy, T. M., Dube, D., Mitchell, K. A., & SoRelle, M. (2021a). *What inclusive instructors do: Principles and practices for excellence in college teaching*. Sterling, VA: Stylus Publishing.

Addy, T. M., Reeves, P. M., Dube, D., & Mitchell, K. A. (2021b). What really matters for instructors implementing equitable and inclusive teaching approaches. *To Improve the Academy: A Journal of Educational Development*, 40(1), Article 1. doi:10.3998/tia.182.

Bishop-Clark, C., & Dietz-Uhler, B. (2012). *Engaging in the scholarship of teaching and learning: A guide to the process, and how to develop a project from start to finish*. New York and London: Routledge.

Byars-Winston, A., Rogers, J. G., Thayer-Hart, N., Black, S., Branchaw, J., & Pfund, C. (2023). A randomized controlled trial of an intervention to increase cultural diversity awareness of research mentors of undergraduate students. *Science Advances*, 9(21), eadf9705. doi:10.1126/sciadv.adf9705.

Dewsbury, B. M., Swanson, H. J., Moseman-Valtierra, S., & Caulkins, J. (2022). Inclusive and active pedagogies reduce academic outcome gaps and improve long-term performance. *PLOS ONE*, 17(6), e0268620. doi:10.1371/journal.pone.0268620.

EQUIP App. (n.d.). Retrieved June 13, 2023, from https://www.equip.ninja/.

Espasa, A., Mayordomo, R. M., Guasch, T., & Martinez-Melo, M. (2022). Does the type of feedback channel used in online learning environments matter? Students' perceptions and impact on learning. *Active Learning in Higher Education, 23*(1), 49–63. doi:10.1177/1469787419891307.

Gillis, A. (2019). Reconceptualizing participation grading as skill building. *Teaching Sociology*, 47(1), 10–21. doi:10.1177/0092055X18798006.

Gopalan, M., & Brady, S. T. (2020). College students' sense of belonging: A national perspective. *Educational Researcher, 49*(2), 134–137. doi:10.3102/0013189X19897622.

Intercultural Development Inventory (IDI). (n.d.). Retrieved August 30, 2023, from https://www.idiinventory.com/.

Knekta, E., Chatzikyriakidou, K., & McCartney, M. (2020). Evaluation of a questionnaire measuring university students' sense of belonging to and involvement in a biology department. *CBE—Life Sciences Education*, 19(3), article 27. doi:10.1187/cbe.19-09-0166.

Kohn, A., & Blum, S. D. (2020). *Ungrading: Why rating students undermines learning (and what to do instead).* Morgantown, WV: West Virginia University Press. https://muse.jhu.edu/pub/20/edited_volume/book/78367.

Kumar, R., & Refaei, B. (Eds.). (2021). *Equity and inclusion in higher education: Strategies for teaching.* Cincinnati, OH: University of Cincinnati Press. https://press.uchicago.edu/ucp/books/book/distributed/E/bo135973059.html.

Mayes-Tang, S. (2022). Sharing our stories to build community, highlight bias, and address challenges to authority. In J. Neuhaus (Ed.), *Picture a professor: Interrupting biases about faculty and increasing student learning.* Morgantown, WV: West Virginia University Press.

Mojarad, S. N., & Cruz, L. (2022). MegaSoTL: Supporting pedagogical research across multiple institutions. *To Improve the Academy: A Journal of Educational Development*, 41(2), article 2. doi:10.3998/tia.470.

Neuhaus, J. (Ed.) (2022). *Picture a professor: Interrupting biases about faculty and increasing student learning.* Morgantown, WV: West Virginia University Press. http://wvupressonline.com/picture-a-professor.

Tan, T. M., & Venkatesh, M. J. (2023). Reimagining journal clubs for inclusive scientific training. *Trends in Cell Biology*, 33(7), 531–535. doi:10.1016/j.tcb.2023.03.012.

TiLT Higher Ed. (n.d.) Retrieved August 31, 2023, from https://tilthighered.com/.

Tobin, T. J., & Pittman, C. (2022, February 7). Advice | Academe has a lot to learn about how inclusive teaching affects instructors. *The Chronicle of Higher Education.* https://www.chronicle.com/article/academe-has-a-lot-to-learn-about-how-inclusive-teaching-affects-instructors.

Waller, K. L., & Prosser, M. (2023). The rapidly changing teaching and research landscape: The future of SoTL and the Teaching-Research Nexus. In K. Coleman, D. Uzhegova, B. Blaher, & S. Arkoudis (Eds.), *The educational turn: Rethinking the scholarship of teaching and learning in higher education* (pp. 27–41). Singapore: Springer Nature. doi:10.1007/978-981-19-8951-3_3.

Wilcox, P., Winn, S., & Fyvie-Gauld, M. (2005). "It was nothing to do with the university, it was just the people": The role of social support in the first-year experience of higher education. *Studies in Higher Education*, 30(6), 707–722. doi:10.1080/03075070500340036.

Won, S., Hensley, L. C., & Wolters, C. A. (2021). Brief research report: Sense of belonging and academic help-seeking as self-regulated learning. *The Journal of Experimental Education*, 89(1), 112–124. doi:10.1080/00220973.2019.1703095.
Yorke, M. (2016). The development and initial use of a survey of student "belongingness", engagement and self-confidence in UK higher education. *Assessment & Evaluation in Higher Education*, 41, 154–166. doi:10.1080/02602938.2014.990415.

PART III

Critical and Emerging Topics in Higher Education

8

TRANSFORMING DEPARTMENTAL AND INSTITUTIONAL CULTURE

In this chapter we explore how to support the adoption of inclusive teaching beyond the level of the instructor based on the major themes shared in this book. Specifically, we discuss the roles that departments and administrators within institutional leadership can play in advancing inclusive teaching efforts across the institution.

Departmental Approaches

The department is a critical unit for cultivating inclusion within and beyond the course level and more broadly across the curriculum, as there is power in a department that is unified with regards to inclusive teaching. Departments have their own cultures, values, norms, and procedures. If the inclusion of the students who take the departmental courses and the faculty who teach them is a core value, there are actions departments can take that can make a large impact. The collective efforts of multiple instructors have the potential to expand inclusion efforts more than an individual instructor can do on their own and can make a substantial difference to students who take a number of courses within a department. In this chapter we describe how departments can use the information within this book to build more inclusive environments for their learners.

Building Community

The importance of community emerges throughout this book, particularly in discussions around the learning communities within courses. Students expressed how when they feel connected to their instructors and other

DOI: 10.4324/9781003442929-11

students they feel more included in the course. Similarly, at the departmental level, community matters. For departments, community can also be particularly important to create a sense of belonging for students. Departments can foster community with their students in a variety of ways. One example is to create a yearbook or photomontage of all majors to learn their names and their interests. This can help instructors better learn the names of the students within their courses and their learners know the name of their classmates. In addition, retreats or gatherings with students can allow them to meet their peers as well as get to know their professors. Departmental poster sessions or exhibitions can be a great way for students to showcase their learning and skills as well as build community.

While efforts often focus on the importance of building student–student, student–instructor, student–staff communities within departments, critically important is the community that instructors feel within their departmental community. Instructors particularly vulnerable to exclusion are those from historically excluded communities (e.g., women in male-dominated fields, instructors of color in STEM, and disciplines where they are underrepresented) as well as instructors who are not on the tenure-track (Kezar, 2013). When instructors do not feel a sense of community, whether due to the departmental culture or not, their basic human needs are not being met. Departments not only need to take care of their students, but also one another.

Reflection Questions

- In which community-building activities does your department engage?
- Do all members of your department feel a sense of community? If you do not know, how can you find out?

Recruitment and Retention of a Diverse Faculty

First and foremost, departments should strive to recruit and retain a diverse faculty. Such diversity matters with regards to student outcomes for inclusion (Cross & Carman, 2022; Llamas et al., 2021; Sandhu et al., 2022). The benefits are multifaceted and can lead to positive outcomes for diverse students such as increased graduation rates (Bowman & Denson, 2022; Stout et al., 2018). Recruitment strategies include bias training for search committees, cluster hiring multiple faculty from diverse backgrounds, and recruitment of faculty from diverse pools. Retention strategies should focus both on providing structural support and enhancing the social capital of historically excluded faculty members. Examples include creating review committees focused on diversity, equity, and inclusion; aligning missions and actions; creating support systems that hold members accountable for oppressive acts; sharing leadership pipelines for a diverse faculty; and developing communities of practice such as mentorship and affinity groups (Banks, 2022, 194–195).

Departmental Discussions

Various support structures and initiatives within departments can support instructor adoption of inclusive teaching approaches. Collectively reading this book, or other relevant books, and holding discussions as a whole department are a powerful way to continue or start conversations on inclusive teaching. These discussions can allow instructors to share their experiences and knowledge and provide information for departments to develop plans to create more inclusive environments for their learners. Discussion questions might include the following, which could be brought up as ongoing discussion topics at departmental meetings as a thread. Or, alternatively, departments might hold a brown bag or other lunch discussions. A year-end retreat can even focus on action planning for the next year about inclusive teaching.

Reflection Questions

Below are several starter questions for departmental conversations.

- Who are the students who take our courses? What do we know about their backgrounds, experiences, attitudes, and individuality? How are we taking that into account in the course that we teach?
- What do we value as a department with regards to inclusive teaching and learning?
- What are examples of research-supported inclusive teaching strategies within our discipline?
- Are there ableist teaching approaches being utilized that we must reconsider?

Course Design:

- How do we maximize student engagement in our courses?
- What is the average workload for our various courses and is it inclusive for our learners?
- What are course setups that our students have really appreciated that support their success?
- How do we obtain informal student feedback on our courses?
- Which courses integrate diversity or social justice topics?

Welcoming Environment:

- What strategies are we using to create a welcoming environment in our courses?

Conducting Class Sessions:

- What are the different approaches we use to conduct class inclusively?
- Do we give students enough time to complete work while they juggle other classes and activities?

Reflection and Observation:

- How did our inclusive teaching approaches go the last time we taught?
- What are some ways we can informally observe one another to support inclusion efforts?

Endorsement of Inclusive Teaching Approaches

In having conversations around inclusive teaching and the disciplinary context, departments might choose to endorse particular research-supported teaching approaches for instructors to utilize in their course. Oftentimes teaching is viewed as an individual and siloed activity even within a departmental unit. While still allowing for agency for how instructors teach, general approaches might be agreed upon as a values statement. For example, a department might agree upon problem-based learning as an active learning approach as critical to developing students' knowledge and critical thinking skills. Such is not to say that other approaches are not sanctioned by the department, but that particular ones are agreed upon more globally to implement.

A major theme that emerged in the study is students indicating that lecture-only approaches are not inclusive. Such teaching focuses on the delivery of information and may not take into account the science of learning and how diverse students process and make sense of this information. Departments collectively, through their shared values, can counter such approaches and agree upon teaching students in more inclusive manners. Additionally, highlighting examples of instructors implementing inclusive teaching approaches at department meetings and other gatherings can support knowledge-sharing and collaboration. Sometimes such conversations are difficult to have within departments. One promising approach is incorporating student voices as a lever. Students who have taken departmental courses can advocate for the type of learning that most engages them. If newer faculty reach a critical mass, they too can advocate and initiate change. Additionally, senior faculty members of influence within a department can also play the role of advocates. In our previous study we found that data-driven approaches, such as reviewing departmental data on student outcomes, can be seen as a driving factor to change practice (Addy et al., 2021).

Observations of Inclusive Teaching Approaches

There are various departmental usages of the PAITE for instructors to obtain low-stakes observational feedback on their inclusive teaching approaches. Instructors can consider various models based on what makes the most sense for their contexts. Student pedagogical partners can be trained to use the PAITE and be paired with faculty within the department to conduct observations. Trained students might include teaching assistants, supplemental instructors, and advisory committees of student boards. Additionally, if there are educational developers within the institution, they might also be able to conduct the observations and provide feedback. Student pedagogical partners who work with educational developers can also be trained to conduct the observations. Departments can set up spaces where instructors share what they learn from using the PAITE during departmental meetings to advance conversations and actions around inclusive teaching.

Instructor Peer Mentorship

Depending on the departmental context and culture, faculty members can use the PAITE within each other's courses in a mutualistic, reciprocal manner as a peer observation of teaching initiative. Peer mentorship, both formal and informal, can be helpful to connect instructors and allow them to learn from one another. For example, instructors within a department may teach the same courses, the same students, and navigate specific disciplinary teaching issues. Being able to speak with other instructors and brainstorm ideas, and potentially observe one another's courses can support efforts toward inclusion. Instructors within departments with multi-section courses can also partner to implement inclusive approaches. These interactions can help instructors grow in their efforts in a smaller environment with more focused engagement. Pairings need not necessarily be a more and less experienced instructor, although that might be beneficial depending on the context. These mentorship groups can also provide opportunities for reflection on teaching.

Valuing the Scholarship of Teaching and Learning

Taking a scholarly approach to inclusive teaching can look like many things, from reading the literature on research-based practices to engaging in the scholarship of teaching and learning by performing research studies or writing on practices to disseminate efforts much more broadly. There can be value in departmental colleagues collaborating across sections of a course or course topics within the discipline. One of the barriers that instructors can experience when they are interested in sharing their work is that their department or institutional rewards system does not support it; therefore, this type of work might not be prioritized over disciplinary scholarship. Effective teaching, however, is based on a body of peer-reviewed literature. Being knowledgeable about pedagogical approaches that can facilitate equitable learning environments can only make departmental teaching stronger if upheld in practice. It can help mitigate equity gaps and lack of persistence, among other challenges that students within departmental courses can face. Using research-supported approaches and gaining a better understanding of how individual teaching can impact students are not just more effective for advancing equity, they are more efficient teaching. The scholarship of teaching and learning can help give understanding of local contexts within a departmental course.

Departmental Climate

Many departments can benefit from climate studies, which can provide direct insight into the effects that inclusive teaching approaches have had on students as well as other important data. In addition to hearing the voices of students, climate studies can benefit from instructors and academic and research support staff.

Instructor Voice

Critical to any inclusive teaching efforts are the perspectives and well-being of the instructor who teach the students. Understanding any obstacles faculty face in adoption, as well as actions they are taking toward inclusivity is essential to the further implementation of such practices and resulting outcomes. In addition, hearing the experiences of faculty of color, adjunct faculty, international instructors, and faculty members from additional historically excluded groups and taking action upon any needed areas is particularly important given the systemic and additional barriers these instructors can face in implementing inclusive teaching approaches. If instructors are using inclusive teaching approaches, departmental colleagues can put in a good word for them as advocates.

Academic and Research Support Staff Voice

A second critical voice is that of the staff who support departmental efforts. These might include coordinators, administrative assistants, and others who play such roles within departments. What is their experience like with regards to the support they have to do their work? What are their perceptions of challenges students in the departments face with regards to inclusion?

Student Voice

Asking students about their experiences around belonging, mattering, and inclusivity is important as well as changes that might improve their experiences. Reaching out to specific groups of students at key junctures can be particularly informative. For example, in many disciplines, the foundational courses are critical junctures for students. These include the "Introduction to..." or "Principles of..." series of courses. Learning about students' experiences in those courses can allow any interventions to be undertaken to support inclusive practices. Additionally, there has been work which demonstrates that certain experiences, such as early student involvement in research, can support inclusion (see the Persistence Framework in Graham et al., 2013). Students who are further along in college such as those enrolled in capstone courses can provide valuable, more longitudinal insights into learners' experiences within the department. Departments might choose to reach out to students who changed their major. Another critical group is alumni, who have since graduated from the institution. They can share how their learning impacted their engagements after college.

Listening to the voices of students historically excluded from higher education such as first-generation students, students of color, students with disabilities, and more is particularly important in order to learn about their experiences and to take appropriate action.

Curriculum

We hope that throughout this book we have described how belonging and equity are important and how fostering a sense of belonging and creating equitable experiences is as critical as building students' content knowledge and skills. The curriculum is also a space in which to foster inclusion. This includes the types of course material included for courses that have the potential to resonate with a diversity of learners. For example, instructors can provide diverse examples, authors, and perspectives, as highlighted in Chapter 2. Further, assessment and grading practices are tied to inclusive practices.

Earlier we described the importance of formative assessments and the inequities that can result from the reliance on just a few high-stakes assessments in a course. Some segments in higher education have also more widely come to a moment of reckoning regarding traditional grading practices and instead use alternatives such as ungrading, contract grading, specifications grading, and other approaches. Departmental course mapping that tracks how goals for equity and inclusivity are infused across the curriculum is an intentional act that can support broader integration.

High-Impact Educational Practices

There are a variety of high impact practices that can facilitate more equitable learning for students (Kuh, 2008). These include capstone courses and projects, collaborative assignments and projects, common intellectual experiences, diversity/global learning, ePortfolios, first-year seminars and experiences, internships, learning communities, community engaged learning, undergraduate research, and writing intensive courses. Departments can play a key role in developing and engaging their students to these learning experiences. Throughout this book, students have mentioned the importance of when their instructors set up environments that allow them to connect with other students. Collaborative assignments and projects can facilitate such interactions as well as other high-impact practices. *Delivering on the Promise of High-Impact Practices: Research and Models for Achieving Equity, Fidelity, Impact, and Scale* provides several case examples of how such practices can be integrated to support equitable learning (Zilvinskis et al., 2022).

Assessment of Progress

Data-driven approaches, through regular cycles of informal and formal feedback, can be useful for departments to identify needed inclusion efforts (Addy et al., 2021). How to gather this feedback is context dependent. Department meeting discussions, one-on-one interviews, surveys, or focus groups are each possibilities. When feedback solicited is more for formal processes, involving an external source or evaluator, or entity outside of the department, allows for confidentiality and an outside perspective or outside advice. Departments can also request external evaluators to address DEI efforts when regular external reviews occur. These types of climate studies and investigations should capture the experiences of students enrolled within the department as well as faculty. Formalizing this process might involve a department creating a strategic plan for inclusion. Departments can also consider forming subcommittees tasked to create such a plan. Plans might focus on the outcomes that they want to see with regards to their students and the ways that they will alter the curriculum and pedagogy, or create other structures and resources that can advance such outcomes. Hearing from multiple voices is critical, including instructors, support staff, and students.

Ongoing Professional Development

Continuous development is an integral part of being an effective instructor. Departments can engage with available on-campus supports if there are educational developers present or external support to learn more about how to be an effective instructor. As revealed through the COVID-19 pandemic, as well as the sophistication of, and increased access to, generative artificial intelligence, higher education is impacted by circumstances and society. Instructors must come to expect change, and that they will also continue to learn and grow. In many professions, such as business to healthcare, change is constantly occurring. Higher education is not immune to such change as well, and ongoing learning and adaptability remain a critical aspect of the profession. Having a departmental community as a support structure through such changes can make a difference.

Reflection Questions

- If you had to focus your efforts on a few departmental approaches for inclusion as discussed above, which would you choose, why, and how could you go about making progress?
- How can you collectively as a department advance inclusive teaching and learning?

Institutional Efforts

A Culture of Cultural Competence and Humility

Being able to appreciate a diversity of people and work across different cultures is critical for any institution of higher education in educating a diverse student population. Such cultural competence is important for students as they interact with others who are different from themselves, as well as take classes from potentially a diverse faculty. Students might enter the institution with much variability in their cultural competence. Instructors and staff might vary as well. We cannot assume that all students have had an opportunity to develop such mindsets and skill sets. Lack of cultural competence and humility can result in lack of inclusion and members of the institutional community feeling as if they do not belong or matter. For an institution to more successfully build an inclusive campus, either virtual or online, there should be a prevailing culture wherein the "isms," such as sexism and racism, are not acceptable, and members of the community work together to ensure that all will be treated with respect. Cultural competence and humility are foundational for positive student–student and student–instructor interactions in every course.

There has been some work demonstrating that online modules can support first-year undergraduate students from majority group backgrounds in developing cultural competence (Robey & Dickter, 2022). There is also evidence that similar development for faculty and staff can lead to positive outcomes (Goldstein Hode et al., 2018; Hutchins & Goldstein Hode, 2021). Institutions should consider how they can support such development, whether through Student Affairs or Academic Affairs initiatives, whichever institutional structures are the most appropriate for the context.

Early Student Social Belonging Interventions

Institutions can implement interventions that may help first-year students to thrive at the institution. One notable initiative is the Social Belonging for College Students project (Walton et al., 2023). This intervention involved over 20,000 incoming students at more than 20 institutions who completed an online exercise prior to starting college. The exercise normalized the challenges that college students can face using survey data and the testimonials of current or previous students. The first-year students wrote reflections to future students on what they had learned. The students within institutions with more resources that supported learners' sense of belonging experienced greater positive outcomes related to persistence and belonging. Other institutions can learn from these types of interventions in conjunction with the efforts that instructors can play at the level of the classroom during key college junctures. These types of interventions can further enhance the inclusive teaching approaches being implemented in courses, tackling the issues at multiple levels.

Data-Informed Institutional Assessments

In general, institutions can use assessment to better understand the culture around inclusion in courses. They can hire an external consultant to conduct a climate study and disaggregate the data to gain insights into the experiences of students, faculty, and staff members. A variety of established instruments might be considered depending on the goals and objectives of the institutional assessment. For example, the USC Race and Equity Center administers different versions of the National Assessment of Collegiate Campus Climates (NACCC) for students, faculty, and staff—multiple key voices across an institution. The focus of these climate studies is on racial equity (USC Race and Equity Center, n.d.). One content area of the NACCC student survey is Mattering and Affirmation. These questions assess students' perspectives on mattering both in classroom and other spaces and how they are affirmed by their instructors. Recall that the PAITE contains the code "AFFIRM," which focuses on the affirmative language that an instructor uses with their learners. Imagining the usage of this code quite frequently could lead to students as a whole at the institution responding that their instructors frequently use such language. Other content areas on the NACCC student survey include Cross-Racial Engagement, Racial Learning and Literacy, Encounters with Racial Stress, Appraisals of Institutional Commitment, and Impact of External Environments. For Cross-Racial Engagement, the usage of more collaborative course activities, such as group work where students can engage with other students from diverse backgrounds, can increase such engagement. Growing in cultural competence skills can support more positive interactions between students. Similarly, Racial Learning and Literacy questions implicate course design and curricula. Using diverse course content can speak to a more diverse student population. Imagine an institution where inclusive teaching practices are predominant across courses with some expected variation. Findings of this survey would ideally demonstrate that students, especially those from groups historically excluded when the data are disaggregated, are being affirmed, feel as if they matter, are engaging in positive collaborative activities with other students, and the curriculum resonates with them.

Another established instrument that can provide institutions with more global measures of the student experience is the National Survey of Student Engagement (NSSE) (*NSSE*, n.d.). The NSSE has questions categorized into the following major themes, each with their own indicators: Academic Challenge, Learning with Peers, Experiences with Faculty, and Campus Environment. Under the theme Learning with Peers, there is a heavy emphasis on collaborative learning, much aligned with our student voices findings where they perceived group work to be a more inclusive approach to learning. Regarding the second theme, Learning with Others, discussions with diverse individuals within and outside of the classroom, has the potential to support students in their cultural competence abilities to work across differences. The real-world connections code on the PAITE aligns with Reflective & Integrative Learning within the Academic Challenge theme. Sample questions on the 2023 NSSE that distill key aspects of diversity and inclusion on a more global scale include:

1. To what extent do you agree or disagree with the following statements?
   - I feel comfortable being myself at this institution.
   - I feel valued by this institution.
   - I feel like part of the community at this institution.
2. How much has your experience at this institution contributed to your knowledge, skills, and personal development in the following areas?
   - Understanding people of other backgrounds (economic, racial/ethnic, political, religious, nationality, etc.).

So far we have discussed various instruments that focus on students' experience. The faculty NACCC also asks questions that focus on workplace mattering, equity, and encounters with racial stress, which we previously mentioned as critical for instructors within departments to do their best work. Additionally, there are questions that address instructors' attitudes and implementation of inclusive teaching approaches. Institutions with a true commitment to inclusion would be expected to have prominent findings that demonstrate that their employees feel valued and that they espouse inclusive mindsets and implement such approaches. The Collaborative on Academic Careers in Higher Education (COACHE) Faculty Job Satisfaction Survey is another instrument that can be used to provide an understanding of the experiences of instructors at an institution with regards to the many facets of the work that they do including teaching (Collaborative on Academic Careers in Higher Education, n.d.).

Some institutions might prefer to design and administer their own survey instruments, if they have the capacity, or add questions to the established instruments. Some examples of institutional surveys are Stanford's IDEAL study (Stanford University, n.d.) and Penn State's PULSE survey (Penn State University Student Affairs, n.d.).

Reflection Questions

Below are several starter questions for institutional conversations, mirroring those provided for departments.

- Who are the students at our institution? What do we know about their backgrounds, experiences, attitudes, and individuality? How are we taking that into account in the learning experiences that we design?
- What do we value as an institution with regards to inclusive teaching and learning?
- What are examples of research-supported inclusive teaching strategies within our institution?
- Are there any ableist teaching approaches being utilized that we must reconsider?

Curriculum:

- How do we maximize student engagement in our core curriculum if one exists?
- How do we obtain informal student feedback on our core curriculum?
- Which courses integrate diversity or social justice topics?

Welcoming Environment:

- What strategies are we using to create a welcoming environment across learning experiences?

Reflection and Observation:

- How can we hold ourselves accountable for making these changes?

Advice for Department Chairs, Allies, and Advocates

When engaging in departmental climate studies or other assessments related to inclusion, be mindful of who you ask to engage in these roles. If there are few instructors from groups historically excluded, take care to not always ask them for extra service and consider other colleagues who would also thoughtfully invest in such work. Be aware of the challenges that instructors from groups historically excluded can face in classroom teaching, including bias. Believe instructors if they tell you that they have been experiencing challenges and take them seriously.

Conclusion

Departments and programs are critical units within institutions where much change can occur to support the inclusion of students. This chapter presents a number of strategies to support such efforts. Change at the institution level is also discussed and critical for fostering inclusion within higher education.

References

Addy, T. M., Reeves, P. M., Dube, D., & Mitchell, K. A. (2021). What really matters for instructors implementing equitable and inclusive teaching approaches. *To Improve the Academy: A Journal of Educational Development*, 40(1), article 1. doi:10.3998/tia.182.

Banks, T. M. (2022). Black talent: Practical retention strategies. In A. M. Allen & J. T. Stewart (Eds.), *We're not okay: Black faculty experiences and higher education strategies* (pp. 194–195). Cambridge: Cambridge University Press.

Bowman, N. A., & Denson, N. (2022). Institutional racial representation and equity gaps in college graduation. *The Journal of Higher Education*, 93(3), 399–423. doi:10.1080/00221546.2021.1971487.

Collaborative on Academic Careers in Higher Education, H. U. G. S. of E. (n.d.). *Faculty Job Satisfaction Survey*. Retrieved June 26, 2023, from https://coache.gse.harvard.edu/faculty-job-satisfaction-survey.

Cross, J. D., & Carman, C. A. (2022). The relationship between faculty diversity and student success in public community colleges. *Community College Journal of Research and Practice*, 46(12), 855–868. doi:10.1080/10668926.2021.1910595.

Goldstein Hode, M., Behm-Morawitz, E., & Hays, A. (2018). Testing the effectiveness of an online diversity course for faculty and staff. *Journal of Diversity in Higher Education*, 11(3), 347–365. doi:10.1037/dhe0000063.

Graham, M. J., Frederick, J., Byars-Winston, A., Hunter, A. B., & Handelsman J. (2013). Science education. Increasing persistence of college students in STEM. *Science*, 341(6153), 1455–1456. doi:10.1126/science.1240487. PMID: 24072909; PMCID: PMC10167736.

Hutchins, D., & Goldstein Hode, M. (2021). Exploring faculty and staff development of cultural competence through communicative learning in an online diversity course. *Journal of Diversity in Higher Education*, 14(4), 468–479. doi:10.1037/dhe0000162.

Kezar, A. (2013). Departmental cultures and non-tenure-track faculty: Willingness, capacity, and opportunity to perform at four-year institutions. *The Journal of Higher Education*, 84(2), 153–188. doi:10.1080/00221546.2013.11777284.

Kuh, G. D. (2008, October 31). *High-Impact Educational Practices: What They Are, Who Has Access to Them, and Why They Matter.* https://www.semanticscholar.org/paper/High-Impact-Educational-Practices%3A-What-They-Are%2C-Kuh/0b9ee16ec488c30ebf46d3cd705f54b68fdc54b7.

Llamas, J. D., Nguyen, K., & Tran, A. G. T. T. (2021). The case for greater faculty diversity: Examining the educational impacts of student-faculty racial/ethnic match. *Race Ethnicity and Education*, 24(3), 375–391. doi:10.1080/13613324.2019.1679759.

NSSE. (n.d.). *Evidence-Based Improvement in Higher Education.* Retrieved June 26, 2023, from https://nsse.indiana.edu//nsse/index.html.

Penn State University Student Affairs. (n.d.). *PULSE Diversity & Inclusion Survey.* Retrieved June 26, 2023, from https://studentaffairs.psu.edu/student-affairs-staff/research-assessment/research-assessment-analysis-and-reports/penn-state-2.

Robey, N., & Dickter, C. (2022). Internet-based cultural competence training for White undergraduate students at a predominantly White university. *Journal of Applied Social Psychology*, 52(9), 837–850. doi:10.1111/jasp.12881.

Sandhu, H. S., Chen, R., & Wong, A. (2022). Faculty diversity matters: A scoping review of student perspectives in North America. *Perspectives: Policy and Practice in Higher Education*, 26(4), 130–139. doi:10.1080/13603108.2022.2048720.

Stanford University. (n.d.). *IDEAL Diversity Equity and Inclusion Survey.* Retrieved June 26, 2023, from https://idealdeisurvey.stanford.edu/.

Stout, R., Archie, C., Cross, D., & Carman, C. A. (2018). The relationship between faculty diversity and graduation rates in higher education. *Intercultural Education*, 29(3), 399–417. doi:10.1080/14675986.2018.1437997.

USC Race and Equity Center. (n.d.). *National Assessment of Collegiate Campus Climates (NACCC).* Retrieved June 26, 2023, from https://race.usc.edu/colleges/naccc/.

Walton, G. M., Murphy, M. C., Logel, C., Yeager, D. S., Goyer, J. P., Brady, S. T., Emerson, K. T. U., Paunesku, D., Fotuhi, O., Blodorn, A., Boucher, K. L., Carter, E. R., Gopalan, M., Henderson, A., Kroeper, K. M., Murdock Perriera, L.

A., Reeves, S. L., Ablorh, T. T., Ansari, S., ... Krol, N. (2023). Where and with whom does a brief social-belonging intervention promote progress in college? *Science*, 380(6644), 499–505. doi:10.1126/science.ade4420.

Zilvinskis, J., Kinzie, J., Daday, J., O'Donnell, K., & Zande, C. V. (Eds.) (2022). *Delivering on the promise of high-impact practices: research and models for achieving equity, fidelity, impact, and scale*. London and New York: Routledge.

9

ADVICE FOR HISTORICALLY EXCLUDED INSTRUCTORS AND THEIR ALLIES

Have you ever had the experience of someone telling you, "I do this in my course and it works wonders," but then find when you implement the same practices that it doesn't go so well? If you are an instructor who identifies from a group or groups historically excluded there might be times you read portions of this book and think, well this is all good but.... This chapter acknowledges that not all instructors have the same privileges when it comes to implementing inclusive teaching approaches, and provides specific guidance for historically excluded instructors and their allies. We envision such allies to be their colleagues within and outside of their departments and include other instructors and administrative staff within the institution. Examples of instructors from groups historically excluded include instructors of color within disciplines and institutions where they are the minority, female-identifying instructors in male-dominated fields, instructors not on the tenure track, international instructors, neurodivergent instructors, instructors with disabilities, instructors who identify as LGBTQ+, and those with various intersectional identities. These are only examples and this list is not expansive of all who identity from groups historically excluded.

Below we articulate a variety of strategies for being an inclusive instructor while protecting one's peace, embracing one's identities, and navigating power and privilege in academia. First and foremost, we recognize that much of the burden is unduly placed on such instructors but there should be spaces within academia where they are included and can be their authentic selves in their courses and teach effectively. Such is context dependent, as an instructor teaching students who mostly share similar identities to them might have different experiences from those dissimilar, of which there are societal stigmas.

DOI: 10.4324/9781003442929-12

In general, more work is needed to better understand how to support instructors historically excluded, but we know from the experiences of instructors who are successful, how they navigate their circumstances. For example, Black female sociology instructors have been described as being impacted by impression management; as members of minoritized groups, they change their behavior so that others form a favorable impression of them (Atkins & Kalel, n.d.). They are challenged by controlling images, which are prevailing stereotypical views of how others, such as their students and colleagues, perceive them. There is also evidence that students might have better impressions of Black professors if they are dressed in formal rather than casual attire (Aruguete et al, 2017). Because of this, when implementing inclusive approaches in their courses, they must navigate that students might not see them as the authority as compared with colleagues from majority group backgrounds, and if their teaching approaches do not go well they might be thought of as being subpar.

Student exposure to diverse international faculty can be an enriching experience (Kim et al., 2011). International instructors can face challenges with being perceived as foreigners and in communication, which can negatively impact their ability to implement inclusive instruction (Hu & Chen, 2021). These include faculty who were born abroad and attended college outside or within the United States. Each might have different experiences (Kim et al., 2011). Their integration into learning the cultural norms and expectations of their new institutions is critical (Lee, 2021).

Instructors from any groups that differ from the perceived stereotypical professor can face these challenges. So, then, how can instructors get students on board with their inclusive teaching approaches? How do they navigate obtaining feedback, assessing impacts, and reflection on practice? We articulate several pieces of guidance below that instructors can consider within their own contexts.

Advice for Engaging Students in Learning

Teaching is a two-way partnership between students and instructors. A dynamic, effective course will involve the respectful engagement of both parties. Sometimes this is referred to as student buy-in or getting students on board for instruction. If such does not occur, the social and learning environment can be negatively impacted. In this section we describe general strategies that instructors from historically excluded groups can utilize to engage their students in inclusive learning practices. Below we highlight several powerful instructor actions: learning the culture; demonstrations of care; establishing community guidelines; communication; storytelling; and engaging advocates.

Learn the Cultural Norms

A critical step for any new instructor is being familiar with the culture of the institution and how students interact with their instructors. These insights can be gained through observation as well as soliciting the perspectives of a variety of individuals at the institution, and ideally also students. For example, if you have the opportunity to ask such questions during the search process, ideally from other faculty from historically excluded groups if possible, such can help you start to gain a better sense of what you might experience. Additionally, if you are currently at the institution, asking trusted colleagues what they have done to form positive relationships with their students can also be beneficial. Knowing the cultural norms and some examples of how other instructors have worked them in their courses can allow you to reflect upon what you can do to still be your authentic self and successful within that institutional context.

Demonstrations of Care for Students

No matter one's background as an instructor, a theme that we noticed throughout the students' perspectives study responses was the importance of an instructor demonstrating care. Several respondents' quotes are included below, both in response to students being asked why particular teaching approaches used by their instructors were or were not effective.

> *These approaches were effective because it made me feel as if the teacher really cared about what was going on in my life and my peers which made the environment more comfortable to ask questions in and to just be yourself in.*
>
> *—A private university student who identifies as White and female*

> *Because they [the inclusive teaching approaches] showed that the instructor cared more about the students than the work.*
>
> *—A student with an undisclosed background*

> *These approaches were not effective simply because the professor did not care.*
>
> *—A private university student from a private university who identifies as White, male, and straight*

> *The Teachers clearly cared about the student succeeding and learning effectively, and not just about their jobs, and getting students through the course like trained cattle.*
>
> *—A community college student who identifies as non-binary/queer*

> *Most teachers do not care much for the students, especially noticeable in gen-ed classes. They would not acknowledge issues students had and usually try to defer as many potential issues as possible to not be burdened. Many of the more established teachers refuse to change course design and format.*
>
> *—A student who identifies as White, male, and straight*

> *I felt a disconnect of sorts with this professor. May just be me, but if someone shows lack of enthusiasm for what they are teaching and do[es] not seem to care for students, I feel less confident in asking for help, and less welcome or engaged in the classroom.*
>
> *—A private university student who identifies as White, female, and straight*

Although these responses do not parse out the identities of the instructors described in the courses they teach (we intentionally did not ask such information to uphold anonymity), they send a clear message that when students perceive that their instructor's approaches truly demonstrate care toward them and their success, they perceive such methods as being effective. For instructors from groups historically excluded, demonstrations of care can be more complex. For example, because of negative societal stereotypes (e.g., Black men as uneducated or violent, Black women as angry, or instructors with accents as not comprehendible), additional time and care might be needed to rework any internal biases that are barriers to students' own learning.

Acts of care can be powerful levers that promote student learning. They can be demonstrated through the words, body language, and actions of an instructor. For example, instructors who let their students know that they care about their success and demonstrate such care through their actions and ways that they can understand and see have already made a critical contribution to fostering an inclusive course environment. Such care is not about making a course easy; a major goal of higher education is to challenge students. Such care still involves having boundaries. If instructors are unsure about how they can demonstrate such care in ways that students comprehend, they can ask their classes at the beginning of the semester what an inclusive classroom looks like to them, especially with regards to how the instructor demonstrates care. This could potentially be among the most important questions they ask their students during the course to facilitate an inclusive course environment.

Establishing Community Guidelines the First Day of Class

Sometimes in college courses instructors might want to get to the business of teaching quickly. Instructors from groups historically excluded should early on in a course discuss how respectful dialogue can occur on the first day of the course, as described in previous chapters. Even further, they can engage their students with coming up with such guidelines in partnership. This proactive approach has the potential to mitigate problematic scenarios. Such is always a helpful approach and can be particularly useful when teaching courses that have content which students perceive as unfamiliar or uncomfortable to discuss.

Effective Communication

For some international faculty members, students' responses to their accents and communication can be perceived as a barrier. However, international faculty can be empowered toward effective communication as they implement inclusive instruction. In Chapter 4 we highlighted how students valued their instructors creating learning experiences with a variety of approaches (Kavas & Kavas, 2008). In order to effectively communicate course material, international instructors can leverage Universal Design for Learning approaches to teach course material in multiple ways to support student learning (*About Universal Design for Learning*, n.d.). Speaking slower, having an organized presentation (also mentioned by students in our study), as well as using substantial wait-time or giving learners time to reflect on their learning, can support students' learning when the instructor's accent is unfamiliar to them (Kavas & Kavas, 2008). By focusing on effective communication, instructors from diverse backgrounds in general can advance inclusion in their courses.

Storytelling

Stories can be very powerful. Another instructor tool for confronting bias is storytelling. In *Picture a Professor*, Dr. Sarah Mayes-Tang, who identifies as a White female math professor, describes using storytelling in her courses to build community and confront biases to engage students in learning in mathematics, a male-dominated discipline (Mayes-Tang, 2022). She shares a challenging situation that she faced where she taught a course in which another section was led by a White male professor who represented the stereotypical image of a math professor. After the first day of classes, students transferred into the other professor's course and continually compared her with the other instructor. She shares how:

> One morning near the end of the term, students prepared to leave class to participate in a campus-wide class walkout as a feminine protest. I decided to point out the feminist issue shaping our own class by sharing some of my stories about working in the institution and teaching our class. Rather than simply recounting the facts, I told them the story

> from my perspective: how I anticipated the problems, how I worked to prevent them, and most importantly how I felt throughout all of this. I told them that I felt embarrassed and betrayed. I even told them that I cried. I went on to show my students quotes from their writing about different professors at the institution that spoke of the knowledge of male professors frequently and about how "nice" or "not nice" the female professors were. I read them quotes from my end-of-term evaluations. I told them about the desperation of feeling like I was playing a losing game and how I didn't think that situation would ever resolve. I could not both be myself and be a successful professor at the institution.
>
> Rather than making me weak, being vulnerable allowed me to claim some of the authority and strength I deserved. The things that I was ashamed of were out in the open. Surprisingly, I felt in complete control of the class from that day forward. Students listened to me and really seemed to respect what I had to say. I received notes and comments from several students in the class about how impactful this moment had been.
>
> *(Mayes-Tang, 2022, 262–263)*

Such storytelling requires vulnerability on behalf of the instructor and, as she mentions, comes with risks. However, this instructor witnessed the rewards of this approach. Not everyone might feel comfortable with this method, however; sharing stories can humanize the instructor in the eyes of the students and increase their empathy by building awareness of their own biases and their harmful impacts, of which some learners might not even be aware.

Instructors from groups historically excluded might also share stigmatized identities with their students in an effort to be role models. Women in science and engineering disciplines were found to be more likely than men to disclose their disabilities and experiences with depression and anxiety with students (Busch et al., 2023). Such disclosures may have a positive effect on normalizing.

Engaging Respected Advocates and Allies

Instructors from groups historically excluded who are new to an institution might not have established a reputation or presence with students, and can benefit from advocacy. Instructors can engage trusted colleagues who are respected on campus and are allies or advocates to put in a good word about their teaching. Depending on institutional approaches for advising (whether through faculty or staff), course registration meetings can be opportunistic times for advocates to hold these conversations with students. Additionally, department chairs can also engage in such dialogues with students as well as other instructors through informal conversations. Centers for teaching and learning and Communications offices can also highlight the efforts of instructors more publicly. When students observe that their instructors' efforts are respected by other instructors and staff members whom they respect, this has the potential to challenge any biases.

International instructors can benefit by working with advocates to support their integration into the culture of the institution and learn cultural norms and expectations (Véliz et al., 2020). In general, being able to understand and work across cultural differences is important for instructors. In our previous study, an instructor identifying as Asian from a baccalaureate college shared: "Not being able to understand various students' backgrounds is challenging for me."

A Note on the Perceptions of Students Sharing Similar Identities

Understanding the perspectives of students who share similar identities as their instructors is also critical. For example, in a qualitative study, researchers found that Black faculty expressed that students who are in their earlier years were most concerned with how they "speak, sit, and use body gestures" (Moore & Toliver, 2010, 939). They indicated that "Students were described as checking out professors' accents, skin color, and ethnicity to see if they were consistent with their expectations and level of emotional compatibility." Thus, students even sharing (some) similar identities might still judge the efficacy of their instructors, with potential implications on degree of connectedness based on the differences between the socioeconomic status of the instructors and their students.

Advice for Obtaining Observational Feedback

For observational feedback, instructors can seek out trusted advocates to perform classroom observations of teaching who might also be willing to promote their good teaching efforts through various academic circles, such as within their department or more broadly at the institution. For example, even during an observation itself, an observer could take time to share positive comments about their teaching to the class and indicate that this observation is being conducted because of their commitment to teaching, but not for evaluative purposes.

Instructors might also consider setting up reciprocal classroom observations with colleagues from groups historically excluded, in addition to majority groups, to discuss what they have found to be effective in their inclusive teaching efforts through peer mentorship (Bhopal, 2020).

Tracie has worked with many instructors of diverse backgrounds who have successfully implemented inclusive teaching approaches described in this book. She has also noticed that, at times, but not always, students may react in negative nuanced ways to the inclusive teaching efforts utilized by diverse instructors with dissimilar backgrounds. For example, there might be some initial push back. Such circumstances problematically highlight the systemic nature of bias in our society and lack of representation and exposure to a diverse faculty. Instructors can ask observers if they notice whether student reactions seem different from expected and what they are seeing, and brainstorm possible ways to address such scenarios. Building trust with students sometimes takes longer, and being transparent can sometimes go a long way about why an instructor uses particular approaches in the course. PAITE observational data also serves as documentation of the efforts that they are making and how they are taking a reflective, scholarly approach to teaching that can be described in a teaching portfolio. Additionally, if instructors have taught in the past, they could choose to take time to share with current students what previous students have appreciated about their teaching. Additionally, having a diverse circle of colleagues to whom instructors can talk about their teaching efforts can be helpful. These might include staff at a center for teaching and learning, if available, or other colleagues.

At all times instructors should protect their peace—they have amazing learning experiences to offer to their students—and trust their gut. If something does not feel right, which might not emerge in classroom observation data given that they are announced observations by outside observers, instructors can determine if there are those whom they can trust to discuss these concerns with who are willing to brainstorm with them or to take action.

Advice for Measuring and Sharing Outcomes of Inclusive Teaching Efforts

Instructors' reactions might vary when reviewing outcomes data. For some it may empower them to create learning environments that support students of diverse backgrounds. For others, especially those sharing similar identity backgrounds as their learners, it might bring back memories of how they have navigated similar academic scenarios. Some might feel empathy through shared experience. Some might feel frustrated or as if situations still have not changed since they were in college. Instructors can take time to allow themselves to process this information and any emotional responses to it. If they have a trusted colleague, they might consider sharing their thoughts with them, and consider peer or more experienced mentorship that they might be able to receive from minoritized instructors whom they look up to. Instructors from groups historically excluded can cultivate a sense of belonging for learners because of the power of students seeing someone who looks like them who may have also navigated similar scenarios as a learner.

As illustrated in this example, sometimes students from backgrounds historically excluded might gravitate more toward instructors from groups historically excluded and seek their mentorship and support. Instructors should document any informal mentorship they engage in with these students as an extension of the classroom experience. It is important to set boundaries for how instructors can support all learners. The rewards are many, but burnout can be real. Simultaneously, just because students have similar identities does not necessarily mean that they may choose an instructor from a group historically excluded for a mentor even if the instructor reaches out to them (Moore & Toliver, 2010). There is complexity in these relationships, which must be acknowledged and respected.

Additionally in *Picture a Professor*, Dr. Chavella Pittman describes the importance of historically excluded instructors collecting evidence of student learning (Pittman, 2022). This evidence can be used for individual assessment purposes by the instructor as well as documentation to demonstrate that students are learning in their courses, and their teaching practices are making a difference.

Advice for Reflecting on Practice

Worth noting are the studies which show that historically excluded faculty can be subject to bias in student evaluations leading to lower scores than those in the contextual majority (often, but not always White males) (Deo, 2015; Fan et al., 2019; Ghorpade & Lackritz, 1991; Huston, 2006; Santisteban & Egues, 2022). It is not then illogical to think that some of these biases may also find their way into other means of student feedback that is collected for the purposes of reflection and improving teaching, and not solely instructor evaluation. However, this may in fact be one of the strongest arguments for incorporating formative student feedback into courses prior to the end of the term, so that such biases can be acknowledged and addressed in real time. Further, some strategies for mitigating biases in student evaluation results have been published, including directly discussing implicit bias, noting the importance of student evaluations, and ensuring that evaluation questions are not vaguely worded and thus eliciting bias (Genetin et al., 2022; Wolfe, 2022). More systemically, and beyond an individual instructor's control within a single class, enhancing representation of historically excluded groups in the faculty ranks and incentivizing faculty and course evaluation developers to research ways to mitigate bias in teaching evaluations and feedback forms, are strategies that could help in this arena. Course evaluations remain an imperfect measure, and faculty from historically excluded groups should consider multiple forms of evidence when they reflect on their teaching.

Advice for Working with Departments and Institutions at Large

If instructors are, or will soon be, on the job market, they can keep a look out for departments with openings that have a track record of supporting a diverse faculty and being inclusive of students. The job market is increasingly competitive, but such departments might be more likely to have a culture of inclusion. Instructors should ask around about the department, and where possible, solicit insights from colleagues from historically excluded backgrounds who are willing to give their confidential perspectives. When securing such positions they should also not feel obligated to take on the work of a diversity champion and be careful about the service to which they commit. If they are searching for support structures on campus outside of their department, consider Faculty Affairs; Diversity, Equity, and Inclusion Committees; and Offices of Intercultural Development. In mentoring relationships, instructors can share their stories with students about how they have confronted obstacles and where they find joy.

Words of Encouragement

We acknowledge that instructors from groups historically excluded in higher education might have experiences with inclusive teaching that differ from those of majority groups. Simultaneously, many instructors from groups historically excluded who participated in our study for *What Inclusive Instructors Do* noted that they felt empowered to use a variety of inclusive teaching approaches in their various contexts. Such efforts can be very impactful for students. See the quotes below.

> *Citing diverse authors, including the contributions of diverse communities, and allowing students to contribute to the teaching and learning.*
>
> *—A part-time instructor from a doctorate-granting university who identifies as Black or African American and male*

> *I use transparent assignment design using the TILT [Transparency in Learning and Teaching] interventional methodologies. I teach only in active learning classrooms which facilitates active participation. All of my learning activities for students are aligned with the course and module learning outcomes, and I ensure that students understand them and can relate them to their own goals. I conduct pre-semester surveys of all students in my classes, in which I ask about their goals, learning preferences, etc. I ensure that all students feel safe in class, monitor their levels of comfort and intervene where necessary to ensure a safe and healthy place for learning. I work with students who are homeless, hungry and some who work 40–60 hours a week; I try to connect students to*

services and am not a jerk about late work. Also promote student wellness (mindfulness) practices in class.

—A full professor (tenured) at a large urban Minority serving master's college or university who identifies as female, and both Black or African American and White

Informal surveys of their cultural background, work experience, education, languages spoken, preferred foods/music/readings/sports/etc, family education, etc. I also OPENLY share with them my multiethnic background, places I have lived, languages I speak, known genetic profile/predisposition to different diseases in my family, how my cultural upbringing influenced perceptions of different careers and life "styles", etc. It's been very important to "introduce" myself openly to them and make it a safe environment by example.

—A full professor (tenured) at a doctoral-granting university who self-identifies as female and Asian

Reflection Question

- What challenges, if any, have you confronted as an instructor from a historically excluded group?
- Who are the advocates and allies that can support you?
- What advice most resonates with you from this chapter?
- If you are an instructor who is not from a historically marginalized group, how can you acknowledge the privileges you may have while also being an ally for your colleagues?

Conclusion

We acknowledge in this chapter that instructors from groups historically excluded might face distinct challenges to implementing inclusive teaching practices compared with those from majority groups. There are a variety of approaches that can help such instructors navigate their circumstances to ultimately build more inclusive courses and protect their well-being.

References

About Universal Design for Learning. (n.d.). *CAST.* Retrieved May 20, 2023, from https://www.cast.org/impact/universal-design-for-learning-udl.

Atkins, C., & Kalel, C. (n.d.). Teaching up: The intersection of impression management and controlling images for black, cisgender, women faculty. *Symbolic Interaction.* doi:10.1002/symb.655.

Aruguete, M. S., Slater, J., & Mwaikinda, S. R. (2017). The effects of professors' race and clothing style on student evaluations. *The Journal of Negro Education*, 86(4), 494–502. http://www.jstor.org/stable/10.7709/jnegroeducation.86.4.0494.

Bhopal, K. (2020). Success against the odds: The effect of mentoring on the careers of senior black and minority ethnic academics in the UK. *British Journal of Educational Studies*, 68(1), 79–95. doi:10.1080/00071005.2019.1581127.

Busch, C. A., Cooper, K. M., & Brownell, S. E. (2023) Women drive efforts to highlight concealable stigmatized identities in U.S. academic science and engineering. *PLoS ONE*, 18(7): e0287795. doi:10.1371/journal.pone.0287795.

Deo, M. E. (2015). A better tenure battle: Fighting bias in teaching evaluations. *Columbia Journal of Gender and Law*, 31, 7.

Fan, Y., Shepherd, L. J., Slavich, E., Waters, D., Stone, M., Abel, R., & Johnston, E. L. (2019). Gender and cultural bias in student evaluations: Why representation matters. *PLOS ONE*, 14(2), e0209749. doi:10.1371/journal.pone.0209749.

Genetin, B., Chen, J., Kogan, V., & Kalish, A. (2022). Mitigating implicit bias in student evaluations: A randomized intervention. *Applied Economic Perspectives and Policy*, 44(1), 110–128. doi:10.1002/aepp.13217.

Ghorpade, J., & Lackritz, J. R. (1991). Student evaluations: Equal opportunity concerns. *Thought and Action*, 7(1), 61–72.

Hu, R., & Chen, X. (2021). Challenges and potentials of international faculty in U.S. higher education: Perspectives from two Chinese female faculty. In C. R. Glass, Krishna Bista, & Xi Lin (Eds.), *The experiences of international faculty in institutions of higher education: enhancing recruitment, retention, and integration of international talent* (pp. 57–72). London and New York: Routledge. doi:10.4324/9781003081562.

Huston, T. A. (2006). Race and gender bias in higher education: could faculty course evaluations impede further progress toward parity? *Seattle Journal for Social Justice*, 4(2).

Kavas, A., & Kavas, A. (2008). An exploratory study of undergraduate college students' perceptions and attitudes toward foreign accented faculty. *College Student Journal*, 42(3), 879–891.

Kim, D., Wolf-Wendel, L., & Twombly, S. (2011). International faculty: Experiences of academic life and productivity in U.S. universities. *The Journal of Higher Education*, 82(6), 720–747. doi:10.1080/00221546.2011.11777225.

Lee, T. (2021). Integration of foreign-born faculty in US higher education. In C. R. Glass, Krishna Bista, & Xi Lin (Eds.), *The experiences of international faculty in institutions of higher education: enhancing recruitment, retention, and integration of international talent* (pp. 163–173). London and New York: Routledge. doi:10.4324/9781003081562.

Mayes-Tang, S. (2022). Sharing our stories to build community, highlight bias, and address challenges to authority. In J. Neuhaus (Ed.), *Picture a professor: Interrupting biases about faculty and increasing student learning* (pp. 254–270). Morgantown, WV: West Virginia University Press.

Moore, P. J., & Toliver, S. D. (2010). Intraracial dynamics of black professors' and black students' communication in traditionally white colleges and universities. *Journal of Black Studies*, 40(5), 932–945. doi:10.1177/0021934708321107.

Pittman, C. T. (2022). Empowered strategies for women faculty of color navigating teaching inequities in higher ed. In J. Neuhaus (Ed.), *Picture a professor:*

Interrupting biases about faculty and increasing student learning (pp. 285–305). Morgantown, WV: West Virginia University Press.

Santisteban, L., & Egues, A. L. (2022). How student evaluations of teaching contribute to hindrance of faculty diversity? *Teaching and Learning in Nursing*, 17 (4), 455–459. doi:10.1016/j.teln.2022.04.007.

Véliz, D., Guizman-Valenzuela, C., & Pickenpack, A. (2020). Becoming a successful international faculty member in a striving university. *Current Issues in Education*, 21(3), 1–22.

Wolfe, J. (2022). Let's stop relying on biased teaching evaluations. *Inside Higher Education*. https://www.insidehighered.com/advice/2022/01/21/teaching-evaluations-reflect-colleges-commitment-diversity-opinion.

10

GENERATIVE ARTIFICIAL INTELLIGENCE AND EQUITY

As we write this book we are in the middle of a technological storm where more sophisticated generative artificial intelligence (AI) technologies continue to impact higher education and other industries at what seems like an exponential rate. These technologies, when prompted, can summarize existing text, query large datasets to produce written text, and create media, and more. Companies constantly develop new tools with these technologies or integrate them into existing applications, giving them the capacity to generate output in various forms and levels of sophistication. The world is taken aback by the possibilities to decrease workflows, improve existing text, as well as make novel products. The possibilities and impacts on higher education are multitudinal, and will continue to be realized, as more people use the technologies and become even more capable of carrying out relevant tasks, and students, faculty, and staff learn to use them (Addy et al., forthcoming).

Given such promise, it is imperative to consider how generative artificial intelligence impacts equity work in teaching and learning spaces. Here we revisit several major findings from our student perspectives study to explore how instructors can leverage these tools to create more equitable learning experiences for their learners, and cautions for them to consider. We also discuss how the technologies open up possibilities for all learners, with special considerations to neurodivergent learners and students with specific learning disabilities. In general, these tools can expand the capacity of an instructor to facilitate an inclusive learning environment with appropriate cautions.

Our study findings revealed that student respondents perceived embedding structure and having clear expectations as inclusive instruction. Toward these ends, having explicit course policies on students' usage of generative

DOI: 10.4324/9781003442929-13

artificial intelligence in coursework, discussing them with students, and highlighting the benefits and limitations of the technologies have the potential to support a more inclusive learning environment.

More Efficient Learning Experiences

A major theme that emerged from the study findings was that students expressed that their instructors were inclusive when they designed courses that acknowledged and respected students' time. This theme is aligned with having a holistic approach to teaching, highlighted in *What Inclusive Instructors Do* in describing the mindsets of inclusive instructors (Addy et al., 2021). Instructors who embrace these mindsets are aware that students are balancing the work of other courses, co-curricular activities, or life demands, and are intentional about how they design learning experiences that maximize the best usage of students' time while simultaneously supporting students in achieving learning outcomes.

With the sophistication of generative AI, instructors can reflect on the types of learning activities they assign and how such technologies can augment and add appropriate efficiencies while simultaneously supporting students' learning. For example, if a goal is for students to complete an experiential learning project that emphasizes what students learn through the process, they might use the technologies to support their process by brainstorming topic ideas to help them narrow down their focal area. Such can be especially helpful for students who generally might need more processing time and scaffolding. Furthermore, such usage of AI has the benefit of supporting learners who do not enter the course with prior knowledge of the content because they were not previously exposed to it, allowing them to focus on critical thinking and action while completing the project. Such applications of usage can enhance equity but should be carefully designed to ensure that students are still meeting expected outcomes, and will lend themselves to experimentation to what better facilitates learning.

A major pitfall for generative AI is if it is used as a shortcut to learning rather than as a support. For example, if students can generate an entire assignment through generative AI without critical thought and engagement, and such actions do not help them accomplish learning objectives, then such usages of the tools can be barriers to learning. Further, the tools can hallucinate, or produce inaccurate outputs. Their outputs can also be biased. Generative AI tools are not infallible.

Yet, simultaneously, generative artificial intelligence can benefit multilingual learners to more efficiently and effectively write outside of their native tongue, learn the new language, and better understand written information in the new language. They can prompt the tool to proofread writing, ask it to say a particular phrase, or summarize text, with caution, bearing in mind that some languages might not be optimized in various technologies. One major concern, however, is that generative AI tools might perpetuate linguistic biases as a result of the information on which they are trained. Neurodivergent students and students with disabilities may use generative AI to address barriers they face that impede their ability to effectively learn. Perhaps coming up with a topic or idea for an assignment is a barrier that slows down their learning. Generative AI might have the potential to support their process.

More Equitable Personalized Learning Opportunities

Another theme that emerged through our student voices study is instructors facilitating more personalized learning experiences for students. There is promise in how generative AI tools can enhance these opportunities. For example, students who find particular concepts difficult in the course might be able to use the tools as aids to their learning and understanding in addition to instructor explanations and peer–peer learning.

For example, imagine that an instructor asks students their "muddiest points" after a class session as a formative assessment to track their progress and help create a more responsive learning or personalized learning environment. The instructor uncovers several themes in the students' responses that fall on various levels of Bloom's taxonomy; most students have difficulty understanding a particular concept and others are challenged by applying the concept. The instructor, having previously asked students what they already knew about the topic, sees how students with prior knowledge were at a clear advantage in their understanding of the topic. Students needing more clarity could potentially use generative artificial intelligence as a supplementary aid to explain the concept in several different ways to support their learning. Further, depending on the topic, they might be able to query the tools to help them better understand how to transfer their knowledge to multiple other scenarios, thus understanding how the concept can be applied. They are then challenged to create a new scenario where this concept is applied to monitor their understanding. One of the limitations to this approach is that the quality of the output generated by AI might not have been vetted by the instructor.

All students, including neurodivergent students and students with disabilities, may benefit from using such tools to help them summarize and gather the main ideas of a course or other course material, or in other ways to support their learning.

Increased Potential for Inclusive Teaching Ideation

Instructors can leverage generative artificial intelligence technologies to create more welcoming environments for students as well as have a starting point for various teaching and learning scenarios. As one example, an instructor might input the following prompt to generate a variety of ideas that can support a more inclusive classroom climate:

> Act as a college professor teaching a discussion-based course. What are sample course expectations that can help foster an inclusive classroom environment?

ChatGPT Output:

> Certainly, creating an inclusive classroom environment is crucial for promoting productive discussions and ensuring that all students feel valued and heard. Here are some sample course expectations that can help foster inclusivity:
>
> 1. **Respect for Diverse Perspectives:** All students should be encouraged to share their viewpoints, and it's important that we respect and value the diversity of perspectives in our class.
> 2. **Active Listening:** We should practice active listening, which means giving our full attention to the speaker without interrupting, and avoid making assumptions about their experiences.
> 3. **Speak Thoughtfully:** When you speak, take a moment to think about how your words might impact others. Be aware of the potential biases in your statements.
> 4. **Use Inclusive Language:** Be mindful of the language you use. Avoid stereotypes, derogatory language, or any form of hate speech. Use gender-neutral terms when appropriate.
> 5. **Participation Encouragement:** Encourage all students to participate, but don't pressure anyone. Some students may be more comfortable writing their thoughts instead of speaking aloud.
> 6. **Respect for Pronouns:** Respect and use the correct gender pronouns for your peers. If you're unsure, ask in a respectful and private manner.
> 7. **Challenging Ideas, Not Individuals:** It's perfectly fine to challenge ideas and concepts, but avoid attacking or demeaning individuals personally.
> 8. **Provide Trigger Warnings:** If a discussion topic or content might be emotionally triggering for some students, let me know privately so we can find an alternative or provide warnings.
> 9. **Create Safe Spaces:** Ensure that everyone feels safe sharing their experiences and emotions. What's shared in this class should stay confidential.

10. **Open-mindedness:** Be open to learning from your peers. We all come from different backgrounds, and this class is an opportunity to broaden your understanding.
11. **Feedback:** Constructive feedback is valuable. If you have suggestions on how to improve the class's inclusivity, please feel free to share them with me privately.
12. **Accommodations:** If you have specific accommodation needs, please communicate them with me early in the semester so we can make appropriate arrangements.

> Remember, the goal is to create an environment where everyone can learn from each other and grow, while feeling respected and valued. Your active participation in fostering inclusivity in this classroom is vital.
>
> *(Queried September 6, 2023)*

The instructor could use this list as a starting point to create or co-create classroom guidelines for discussion for their courses to help facilitate more welcoming environments. For example, the instructor could ask the class to review this list and consider what to keep, add, or remove. This list could become a collaborative guideline document for usage in their courses.

Instructors interested in informal community-building activities can query ChatGPT with the following prompt:

> Act as a college professor interested in implementing informal activities that build community. What are some sample activities appropriate for this level?

ChatGPT Output:

> Certainly! Building a strong sense of community in a college classroom can enhance the learning experience and create a supportive environment for students. Here are some sample classroom activities appropriate for college-level students:

1. **Small Group Discussions:** Divide the class into small groups and give them a thought-provoking question or topic related to the course material to discuss. Afterward, each group shares their insights with the whole class.
2. **Peer Introductions:** At the beginning of the semester, ask each student to introduce themselves briefly, including their major, interests, and one fun fact. This helps students get to know each other.

3. **Course-Related Debates:** Organize a structured debate on a controversial topic related to the course content. Assign students to argue both sides, encouraging critical thinking and discussion.
4. **Student-led Mini-Workshops:** Allow students to take turns leading short workshops or discussions on topics of their choice, related to the course. This promotes leadership and peer learning.
5. **Collaborative Problem Solving:** Present a real-world problem or case study relevant to the course. Have students work in teams to analyze the problem and propose solutions, fostering teamwork and critical thinking.
6. **Guest Speaker Q&A:** Invite a guest speaker related to the course material and allow students to ask questions and engage in a discussion afterward. This provides exposure to real-world perspectives.
7. **Class Polls and Surveys:** Use technology to conduct real-time polls or surveys on course-related topics. Discuss the results, encouraging students to consider different viewpoints.
8. **Role-Playing Exercises:** Create scenarios where students take on roles relevant to the course material and act out interactions. This helps students apply theoretical concepts to practical situations.
9. **Student Panels:** Form panels of students who excel in specific areas of the course and have them share their insights, study tips, and strategies with the class.
10. **Reflection Journals:** Assign periodic reflection journals where students can write about their learning experiences, challenges, and personal growth throughout the course. Share excerpts anonymously for discussion.
11. **Group Projects:** Assign collaborative projects that require students to work together over an extended period. Encourage them to share their progress and challenges with the class.
12. **In-class Quizzes or Games:** Incorporate quizzes, Kahoot! quizzes, or other educational games related to the course content. It adds an element of fun and competition while reinforcing learning.
13. **Themed Discussions:** Dedicate specific class sessions to discussing relevant current events or themes related to the course material, encouraging students to apply what they've learned.
14. **Mindfulness or Stress-Reduction Exercises:** Occasionally, incorporate mindfulness exercises or stress-reduction techniques into the class to support students' well-being.
15. **Open-Ended Questions:** Encourage open-ended questions from students during lectures or discussions to stimulate critical thinking and deeper exploration of topics.

Remember to adapt these activities to suit your specific course and learning objectives. The key is to create opportunities for students to engage with each other and the course material in a meaningful way, fostering a sense of belonging and community within the classroom.

(Queried September 6, 2023)

Act as a college writing instructor who teaches students with varied incoming writing skills. What different approaches might you use to teach college level writing?

ChatGPT Output:

Teaching college-level writing to a diverse group of students requires a flexible approach that can accommodate varying skill levels. Here are some different approaches you can use:

1. **Diagnostic Assessments:** Begin the semester with a diagnostic writing assessment. This can help you gauge each student's writing proficiency and tailor your instruction accordingly.
2. **Differentiated Assignments:** Assign different writing tasks or essay prompts that allow students to choose topics or approaches that align with their interests and skill levels. Provide clear grading criteria for each assignment type.
3. **Peer Workshops:** Organize peer review workshops where students can provide feedback on each other's work. Pair students strategically, mixing those with stronger writing skills with those who need more support.
4. **Individualized Feedback:** Provide personalized feedback on assignments, focusing on specific areas where each student can improve. Encourage students to schedule one-on-one conferences to discuss their writing and receive guidance.
5. **Writing Centers:** Encourage students to visit the campus writing center for additional support and tutoring. Familiarize them with available resources.
6. **Writing Process Emphasis:** Highlight the writing process, including prewriting, drafting, revising, and editing. Encourage multiple drafts and revisions as a means of improvement.
7. **Modeling:** Share well-written sample essays or papers as models for effective writing. Analyze these models as a class to identify key elements and techniques.
8. **Genre Analysis:** Explore different types of writing genres and their conventions. Have students practice writing in various genres to develop versatility.

9. **Grammar and Style Workshops:** Offer workshops or tutorials focusing on grammar, punctuation, and style issues. Students can choose to attend sessions that address their specific needs.
10. **In-Class Writing Exercises:** Incorporate regular in-class writing exercises that target specific writing skills, such as sentence structure, paragraph development, or argumentation.
11. **Revision Portfolios:** Implement revision portfolios where students compile multiple drafts of their work alongside reflective statements that discuss their writing choices and growth.
12. **Collaborative Writing:** Assign group writing projects, encouraging students to collaborate on a single piece of writing. This promotes peer learning and teamwork.
13. **Self-Assessment and Goal Setting:** Encourage students to self-assess their writing and set achievable goals for improvement. Regularly revisit these goals throughout the semester.
14. **Technology Integration:** Utilize writing tools and software that provide grammar and spell-check assistance, as well as plagiarism detection. Teach students how to use these tools effectively.
15. **Cultural Sensitivity:** Foster an inclusive classroom environment by acknowledging and respecting the diverse cultural backgrounds and perspectives of your students. Discuss how different cultures may influence writing styles and communication.
16. **Critical Reading:** Emphasize the importance of critical reading as a foundation for strong writing. Analyze texts and articles in class to develop analytical skills.
17. **Reflection and Metacognition:** Encourage students to reflect on their writing process and choices. Help them develop metacognitive awareness about their strengths and areas for improvement.

Remember that flexibility and adaptability are key when teaching college-level writing to students with varied skills. Creating a supportive and inclusive classroom environment can also enhance the learning experience for all students.

(Queried September 6, 2023)

Another example is below:

> Act as a college chemistry instructor. How could you use Universal Design for Learning to teach a class on the topic of diffusion?

ChatGPT Output:

Incorporating Universal Design for Learning (UDL) principles into teaching a college chemistry class on the topic of diffusion can make the material more accessible and engaging for a diverse range of students. Here's how I would apply UDL to teach diffusion:

1. **Multiple Means of Representation:**

   -**Lecture with Visual Aids:** Begin with a lecture using clear and concise explanations. Supplement this with visual aids like diagrams, animations, and molecular models to illustrate diffusion at the molecular level.

   -**Interactive Simulations:** Integrate interactive simulations or virtual experiments that allow students to visualize and manipulate variables related to diffusion. This provides a dynamic representation of the concept.

   -**Real-World Examples:** Share real-world examples of diffusion, such as its role in biological processes, environmental science, or industry applications, to demonstrate its relevance.

2. **Multiple Means of Engagement:**

   -**Hands-On Experiments:** Conduct hands-on experiments in the lab where students can observe and measure diffusion rates directly. This engages kinesthetic learners and reinforces theoretical knowledge.

   -**Class Discussions:** Encourage class discussions by posing thought-provoking questions related to diffusion. Use clicker questions to gather instant feedback and stimulate discussion.

   -**Group Activities:** Organize group activities or problem-solving exercises that require collaboration. This fosters social interaction and allows students to learn from each other.

3. ***Multiple Means of Expression:**

   -**Varied Assessment Methods:** Provide a range of assessment options, such as traditional exams, lab reports, presentations, and concept maps. Allow students to choose the format that best aligns with their strengths.

-**Revision Opportunities:** Offer students the chance to revise and resubmit assignments to improve their understanding of diffusion concepts.

-**Supportive Feedback:** Provide timely and constructive feedback on assignments to help students identify areas of improvement.

4. **Flexibility and Accessibility:**

-**Accessible Materials:** Ensure that all course materials, including lecture slides, online resources, and textbooks, are accessible to students with disabilities. Use accessible document formats and provide alternative formats when needed.

-**Accommodations:** Work closely with the campus disability services office to accommodate students with disabilities and provide necessary accommodations, such as extended exam time or accessible lab equipment.

5. **Supportive Learning Environment:**

-**Inclusive Language:** Use inclusive language and create a classroom environment where all students feel valued and respected.

-**Office Hours and Communication:** Offer regular office hours and open channels of communication to address individual student needs and concerns.

By incorporating these UDL principles, the diffusion topic in the chemistry class becomes more accessible, engaging, and inclusive, catering to the diverse learning needs and abilities of all students.

(Queried September 6, 2023)

There might be some outputs with which instructors disagree, as they do not align with their teaching philosophies or evidence. For example, the output above refers to catering to students' learning styles, yet there is insufficient evidence to support that such approaches lead to effective learning highlighting how generative AI outputs should always be treated with caution and multiple sources utilized for fact-checking purposes (Kirschner, 2017). Instructors (and their students) should recognize that the output should not be considered infallible but rather a place for ideation, and to always have a critical lens when reading it. Further, these tools are as good as the datasets they draw from. In higher education, scholarly, peer-reviewed sources are valued. Right now, the bot cannot replace these, but perhaps might become even more sophisticated to draw more heavily from such sources during a query.

Below is another sample prompt to provide instructors with a starting point for working with neurodivergent learners. Cross-checking these suggestions with the learners themselves and accessibility offices will be critical.

How can I support neurodivergent students as a college professor?

ChatGPT Output:

Supporting neurodivergent students as a college professor involves creating an inclusive and accessible learning environment. Here are some strategies to consider:

1. Educate Yourself: Familiarize yourself with different neurodivergent conditions such as autism, ADHD, dyslexia, and anxiety disorders. Understand the strengths, challenges, and common accommodations for these conditions. This knowledge will help you better support your neurodivergent students.
2. Clear Communication and Instructions: Provide clear and explicit instructions for assignments, expectations, and classroom activities. Break down complex tasks into smaller, manageable steps. Use visual aids, written summaries, or multimedia materials to supplement verbal instructions.
3. Flexible Assignments and Assessments: Consider providing flexibility in assignments and assessments. Offer alternative formats for exams or assignments, such as extended time, allowing for assistive technology, or allowing students to present their knowledge in different ways (e.g., written, oral, or multimedia presentations).
4. Accommodations and Accessibility: Familiarize yourself with disability services on campus and ensure that students are aware of the available accommodations. Be open to discussing individualized accommodations with students and collaborating with disability service providers.
5. Sensory Considerations: Be mindful of the classroom environment and its potential sensory stimuli. Reduce distractions, provide seating options, and be understanding of sensory sensitivities that students may have. If possible, offer quiet spaces or provide noise-canceling headphones for students who may benefit from them.
6. Universal Design for Learning (UDL): Incorporate UDL principles into your teaching approach. Offer multiple means of representation, engagement, and expression to accommodate diverse learning styles and needs. Provide a range of resources, such as visual materials, hands-on activities, and opportunities for peer collaboration.

7. Build Rapport and Open Communication: Foster a supportive and inclusive classroom atmosphere. Encourage open communication with your students, including one-on-one check-ins or office hours. Create opportunities for students to provide anonymous feedback or suggestions for improving the learning environment.
8. Sensitivity and Respect: Treat all students with respect and avoid making assumptions or generalizations about neurodivergent conditions. Be sensitive to their individual needs, privacy, and confidentiality. Use person-first language and ask students how they prefer to be supported.

Remember, every student is unique, and their needs may vary. It's crucial to approach neurodivergent students as individuals and collaborate with them to determine the best ways to support their learning experience. By creating an inclusive and accessible learning environment, you can help neurodivergent students thrive academically and personally.

(Queried June 17, 2023)

Reflection on Practice

As described earlier in the book, reflecting on practice is critical to the growth of an inclusive instructor. After implementing various inclusive teaching practices and perhaps not seeing the desired outcomes, instructors might leverage generative AI tools to query other approaches to consider.

For example, suppose an instructor learns through observational feedback that students are not equitably engaging in their course. They want to know other approaches to helping students participate and ask the following prompt:

What are strategies for distributing participation in a college course?

ChatGPT Output:

Distributing participation in a college course can be achieved through various strategies. Here are some effective methods:

1. Randomized selection: Use a random selection process to determine who will contribute during class discussions. You can accomplish this by using tools like random name generators or index cards with students' names to ensure everyone has an equal chance to participate.
2. Small group activities: Divide students into small groups for discussions or collaborative activities. This approach provides a

more comfortable and inclusive environment for participation, allowing each student to contribute to the group's overall discussion or project.

3. Discussion roles or prompts: Assign specific discussion roles or provide prompts to guide participation. For example, you can designate a facilitator, a note-taker, and a devil's advocate for each discussion session. This approach ensures that different students take on active roles and contribute to the conversation.
4. Pre-assigned discussion points: Before a class discussion, provide students with pre-assigned discussion points or questions. This way, each student knows they will be responsible for contributing to the discussion on a particular topic or question.
5. Think-pair-share: Incorporate the think-pair-share technique, where students first think independently about a question or prompt, then pair up with a partner to discuss their thoughts, and finally share their ideas with the larger class. This strategy encourages all students to engage in the initial reflection and discussion process.
6. Online discussion forums: Utilize online platforms or discussion forums where students can contribute their thoughts asynchronously. This allows quieter or more introverted students to participate and express their ideas in writing at their own pace.
7. Anonymous participation: Use anonymous participation tools or platforms to encourage students to share their opinions without the fear of judgment or bias. This can promote more open and honest discussions, especially on sensitive or controversial topics.
8. Regular check-ins: Schedule individual or small group check-ins with students to gauge their understanding and encourage their participation. By providing personalized attention, you can help students overcome any barriers or challenges they might be facing.

Remember, it is essential to create a supportive and inclusive classroom environment where all students feel comfortable participating. By implementing these strategies, you can distribute participation more equitably and promote a richer learning experience for everyone in your college course.

(Queried June 28, 2023)

This query provides a variety of different approaches that instructors might use, a number of which have been discussed within this book and *What Inclusive Instructors Do*. Again, drawing from the literature is also critical here, and with the hopes that these tools improve upon their attribution so that we know the information is coming from trusted sources as well as the scholarly literature; then they are starting points but not end points to information gathering.

In general, there is promise in how generative AI technologies can support more inclusive classroom experiences. Yet, while this technology evolves, instructors and learners must also be aware of issues of privacy as well as bias in outputs. Students, instructors, and staff should be aware of the privacy policies of these tools and what they consider as acceptable with the type of information they collect, avoiding inputting private or confidential information and keeping in mind policies that are in place.

The datasets drawn from could potentially include biased or inaccurate information. With the increased importance of information literacy, a critical eye must be applied to all outputs. Such can be particularly problematic for all students and particularly harmful to those from minoritized backgrounds. Lack of regulation of these tools is currently an important concern.

Further, while we previously highlighted the many positives of these technologies in advancing equity, they can also perpetuate inequities if there are issues of access and affordability. Not all of the technologies are, or will be, free to students, which poses issues around equitable access. Also, care must be taken to ensure that the technologies are not used in punitive ways such as focusing on "catching students," as this can result in students from particular backgrounds such as multilingual learners being targeted more frequently than others (Liang et al., 2023). Additionally, we currently have only an early understanding of more global challenges, such as how such technologies can impact the environment.

Reflection Question

- Have you incorporated generative artificial intelligence technologies into any courses to build a more inclusive classroom environment? If so, how? If not, what do you foresee as possibilities or challenges to doing such?

Conclusion

We anticipate that inclusive instructors and their learners will continue to adapt their teaching practices as the technologies evolve. Generative AI tools have their limitations but also hold some promise in equity work. We'll need to continue to discuss, track, and consider their impacts in higher education.

References

Addy, T. M., Kang, T., & Laquintano, T. (forthcoming). Who benefits from generative AI and who is excluded?

Addy, T. M., Dube, D., Mitchell, K. A., & SoRelle, M. (2021). *What inclusive instructors do: Principles and practices for excellence in college teaching*. Sterling, VA: Stylus Publishing.

Kirschner, P. A. (2017). Stop propagating the learning styles myth. *Computers & Education*, 106, 166–171. doi:10.1016/j.compedu.2016.12.006.

Liang, W., Yuksekgonul, M., Mao, Y., Wu, E., & Zou, J. (2023). GPT detectors are biased against non-native English writers. *arXiv:2304.02819.* https://arxiv.org/pdf/2304.02819.pdf https://doi.org/10.1016/j.patter.2023.100779.

11

CONCLUDING REMARKS

Students are critical partners in creating inclusive learning environments. In our student voices study, we found that to learners, effective, inclusive course design:

- Maximizes their engagement in their learning
- Respects their time and workload
- Has a clear structure that is easy to follow
- Facilitates more personalized learning experiences and is equity-minded for all students including neurodivergent students and students with disabilities
- Allows them to obtain input from their peers and the instructor
- Includes diverse materials and demonstrates value for their experiences, and
- Accounts for course format

For learners in the study, an inclusive course:

- Is welcoming
- Acknowledges and respects student differences
- Involves equitable participation by students, and
- Includes relationship-building as a core component

Instructors who actively foster inclusive classrooms:

- Implement a variety of teaching approaches to help students learn
- Provide opportunities to hear student voices

DOI: 10.4324/9781003442929-14

- Allocate sufficient class time to student learning
- Conduct class in a variety of ways, some of which students consider better than others

The students in our study described courses that were not inclusive as those involving the instructor lecturing the entire time and not facilitating interactive lessons or opportunities for students to engage with one another. When instructors criticized students, were condescending, or did not try to get to know the students, respondents described feeling more excluded. The participants seemed to perceive these instructional behaviors as demonstrating a lack of care or investment in students, and thus not inclusive.

Reflection Questions

- Reflect on the key themes from this book. Where do you see opportunities for growth?
- How can you use student voice to enhance your inclusive teaching efforts?

In addition to the student voices embedded throughout the book, including this chapter, are intentionally designed opportunities to reflect on the content. Further, we described in Chapter 5 how critical it is for all instructors endeavoring to be more inclusive to reflect on their practices and to use student feedback as one data source among others to inform reflection. The benefits of reflection can be likened to an investment. If an instructor reflects in small amounts, consistently over time, such can make a large longer-term impact on their teaching if they take their thoughts to action. We encourage all instructors to engage in some form of reflection and to obtain feedback from their learners on their teaching.

One very powerful data source for reflection is observational feedback. In Chapter 6 we described current observational tools for obtaining feedback on inclusive teaching efforts such as the Protocol for Advancing Inclusive Teaching (PAITE). Such can be used in tandem with student voices data and instructor reflections to advance inclusive teaching efforts. We draw several parallels between the PAITE and the student voice data, such as creating a welcoming classroom climate through affirmation, using students' names, as well as engaging students in their learning through active learning, real-world applications, and check-ins.

Knowing that, as instructors engage in this journey, they may want to know what difference their inclusive teaching efforts are making, we provided guidance for how to assess outcomes at the course level and a variety of factors to measure. We also discussed how the scholarship of teaching and learning can be particularly useful for individual instructors as well as teaching and learning. To truly create inclusive learning environments across the institution, we highlight that the roles of departments and institutions are critical and create the conditions for cultivating inclusive environments.

If we truly want to advance inclusive teaching and learning in higher education we need to listen to students, reflect on our practices, assess their impact, engage in observational feedback, and provide support at the departmental and institutional levels. Support is needed for all instructors, especially those from groups historically excluded. We hope that you are empowered to continue this journey.

APPENDIX I: SURVEY: STUDENTS' PERSPECTIVES ON INCLUSIVE TEACHING APPROACHES

Please answer the questions to share your perspectives on inclusive teaching in the college or university that you attend. This survey is anonymous.

Please keep in mind the definitions below as you answer the questions.

- **Diversity**—"how learners differ from one another with regard to their social identities, demographics, perspectives, prior experiences, attitudes, knowledge, skills, and other attributes"
- **Equity**—"acknowledges differences between learners, their diversity, and the types of learning environments that help diverse students succeed"
- **Equality**—"suggests that all students should have identical learning experience regardless of their differences", "does not align well with inclusive approaches to instruction"
- **Inclusion**—"creating a welcoming environment and intentionally not excluding any learners"
- **Inclusive teaching**—"designing learning environments that are (a) equitable, where all students have the opportunity to reach their potential, and (b) welcoming, and foster a sense of belonging."

Source: What Inclusive Instructors Do: Principles and Practices for Excellence in College Teaching *(Addy et al., 2021, p. 4)*

Please consider all of the college courses that you have taken thus far in answering the questions below. (Choices: none, few, some, most, all)

How many of your instructors have directly addressed concepts of inclusion and equity in your classes?

How many of your instructors have successfully created an inclusive learning environment in their classes?

In how many of your courses have you felt a sense of belonging?
In how many of your courses have you felt that you have had an equal opportunity to succeed compared with other students in the course?

In how many of your courses have you felt able to express your perspectives on the course content/material?

In how many of your courses have you felt able to express your perspectives on the course setup and format?

In how many of your courses have you felt as if you were a valuable member of the learning community?

In how many of your courses did the instructor know your name by the end of the course?

In how many of your courses do you feel your instructor knew about how your personal background might relate to the course?

In how many of your courses do you feel your instructor knew about how your personal background might affect your ability to succeed in the course?

Give examples of when your instructors did something well with regards to inclusive teaching per the questions that follow. When you are providing responses, please note the type of class to which you are referring with regards to discipline (e.g., Chemistry, Economics, English) and type of delivery (e.g., in-person, online-live, online-asynchronous, etc.).

a In the design of a course
b To create a welcoming environment throughout the course
c In daily class activities

Why were these approaches effective?

Give examples of when your instructors have ***not done well*** with regards to inclusive teaching per the questions that follow. When you are providing responses, please note the type of class to which you are referring with regards to discipline (e.g., Chemistry, Economics, English) and type of delivery (e.g., in-person, online-live, online-asynchronous, etc.).

a In the design of a course
b To create a welcoming environment throughout the course
c In daily class activities

Why were these approaches ***not*** effective?

Which type(s) of courses did you describe above? (select all that apply)

- ▢ STEM (science, technology, engineering, or mathematics)
- ▢ Humanities
- ▢ Social Sciences
- ▢ Other (please specify):

How were these course(s) delivered? (select all that apply)

- ▢ in-person
- ▢ online-live/synchronous
- ▢ online-not live/asynchronous
- ▢ other (please specify):

Interview Questions

Thank you for participating in this interview. Please answer the questions below based on your experiences in your college classes. When you are providing responses, please note the type of class to which you are referring with regards to discipline (e.g., Chemistry, Economics, English) and type of delivery (e.g., in-person, online-live, online-asynchronous, etc.).

Give examples of when your instructors did something "well" with regards to inclusive teaching:

- In the design of a course
- To create a welcoming environment throughout the course
- In daily class activities

Why were these approaches effective?

Give examples of when your instructors have "***not*** done well" with regards to inclusive teaching:

- In the design of a course
- To create a welcoming environment throughout the course
- In daily class activities

Why were these approaches not effective?

What do you recommend that an instructor do to help create an inclusive learning environment?

Which type(s) of course(s) did you describe above?

STEM (science, technology, engineering, or mathematics)
Humanities
Social Sciences
Other (please specify): ____

How were these course(s) delivered?

In-person
Online—live/synchronous
Online—not live/asynchronous
Other (please specify): ____

Demographic Information (Survey and Interview Respondents)

The following demographic questions are being asked to help the research team capture the backgrounds of participants responding to this survey to determine whether there are any trends or themes. Your responses will still be anonymous. Please note that you are not obligated to respond to any questions in this demographics section of the survey.

To the best of your knowledge, which of the following describes the college or university that you attend?

a Community College
b Small, Private Liberal Arts College
c Historically Black College or University or Minority-Serving Institution
d Public University
e Private University
f Master's College or University
g Other (please specify):

Where is the geographic region of your institution?

Northeast
South
Midwest
West
Outside of the United States

With which race(s)/ethnicit(ies) do you identify?

What is your gender identity?

What is your sexual identity?

What is your college major or intended major?

What is your class year/graduation year?

Are you a first-generation college student? (Note: First-generation students are those whose parents or legal guardians have not completed a bachelor's degree.)

FIGURE A.1 Map of the United States showing regions.
Source: Wikimedia Commons. https://commons.wikimedia.org/wiki/File:Map_of_USA_showing_regions.png

a Yes
b No

What is your status as a student?

a full-time
b part-time

What is your age range?

a <18
b 18–24
c 25–34
d 35–44
e 45–54
f 55 +

Are you a veteran?

a Yes
b No

APPENDIX II: HOW'S CLASS GOING? A STUDENT FEEDBACK FORM FOR FOSTERING EQUITY AND INCLUSION

Please respond to each of the following prompts.

Course Design

1. (Likert Scale) The course syllabus clearly provides the necessary information.
2. (Likert Scale) The course content includes diverse perspectives.
3. (Likert Scale) The course materials are offered in an accessible format.
4. (Likert Scale) The cost of course materials did not cause financial hardship.
5. (Likert Scale) The course design respectfully considers students' time.
6. (Likert Scale) Student feedback was considered in how the course was designed.
7. (Likert Scale) The physical (or virtual) classroom space is utilized in an inclusive and equitable manner.
8. (Likert Scale) The overall format of the course is inclusive.
9. (Open Ended) What has been done most successfully in terms of course design related to diversity, equity, and inclusion?
10. (Open Ended) What could be done more successfully in terms of course design related to diversity, equity, and inclusion?

Creating a Welcoming Environment

1. (Likert Scale) My instructor has created a welcoming environment in this class.
2. (Likert Scale) My instructor uses the preferred names of students in the class.

3. (Likert Scale) My instructor treats members of the class as whole individuals, not simply students.
4. (Likert Scale) Student differences are respected and valued in this class.
5. (Likert Scale) Student ideas, opinions, and perspectives are encouraged within learning sessions.
6. (Likert Scale) If or when a violation or disruption to the class expectations occurred, the instructor handled them promptly and appropriately.
7. (Likert Scale) If I need help, I feel that I can approach the instructor.
8. (Likert Scale) I feel like I belong as part of this class.
9. (Open Ended) What has been done most successfully in terms of creating a welcoming environment?
10. (Open Ended) What could be done more successfully in terms of creating a welcoming environment?

Conducting the Course

1. (Likert Scale) Learning activities in the class were varied (i.e., more than just a single format such as instructor lecture, discussion, group work, student presentations, etc.).
2. (Likert Scale) Assessments in the course were varied (i.e., in more than just a single format such as exams, papers, presentations, projects, etc.).
3. (Likert Scale) Sufficient time was allotted to complete learning activities (in-class and out-of-class).
4. (Likert Scale) Sufficient time was allotted to critically think and share thoughts about course topics.
5. (Likert Scale) Student questions were encouraged within learning sessions.
6. (Likert Scale) The instructor was flexible in their daily course implementation, to support the success of diverse students.
7. (Likert Scale) The instructor effectively facilitated student learning in an equitable manner.
8. (Likert Scale) The instructor's behaviors supported inclusive and equitable learning.
9. (Open Ended) What has been done most successfully in terms of conducting the daily activities of the course related to diversity, equity, and inclusion?
10. (Open Ended) What could be done more successfully in terms of conducting the daily activities of the course related to diversity, equity, and inclusion?

APPENDIX III: CHAPTER REFLECTION QUESTIONS

Below are Reflection Questions curated from each chapter that can be used for self-reflection or book discussions.

Chapter 1: Introduction

- Consider the two models presented above (Diversity interventions—resistance to action model and EPIC). Where do you see yourself with regards to your adoption of inclusive teaching approaches?
- For which teaching or learning areas are you most interested in hearing students' perspectives?
- What most stands out to you with regards to the initial study findings presented in this chapter?
- If you designed survey questions to gather students' perspectives, what questions would you ask?

Chapter 2: How My Instructors Design Inclusive Courses

- Do any of these themes surprise you? If so, which ones?
- Which, if any, of these themes have students commented upon in your courses? Was the feedback positive or negative?
- How could you go about gathering student voices to identify relevant themes that apply to your own inclusive course design planning?
- How can you, or do you, design first course assignments that allow your students to engage with you and their peers?
- In what ways do you maximize student engagement throughout your course?

- What are the most likely student engagement pitfalls you may need to avoid?
- If you currently, or in the future, integrate group work in your courses, how can you design it so that it is more inclusive from the start?
- Are you able to provide a syllabus (full or abbreviated) of the course before it starts to your students? If not, is there information you might be able to share beyond the course title and description?
- Could it benefit your students to make all of your course materials and assignments available at the beginning of the course?
- Do you build flexible deadlines and extensions into your courses? If so, does the type of assignment or assessment influence your deadline policy?
- Are you able to incorporate breaks into your courses? Are these short breaks during a class session or entire class periods? Are they movement breaks, mental breaks, or both?
- Which, if any, inclusive syllabus design principles do you use in your syllabus? Are there additional ones that you might be able to use?
- In what ways do you incorporate individual student needs and preferences into your course design while making space for all students?
- How do you educate yourself on student demographic attributes in which you may be unfamiliar?
- How do you account for a variety of student accessibility needs, such as mental health, visible and invisible disabilities, neurodivergence, and diverse socioeconomic status, while designing your courses?
- Do you build in opportunities for students to provide feedback on the overall course design or specific elements (like projects) at the beginning of the course?
- How can you or do you consider diverse scholars in your course materials?
- What strategies do you use, or have you used, to add variety to instructional materials, assignments, and assessment tools?
- John Dewey's Constructivist Learning Theory is based on each student's own perspective and real-world experiences. In what ways do you scaffold your course's learning outcomes based on students' lived experiences?
- Are there options you can provide students who cannot attend a class session in-person? What are they?
- How can you structure the course in a way that maximizes access to hybrid class sessions, whether in-person or online?
- How can you give in-person students online options, or online students opportunities to engage with you in-person?

Chapter 3: How My Instructors Make Me Feel Welcome

- What are verbal and non-verbal ways that you make your students feel welcome?
- What verbal and non-verbal cues do you use to project a good attitude?

- How do cultural views of good and bad attitudes from an instructor and student perspective operate in your classroom?
- Do you use humor in your classroom? If so, do you use affiliative or aggressive humor and how can you be sure?
- When you opt to use humor, how do you account for mixed student perceptions in the same class (i.e., some view joke(s) as affiliative and others view joke(s) as aggressive)?
- What verbal and nonverbal immediacy behaviors do you use to make your students feel included?
- How have you effectively used recognition, acknowledgement, and endorsement to communicate clearly and make students feel welcome?
- How do you learn, and properly pronounce, your students' names?
- How do you handle letting students disclose their pronouns?
- Do you think instructor–student or student–student introductions are better at promoting welcoming through membership and shared emotional connection?
- What strategies do you use to ensure students with disabilities feel like a part of the classroom community?
- Can you use classroom agreements and trigger warnings to encourage respect in your classroom and equitable participation by all of your students? If not, what other strategies do you employ?
- How can you discourage faculty–student and student–student incivility and promote welcoming in your classroom?
- In what ways can you ensure you are encouraging equitable participation and not prioritizing certain students' contributions over others?
- In what ways can you convey care to your students to build positive relationships?
- How have you been proactive in reaching out to your students who need academic assistance?
- What have you done to show empathy and flexibility with assignment due dates and lateness to/absence from class?

Chapter 4: How My Instructors Conduct Class Inclusively

- If you have taught previously, have you seen any of these major themes appear in the feedback you have received from students, either through course evaluations or via other means?
- If so, were they provided as examples of successes or opportunities for growth in your teaching?
- Would you consider your current course(s) varied in terms of teaching approaches? Why or why not?
- Would you consider your current course(s) varied in terms of assessment? Why or why not?

- If you utilize lecturing in your courses, how much do you focus on the organization and clarity of those lectures? Is there something that you could add to your lectures to enhance these features?
- If you teach through lecturing, in which of your courses do you use it most? What approximate percentage of the course time is lecture-based? Considering the information above, do you believe that to be appropriate?
- If you do not utilize lecturing, is there a course where it might be beneficial? How could you implement it in an inclusive manner?
- What specifically could you do to make discussions in your in-person or online courses more inclusive?
- Consider an activity you have had students work on in your course (or if you have not done this, create a hypothetical activity).

  a Was it structured as an independent, paired, or small group assignment?
  b What barriers could that structure present to a learner, considering the neurodiversity found in student populations?
  c How could you design the activity to mitigate this barrier(s) without sacrificing the student's ability to achieve the desired learning outcomes?

- Consider a course you have taught or are planning to teach.

  a What format of assessments did or will you include?
  b If there are only one or two forms of assessment, is there an opportunity to include a broader variety of ways students demonstrate their learning?
  c For any one particular assessment, is there an opportunity to provide the students with choice, to select the format that they prefer to demonstrate their learning?

- What are your personal thoughts around the idea of pop quizzes?
- Do you directly invite student questions in your classes? What language do you use, and what implications might that language have?
- What is a way that you could request questions from your students in your particular class that could increase the number of questions you receive while decreasing the anxiety some students might feel in asking those questions?
- What are your personal feelings about cold-calling? Is it something you utilize in your classes, and what information do you have on how your students respond to it?
- Think about the potential barriers and brainstorm ways that you could incorporate the voices of students with the following:

a Visual impairment
b Hearing impairment
c Motor impairment
d Autism spectrum disorder
e Other impairments or disabilities you have encountered in your student population

- Do you have a particular way in which you start your classes, before immediately jumping into the learning for the day? If not, what could you implement in the future?
- How do you navigate the challenges of limited time in the classroom, while still providing the necessary time for effective student learning?
- Do you have mechanisms for ending your class sessions? If not, how might you end them?
- If you have taught an asynchronous course, how have you navigated student time allotment when you do not meet as a class for specified sessions?
- How do you view your role in the class, specifically related to in-class day-to-day activities?
- How can you serve as a guide for your learners?
- Think about a course that you teach or plan to teach. In what areas within specific class sessions, learning activities, or assessments could increased flexibility benefit your diverse student population?
- What specific challenges do you face as an instructor that can make flexibility in the class difficult? These could be related to course requirements, teaching experience, personal background, time in or out of the class, or other aspects.
- What are aspects of your personality or identity (visible or invisible) that impact your teaching? What challenges might those present? Alternatively, how can you leverage those characteristics within your courses?
- If you teach online, what strategies have you used successfully to connect with your students, or if you have found that connection difficult, what can you try in the future?

Chapter 5: Starting to Reflect on Your Practice

- What do you believe are the main specific benefits of reflecting on one's teaching?
- Do you consider yourself an effective reflective practitioner of teaching? If not, what barriers make reflection difficult for you?
- In regards to reflective teaching, do you feel that you have the three attitudes for effective reflective practice (open-mindedness, responsibility, and wholeheartedness)? If not, which are absent and why?

- Which attribute of reflective practitioners is your strongest? Which is one that could use more development?
- Which lens of reflective teaching, if any, have you most employed? Which lens have you employed the least?
- What is one means or resource for reflection from the options above, if any, that you have used previously? How effective was it for you? What alterations could be made to make it even more effective?
- What is one means or resource reflection from the options above, if any, that you have not used or have only minimally used, and would like to use more? How specifically will you do so?
- What do you believe to be the main specific benefits of acquiring student feedback?
- When you acquire student feedback, do you specifically ask for responses related to inclusion and equity? If not, why not and do you think it would be beneficial to include in the future?
- Do you conduct student feedback surveys in or after your courses, other than your institution's end-of-term course evaluations? If so, are any questions specifically related to diversity, equity, and inclusion?
- Examine the "How's Class Going?" form in Appendix II. Would implementing this tool in your courses be beneficial? If so, consider the following:

  a Would you want to utilize the form in its entirety, or just use selected questions?
  b If you would only use selected questions:

    - Which specifically will you use?
    - Will you ask these in their own survey, or include them as part of a larger survey?

  c Are there other questions not included in the "How's Class Going?" form related to equity and inclusion that you would like to have your students respond to? If so, what are they?

- What benefits and challenges do you see for you and your courses for students having the ability to continuously provide feedback throughout a course, via mechanisms like a physical or digital comment box?
- Do you utilize exit tickets in your teaching?

  a If so, did they focus more on course content or course experience? Do you think it would be practical and beneficial to allow for both types of feedback?
  b If not, do you think exit tickets could be utilized in any of your courses, specifically to address aspects of inclusion and equity? How regularly would you have students complete these exit tickets; every

day, every week, every unit? What specific prompts would you want to include?

- What would be the maximum class size for which you feel you could meet with every student, even just once a semester for five to ten minutes, to discuss their experiences and assess aspects of inclusion and equity?
- When in the term do you believe would be the most appropriate time for one-on-one conferences with students in your courses? Do you feel for your class it would be necessary to meet more than once with each student?
- If you teach larger classes, which of the approaches of collecting student feedback do you find more useful for your classes between the small group or student representatives methods? Alternatively, do you feel that using surveys would be more practical and provide similar benefits?

Chapter 6: Using Observational Feedback

- How do you feel about your teaching being observed?
- If you feel some discomfort, what might help you feel more comfortable?
- What are the resources available to you for reflection on your teaching?
- How can you obtain observational feedback on your inclusive teaching efforts? Who might you ask?
- Which inclusive teaching practices do you implement, if any?
- How might visualizing your inclusive teaching approaches using the PAITE help you enhance your practice?
- Considering the instructional behaviors included on the PAITE, which would you be most interested in focusing on for a classroom observation?
- What type of outcomes would you hope to see?

Chapter 7: Measuring and Sharing Outcomes

- In the last year (or other time frame), what, if any, growth have you noticed, regarding the awareness of your own cultural identity and your students' cultural differences or circumstances?
- What are some opportunities that you have on your own campus to grow in your own cultural competence or humility?
- Reflect on any inclusive teaching practices that you implement in your courses. What types of approaches do you implement? What is the frequency with which you use such approaches? How broad of a scope of approaches do you utilize?
- What might be next steps for you with regards to the frequency with which you use various approaches and the variation of those approaches?
- What, if any, additional instructor-level outcomes would be meaningful to you?

- Consider a course and choose one or two outcomes for inclusive teaching. How might you measure them?
- What might help you better assess outcomes of your teaching efforts?

Chapter 8: Transforming Departmental and Institutional Culture

- In which community-building activities does your department engage?
- Do all members of your department feel a sense of community? If you do not know, how can you find out?

Departmental Reflection Questions

- Who are the students who take our courses? What do we know about their backgrounds, experiences, attitudes, and individuality? How are we taking that into account in the course that we teach?
- What do we value as a department with regards to inclusive teaching and learning?
- What are examples of research-supported inclusive teaching strategies within our discipline?
- Are there any ableist teaching approaches being utilized that we must reconsider?

Course Design:

- How do we maximize student engagement in our courses?
- What is the average workload for our various courses and is it inclusive for our learners?
- What are course setups that our students have really appreciated that support their success?
- How do we obtain informal student feedback on our courses?
- Which courses integrate diversity or social justice topics?

Welcoming Environment:

- What strategies are we using to create a welcoming environment in our courses?

Conducting Class Sessions:

- What are the different approaches we use to conduct class inclusively?
- Do we give students enough time to complete work while they juggle other classes and activities?

- If you had to focus your efforts on a few departmental approaches for inclusion as discussed above, which would you choose, why, and how could you go about making progress?
- How can you collectively as a department advance inclusive teaching and learning?

Institutional Reflection Questions

- Who are the students at our institution? What do we know about their backgrounds, experiences, attitudes, and individuality? How are we taking that into account in the learning experiences that we design?
- What do we value as an institution with regards to inclusive teaching and learning?
- What are examples of research-supported inclusive teaching strategies within our institution?
- Are there any ableist teaching approaches being utilized that we must reconsider?

Curriculum:

- How do we maximize student engagement in our core curriculum if one exists?
- How do we obtain informal student feedback on our core curriculum?
- Which courses integrate diversity or social justice topics?

Welcoming Environment:

- What strategies are we using to create a welcoming environment across learning experiences?

Reflection and Observation:

- How can we hold ourselves accountable for making these changes?

Chapter 9: Advice for Historically Marginalized Instructors and Their Allies

- What challenges, if any, have you confronted as an instructor from a historically excluded group?
- Who are the advocates and allies that can support you?
- What advice most resonates with you from this chapter?

- If you are an instructor who is not from a historically marginalized group, how can you acknowledge the privileges you may have while also being an ally for your colleagues?

Chapter 10: Generative Artificial Intelligence and Equity

- Have you incorporated generative artificial intelligence technologies into any courses to build a more inclusive classroom environment? If so, how? If not, what do you foresee as possibilities or challenges to doing such?

Chapter 11: Concluding Remarks

- Reflect on the key themes from this book. Where do you see opportunities for growth?
- How can you use student voice to enhance your inclusive teaching efforts?

INDEX

Made in the USA
Las Vegas, NV
10 March 2024

86995235R00155